Lecture Notes in Business Information Processing 91

Julia Kotlarsky
Leslie P. Willcocks
Ilan Oshri (Eds.)

New Studies in Global IT and Business Services Outsourcing

5th Global Sourcing Workshop 2011
Courchevel, France, March 14-17, 2011
Revised Selected Papers

Springer

Volume Editors

Julia Kotlarsky
University of Warwick
Warwick Business School
Coventry, UK
E-mail: julia.kotlarsky@wbs.ac.uk

Leslie P. Willcocks
London School of Economics
London, UK
E-mail: l.p.willcocks@lse.ac.uk

Ilan Oshri
Erasmus University
Rotterdam School of Management
Rotterdam, The Netherlands
E-mail: ioshri@rsm.nl

ISSN 1865-1348 e-ISSN 1865-1356
ISBN 978-3-642-24814-6 e-ISBN 978-3-642-24815-3
DOI 10.1007/978-3-642-24815-3
Springer Heidelberg Dordrecht London New York

Library of Congress Control Number: 2011938359

ACM Computing Classification (1998): K.6, K.4.3, D.2

Typesetting: Camera-ready by author, data conversion by Scientific Publishing Services, Chennai, India

Printed on acid-free paper

Springer is part of Springer Science+Business Media (www.springer.com)

Preface

This edited book is intended for use by students, academics and practitioners who take interest in outsourcing and offshoring of information technology and business processes. The book offers a review of the key topics in outsourcing and offshoring, populated with practical frameworks that serve as a tool kit to students and managers. The range of topics covered in this book is wide and diverse. Various governance and coordination mechanisms for managing outsourcing relationships are discussed in great depth and the decision-making processes and considerations regarding sourcing arrangements, including multi-sourcing and cloud services, are examined. Vendors' capabilities for managing global software development are studied in depth. Clients' capabilities and issues related to compliance and culture are also discussed in association with various sourcing models. Topics discussed in this book combine theoretical and practical insights regarding challenges that both clients and vendors face. Case studies from client and vendor organizations are used extensively throughout the book. Last but not least, the book examines current and future trends in outsourcing and offshoring, placing particular attention on the centrality of innovation in sourcing arrangements, and how innovation can be realized in outsourcing.

The book is based on a vast empirical base brought together through years of extensive research by leading researchers in information systems, strategic management and operations.

July 2011

Julia Kotlarsky
Leslie Willcocks
Ilan Oshri

Organization

The Global Sourcing Workshop is an annual gathering of academics and practitioners.

Program Committee

Workshop Chair

Leslie Willcocks	London School of Economics, UK

Workshop Committee

Julia Kotlarsky	Warwick Business School, University of Warwick, UK
Ilan Oshri	Rotterdam School of Management Erasmus University, The Netherlands

Sponsoring Institution

Accenture

Table of Contents

Global Sourcing of Information Technology and Business Processes

Mechanisms to Implement a Global Multisourcing Strategy

Thomas Ph. Herz, Florian Hamel, Falk Uebernickel, and Walter Brenner

University of St. Gallen, Institute of Information Management,
Mueller-Friedberg-Str. 8, 9000 St. Gallen, Switzerland
{thomas.herz,florian.hamel,falk.uebernickel,walter.brenner}@unisg.ch

Abstract. Many multinational enterprises apply multisourcing approaches and both practitioner-related and scholarly literature has identified multisourcing as an emerging key strategy. Multisourcing is described as the blending of services from multiple company-internal and company-external suppliers. Despite its relevance, current literature lacks depth in terms of implementing multisourcing and only a few articles describe multisourcing strategies in detail. Especially, multisourcing in a group-context is scarcely covered. This research study contributes to the body of knowledge by analyzing the case of a worldwide leading financial services provider. This article describes mechanisms that support the implementation of a global multisourcing strategy at a business group with a federal IT organization and provides insights into a real-life example of global multisourcing. Propositions on governance aspects for multisourcing are derived and a split of activities between the group center and the business entities is suggested. In particular, the organizational setup of a business group – with the numerous business entities and the federal governance model – determines the multisourcing strategy and the split of activities. Hence, this research also helps practitioners facing similar challenges.

Keywords: Global multisourcing strategy, IT outsourcing, offshoring, financial services provider, single case study.

1 Introduction

In recent times, it can be observed that IT outsourcing mega-deals – outsourcing deals with a volume greater than one billion USD – under a sole-sourcing approach are less frequent and companies have moved to a more selective outsourcing approach applying multisourcing strategies. The sourcing advisory firm TPI found that during the last years, whilst mega-deals have decreased both in size and prevalence, the number of outsourcing deals signed has increased [1]. Multisourcing has been identified as an emerging key strategy in today's IT outsourcing endeavors by both practitioner-related as well as scholarly literature [2,3,4,5,6,7,8]. Multisourcing is the blending of services from multiple company-internal and company-external suppliers [4]. The main drivers for the emergence

J. Kotlarsky, L.P. Willcocks, and I. Oshri (Eds.): Global Sourcing 2011, LNBIP 91, pp. 1–20, 2011.

of multisourcing strategies are companies' increased needs for cost efficiency, flexibility, and quality in a dynamic and global business environment [5]. Companies face both opportunities and threats while applying multisourcing. On the one hand, companies, who are engaged in multisourcing, gain flexibility and quality, ensure access to specialized expertise and capabilities, foster the competition between the suppliers, mitigate strategic and operational risks and reduce costs [3,5,8,9,10,11,12,13]. But on the other hand, multisourcing may require adoption in the operational model and sets high prerequisites for managerial capabilities [4,5,14]. Moreover, Bapna et al. (2010) claim an increase in cooperation and coordination requirements due to the interdependence between the suppliers in multisourcing compared to single sourcing [3].

Dibbern et al. (2004) identify five major issues of IT outsourcing: (1) why to outsource, (2) what to outsource, (3) which decision process to take, (4) how to implement the sourcing decision, and (5) what is the outcome of the sourcing decision [15]. While the first three questions have been addressed intensively by researchers, the implementation process and the sourcing outcome require further research. Within the fourth area the larger part of IT outsourcing studies have addressed dyadic relationships and little experience-based research has investigated how multisourcing is implemented in large, multinational organizations. Bapna et al. (2010) stress in this context that "linear extensions of dyadic client-vendor IT outsourcing relationships are insufficient to capture the nuances of the multisourced environment" [3]. In addition, organizational aspects such as the group-context or the interplay between company-internal and company-external suppliers have been scarcely covered. Thereby, the group-context describes the organizational form of a business group that encompasses a systematic delegation of duties between the group center and the business entities [16,17]. The purpose of this study is to increase the understanding of how business groups implement multisourcing. Therefore, we have defined one major research question:

[RQ] Which mechanisms support the implementation of multisourcing in a business group?

To answer this research question, we conducted a qualitative single case study to investigate multisourcing at a leading, global financial services provider – in the following organization A. Financial services providers have been in the forefront of outsourcing and offshoring both IT and business processes [5]. This study contributes to research on global multisourcing in three ways. First, it illustrates an extreme and unique case of multisourcing at a financial services provider; second, it reveals mechanisms that support the implementation of multisourcing; and, third, it suggests propositions on governance and sourcing strategy related aspects. This research is also expected to help other organizations facing similar challenges.

The remainder of this paper consists of six sections. The next section provides an overview of fundamental terms. Section three outlines the research method. Section four presents the multisourcing journey of organization A. Section five reveals the main case study findings. In section six we discuss the findings before we conclude in the final section seven.

2 Foundation and Related Research

For a field of research it is important to have a common understanding of basic terms. For this reason, definitions of key terms should be provided [18]. Based on a literature review, we provide an overview about key terms applied in this study.

2.1 The Evolution of the Term Multisourcing

The initial point for the overview on definitions of the term *multisourcing* was set by a practitioner book by Linda Cohen and Allie Young that received great attention during the last years [19]. Additional definitions – explicitly or implicitly – derived for the term multisourcing can be located in the management, information systems (IS) and operations management (OM) literature. Porter (1985) was one of the first authors who implicitly defined multisourcing by describing the competition between suppliers that fosters performance and reduces costs [9]. Sourcing strategies have a long track record in the OM literature; e.g. Treleven and Schweikhart (1988) described multisourcing explicitly in the late 1980's [20]. With IT outsourcing gaining momentum in the 1990's the IS literature has been dealing increasingly with multisourcing ideas. In a recent research study Su and Levina (2011) transfer knowledge of the manufacturing domain with multisourcing to IT outsourcing [8]. Lately, practitioner literature – e.g. provided by the IT research and advisory company Gartner – is expanding the concept to both business and IT services [4]. There seems to be an evolution in the definition of the term multisourcing developing from a management (see, inter alia, [9]) and OM (see, inter alia, [20]) to an IS perspective (see, inter alia, [13]) and finally covering both IT as well as business services (see, inter alia, [4]). Table 1 illustrates relevant definitions of the term multisourcing.

While the basic concept of multiple suppliers is not new [9] and focuses on economies of scale, the multisourcing concept – focusing on services rather than on goods – is beyond the scope of economies of scale mainly concerned with relationships [5]. For this study we apply the definition of Cohen and Young (2006) as suggested by other authors (please see, inter alia, [5]) that describes multisourcing as "the disciplined provisioning and blending of business and IT services from the optimal set of internal and external suppliers in the pursuit of business goals" and is very well in line with other recent definitions (please refer to Table 1) [4].

Table 1. Overview of multisourcing definitions

Year	Author(s)	Definition
2010	Bapna, Barua, Mani and Mehra [3]	[...] the practice of stitching together best-of-breed IT services from multiple, geographically dispersed providers [...]
2009	Janischowsky and Schonenbach [6]	[...] optimizing business, information technology and infrastructure services across external suppliers and internal departments / companies [...]
2006	Cohen and Young [4]	[...] the disciplined provisioning and blending of business and IT services from the optimal set of internal and external suppliers in the pursuit of business goals [...]
2005	Cullen, Seddon and Willcocks [21]	[...] several suppliers are contracted under one contract without a lead supplier [...]
2002	Carmel and Agarwal [22]	[...] longer-term, deeper relationships with a small number of suppliers [...]
1999	Gallivan and Oh [23]	[...] a one-to-many relationship indicates that one client uses multiple outsourcing suppliers to achieve its objectives [...]
1998	Currie [24]	[...] a company signs outsourcing contracts with more than one IT supplier [...]
1998	Currie and Willcocks [25]	[...] a strategy that intends to create an alliance of suppliers who compete with each other [...]
1998	Lacity and Willcocks [13]	[...] one outsourcing contract but multiple suppliers of services [...]
1995	Cross [12]	[...] buy IT services from multiple suppliers and have the pieces delivered as if they came from a single supplier [...]
1988	Treleven and Schweikhart [20]	[...] multiple sourcing refers to a vendee purchasing an identical part from two or more suppliers [...]
1985	Porter [9]	[...] keep the number of sources sufficient to ensure competition [...]

The multisourcing definition covers an optimal set of company-internal and company-external suppliers that are frequently referred to as geographically disperse [3] encompassing both domestic and offshore service delivery [4,5]. While referring to the four major sourcing options of the make-buy matrix as described by Oshri (2011) any combination (Cohen and Young are referring to as the "optimal set") would be possible [26]. In the extreme, a client company applies all four options.

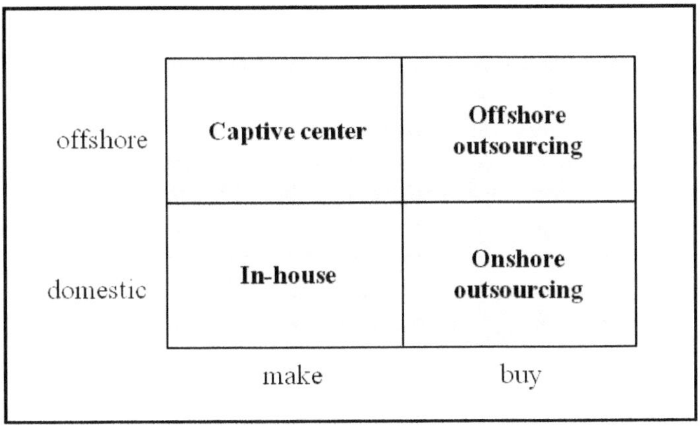

Fig. 1. Sourcing options in the make-buy matrix (according to Oshri (2011) [26])

2.2 Organizational Perspective: Business Groups

For the term *business group* a wide range of definitions exists in scientific literature [16,17,27,28,29,30,31]. Granovetter (1995) considers as business groups "those collection of firms bound together in some formal and/or informal ways, characterized by an intermediate level of binding" [17]. For our research study we follow the suggestion by Granovetter (1994) that also encompasses management

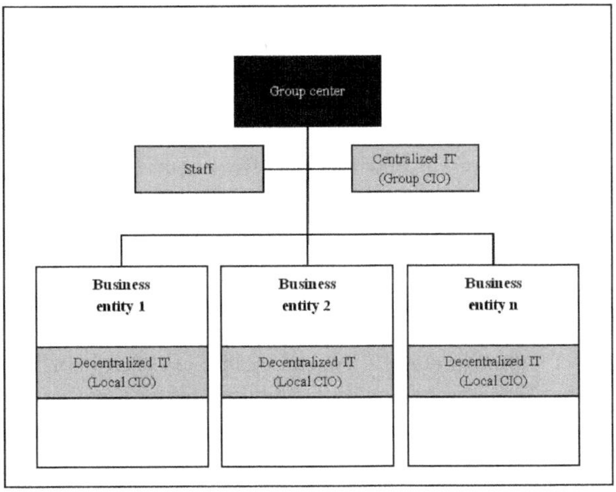

Fig. 2. Illustration of a business group (based on Janssen and Joha (2006)[34])

holdings in which a parent company "confines itself to strategy and finance, and owns operational subsidiaries that are legally separate" [16]. Business groups combine e.g., the advantages of smaller, local companies like flexibility and customer orientation with those of large companies like market presence and power as well as economies of scale [17,32,33].

While referring to Figure 2 (adopted from Janssen and Joha (2006)[34]), a business group can also be described by a systematic delegation of duties between the parent company (also referred to as group center, head office, center, holding, corporate function) and the subsidiaries (also referred to as business entities, business units, daughter company) [16,17,27,28,29,30,31,33]. In our study we apply the terms group center for the parent company and business entity for a subsidiary. The group center typically assumes at a minimum common administrative, financial and managerial coordination. Goold and Campbell (1987) developed a framework on corporate strategic management styles that provides a description of the value a group center can add to the whole group [35]. Three different styles are distinguished in the Goold and Campbell framework: strategic planning, strategic control, and financial control.

2.3 Multisourcing in a Group-Context

Zmud et al. (1986) applied the business group concept to the IT function, whereupon an IT function comprises a federation of several roles, found at the group center and at business entity level [36]. Frequently, a federal governance model is ascertained with the IT function in business groups [37,38,39]. Weill (2004) defines the federal model "as coordinated decision making involving both a center and its business units" and Handy (1992) emphasizes that responsibilities and accountabilities of multiple governing bodies span at least two hierarchical tiers [40,41]. Hodgkinson (1996) identifies four major areas of strategic IT management roles that can be found in a group center: formulation of the group-wide IT strategy and policy, strategic control, functional leadership, and promotion of synergies [38]. Further, Hodgkinson (1996) argues that the extent to which a role is exercised by the group center depends on the management style [38]. Based on the Goold and Campbell framework, Hodgkinson (1996) defines two federal IT management styles: the strategic leadership style and the strategic guidance style [38].

Lacity and Willcocks (2001) identify six phases that characterize the IT outsourcing life cycle: scoping, evaluation, negotiation, transition, middle, and mature phase [42]. In order to implement multisourcing successfully, management and governance related aspects are of vast importance [15,43,44,45]. In this context, certain mechanisms are used to implement and deploy IT governance into organizations [46]. According to Peterson (2004) three types of IT governance mechanisms exist and support the implementation: structures, processes, and relational mechanism [46]. This is very much in line with the mechanisms described by Weill and Ross (2005): decision-making structures, alignment processes, and formal communications [47].

3 Research Method

In order to identify our research focus we conducted expert interviews with IT sourcing managers of seven multinational enterprises and thereby validated the relevance of our research idea. The identified areas of interest built the basis for our research question and the in-depth case study with organization A. In order to answer the research question a holistic single case study [48] was designed to examine the global multisourcing approach of organization A. Case studies facilitate a better understanding of complex phenomena and are preferably better research designs for qualitative research within the field of IS [49,50]. An explorative and qualitative case study research method is appropriate for theory-building [51,52,53]. Organization A was selected because of its complex situation and the enormous number of business entities in the context of its business group structure as well as the extensive, group-wide multisourcing approach. The situation at organization A can be described as an extreme and unique case because it represents a rare situation, where a single case is worth documenting it [48]. Furthermore, since the researchers had the chance to establish close relationships with key stakeholders at organization A [54] and were granted access to key documents the case can be characterized as revelatory because it was previously inaccessible to scientific investigation [48]. Yin (2003) further suggests that single case studies are appropriate if the objective of the research is to explore a previously un-researched area and that a full and rich description of a rare phenomenon contributes to knowledge [48]. In order to gather detailed information on multisourcing at organization A multiple in-depth interviews with representatives of organization A, the captive center of organization A, the preferred external suppliers, and the management consultants supporting organization A with the development of the multisourcing strategy have been conducted (please refer to Table 2).

The data collection process was commenced over a four month period in spring 2010. Each in-depth interview lasted between one and two hours. The interview guidelines for the semi-structured interviews were based on the expert interviews conducted before the single case study and covered the multisourcing approach chosen with a special focus on the group-context as well as the implementation. This encompassed e.g., the objectives of organization A, the sourcing dimensions, the contractual framework, levers of implementation, and governance and performance management related aspects.

Table 2. Overview interview partners

No.	Role	Affiliation	Responsibility
1	Program manager	Group center of organization A	Overall program responsibility
2	Project manager	Group center of organization A	Project responsibility
3	Transition manager A	Group center of organization A	Transition to business entities
4	Transition manager B	Group center of organization A	Transition to business entities
5	Transition manager C	Group center of organization A	Transition to business entities
6	Supplier relationship manager	Group center of organization A	Supplier management, contract management and deals tracking
7	Multisourcing financial controller	Group center of organization A	Financial and multisourcing controlling
8	External supplier representative A	Preferred external supplier	Management of relationship with organization A
9	External supplier representative B	Preferred external supplier	Management of relationship with organization A
10	External supplier representative C	Preferred external supplier	Management of relationship with organization A
11	Representative of organization A's captive	Captive center of organization A	Management of relationship with organization A
12	Multisourcing manager of leading business entity	Large business entity of organization A	Implementation of multisourcing at business entity
13	Management consultant	External management consulting firm	Support for strategy development

For data collection and analysis, guidelines suggested by grounded theory [55] were followed. On the one hand, we intertwined data collection and analysis by evolving the interview guidelines based on previous interviews (theoretical sampling). And, on the other hand, we proceeded with interviews until we reached theoretical saturation. For data analysis we used an open coding approach [56]. All interviews have been transcribed and subsequently challenged in an iterative process between the researchers and the interview partners. The interview transcripts have been analyzed to extract mechanisms that support the implementation of multisourcing. Besides the semi-structured interviews, internal documents of organization A (please refer to Table 3) were examined and the data have been triangulated with the findings from the case study [57,58]. In order to validate our case study findings we presented and discussed them during an expert workshop with sourcing practitioners and IT management consultants. Additionally we performed three follow-up expert discussions to validate selected aspects of our findings.

- The multisourcing master service agreement (MMSA) at group level
- The multisourcing business entity specific service agreement (MBSA) at business entity level
- The multisourcing project specific service agreement (MPSA) at project level

Figure 4 illustrates the contractual framework with its components based on three levels and the involved parties. The MMSA is a comprehensive legal framework covering the global strategic relationship between organization A as a group and each of the preferred external suppliers (group level). Each individual business entity enters into a MBSA with the respective local subsidiary of the preferred external suppliers. This aims to cover local laws and regulations (e.g., country specific laws) at a business entity level. For each project a MPSA is signed between the business entity and the respective subsidiary of the preferred external supplier. The MPSA is strictly project related and does not cover legal topics.

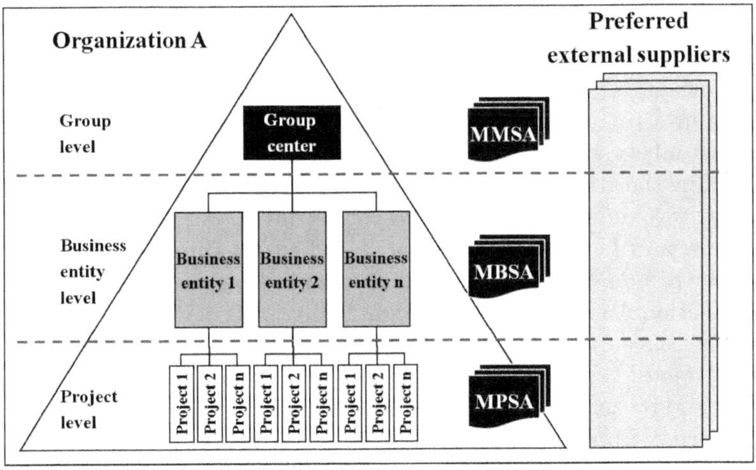

Fig. 4. Contractual framework

5 Case Analysis

We have analyzed the case of organization A and identified six mechanisms that are applied in order to support the implementation of global multisourcing in a business group along the outsourcing life cycle. Thereby we aim to answer our main research question:

[RQ] Which mechanisms support the implementation of multisourcing in a business group?

The six mechanisms that we identified are opportunity assessment, supplier preselection, contractual framework, captive center development, transition to business entities, and governance instruments. The mechanisms follow the phases of the IT outsourcing life cycle as suggested by Lacity and Willcocks (2001)[42].

- *Opportunity assessment:* Usually, the opportunity assessment builds the starting point of a multisourcing strategy and aims to identify core IT capabilities to remain internal and IT activities for potential outsourcing by applying business, economic and technical criteria [42]. Based on the given organizational structure, the current sourcing environment, the business strategy, and best-in-class benchmarks in terms of prices, process standardization, and quality, organization A quantified their multisourcing objectives. Therefore, organization A performed a broad benchmarking initiative with an external consulting company. In addition, a global business case was calculated and localized for each individual business entity. In general, a business case builds the financial baseline, gives orientation for future development, and is used to identify business entities that are suitable for multisourcing. Furthermore, a balanced set of key performance indicators (KPIs) in conjunction with the business case is recommended to be used to monitor and analyze the implementation ex-post on a strategic (group-wide) and operational (business entity) level.
- *Supplier pre-selection:* In order to derive a list of preferred suppliers a vendor selection process has to be initiated. It usually starts with a request for information (RFI) that is followed by a request for proposal (RFP) and results in a list of preferred suppliers with whom the client will enter into contractual agreements [42]. The due diligence of organization A was accomplished by the group center involving some of the business entities in a joined process of evaluation. A cross-functional team of purchasing, legal, sourcing, business, and IT specialists prepared and issued the RFP as well as evaluated the responses of the potential suppliers. Within the evaluation model of organization A monetary aspects build a major criterion in the supplier pre-selection since one of the most relevant objectives of organization A was to achieve factor cost savings by leveraging the company's own captive offshore center and by consolidating the remaining sourcing activities to a few strategic external suppliers with strong offshore delivery capabilities. However, not only monetary aspects were taken into account at organization A, but also soft facts played an important role. Execution quality, ability for process standardization, a global footprint, strong offshore delivery capabilities of the potential suppliers, and the track record with organization A as well as with comparable organizations were important dimensions in the supplier pre-selection. Above this, one should consider potential value add brought in by suppliers, improvements in time-to-market, and scalability [59,60,61]. Since multisourcing is also characterized by interdependencies of suppliers [3] we further recommend to evaluate and select the potential suppliers based on their willingness and capability to cooperate with each other.
- *Contractual framework:* Some researchers place emphasis on the important role of framework agreements in multisourcing (see, inter alia, [12,25]). In accordance with these we have also observed that the contractual framework builds the central piece of global multisourcing at organization A. As described above, it comprises contracts on three levels: group, business entity and project. Accordingly, three major types of documents have been established: the MMSA

on group level, MBSA at business entity level and the MPSA at project level. Within the contractual framework, supplier specific rate cards have been negotiated for each country where organization A is represented with business entities. Thereby, organization A bundles sourcing activities and participates in economies of scale. Additionally, organization A and the suppliers agreed on pre-defined standard skill pyramids that build the basis for the staffing of each project. Therefore, all parties established a standard project process model that was agreed on by each party and is applied for all projects. As a result, the duration of project-specific RFPs could be reduced. Furthermore, the efforts that have to be invested into the agreement on the project process as well as legal and commercial conditions could be reduced substantially. As for the supplier pre-selection an interdisciplinary team consisting of experts in the areas of purchasing, legal, sourcing, business, and IT collaborated in order to implement this holistic contractual framework.

- *Captive center development:* As widely applied in the financial services industry [26] a captive center was one major lever to achieve the defined multisourcing objectives in the sourcing strategy of organization A. Originally, this internal service supplier, located in India, was a subsidiary of one of the business entities. At this time the services were only provided to the parent business entity. While implementing global multisourcing, the services were also offered to all other business entities within the group. The decision for a captive center in addition to external suppliers is based on the fact that organization A aimed to retain key knowledge and core applications internally. In addition, an internal supplier allows for more vertical control [34,62]. However, the challenges related with the development of a captive offshore center are numerous. First, some business entities feared to offshore work to India because of the possible loss of knowledge. Second, the cultural differences appeared to some business entities as another hurdle, e.g. in terms of communication. And, third, the captive offshore center faced enormous competition for talents in India. It was difficult to hire and retain skilled people. According to Oshri (2011) captive centers follow a life cycle with four stages that consist of start-up, value-addition, competence accumulation, and third-party services [26]. The captive center at organization A is currently moving towards the second stage.
- *Transition to business entities:* In the transition phase the contract details are dispensed in the group and post-contract management processes are established [42]. The multisourcing concept at organization A was rolled out to the globally distributed business entities in several waves. It can be observed that two layers of transition were of importance: the strategic and the operational layer. On the strategic layer, aspects related to governance as well as to performance are covered. Organization A decided for low central multisourcing governance. This is based on the federal organizational model. In terms of performance management, a few group-wide agreed KPIs have been selected to steer the multisourcing approach. On the operational layer, the central multisourcing team at the group center supported the business entities with the

implementation on business entity level. Therefore, a number of workshops were organized in order to provide details about the contractual framework as well as governance instruments and performance management.

- *Governance instruments:* Governance is deployed into an organization by applying various governance instruments on a day-by-day basis [46,47]. We ascertained a set of governance instruments that aim to safeguard the implementation of multisourcing in a business group both while deploying multisourcing and also during later phases (middle and mature phase) of the IT outsourcing life cycle [42]. The governance instruments encountered cover two relationship-dimensions: a company-internal dimension that targets the relationship between the group center and the business entities and a supplier-related dimension that focuses on the relationship between the client organization and the multiple external suppliers.

Table 4. Governance instruments

Relationship dimension	**Instruments**
Company-internal	Business entity sourcing plan, group-wide and business entity specific multisourcing business case, multisourcing deals tracking, multisourcing maturity model, CIO committee reporting, multisourcing specific KPIs in financial IT reporting
Supplier-related	Regular supplier meetings, customer satisfaction survey, operational multisourcing KPIs

We could deduct four major areas that are covered by the instruments: baselining and forecasting sourcing opportunities, implementation progress monitoring, management reporting, and supplier management. The first three areas are related to the company-internal relationship dimension and the latter to the supplier-related relationship dimension. In case of the captive center all four areas apply since the captive center is on the one hand an internal business entity and on the other hand comparable to the external suppliers. Table 4 gives an overview of the identified instruments and the allied dimensions. Moreover, we observed that the point of time to define and adjust respectively agree upon governance instruments with all involved stakeholders is crucial. The case of organization A suggests that the definition of governance instruments – in particular the supplier-related once – ideally takes place before issuing the RFP in order to cover governance instruments already in the RFP phase and to contractually agree on them during contract negotiations.

6 Discussion

While there is a growing body of literature on outsourcing and offshoring, there is hardly any account on the implementation of multisourcing in a business group. In addition, in-depth case studies are scarcely published in this research area (see, inter alia, [8,24,25]). This in turn classifies the case study an important finding itself. With this article, we provide not only insights into a real-life example of one of the worldwide leading financial services providers implementing global multisourcing, we also reveal mechanisms that are applied to safeguard the implementation. Based on our findings, we could further deploy propositions in three major areas:

- *Governance:* Organization A has chosen a low central governance approach based on the federal organizational model. This inherits that no strict central governance rules have been put into place and that the group center does not assume the authority to force the business entities to implement the global multisourcing approach. Thus, according to our interview partners, the global multisourcing strategy did not exploit its full potential. Therefore we propose that *clear governance rules should be in place before the implementation.* This proposition is supported by one of our follow-up discussions with sourcing experts. The expert summarizes it as follows:

  > *It is important to define multisourcing governance. Yet, the point of time is crucial. I [the expert] recommend defining the governance even before the RFP is issued. However, I [the expert] observe that many companies define it in a later phase which is one major reason for outsourcing failures.*

  This timely definition of governance is also reflected in the need defined by some researchers that multisourcing requires adoption in the operational model and sets high prerequisites for managerial capabilities [4,5,14].
- *Implementation mechanisms:* Besides our proposition that governance should be in place before the implementation, we suggest that *a balanced set of mechanisms supports the implementation of multisourcing in a business group.* The context of a business group sourcing from multiple company-internal and company-external suppliers inherits a number of specifics to consider. Frequently in a business group, a federal governance model is in place that prohibits central authority of the group center over the globally dispersed business entities. Moreover, the fact of sourcing from multiple suppliers enfolds complexity, might require adoptions in the operational model, sets high prerequisites for managerial capabilities, and increases the requirements for cooperation and coordination due to the interdependence between the suppliers. A balanced set of implementation mechanisms covering the whole sourcing lifecycle – as described above – safeguards the acceptance and utilization of global multisourcing in a business group.
- *Sourcing strategy follows structure:* Overall, we conclude in our study that *the organizational setup with the numerous business entities and low central governance in the context of the federal IT organizational model determines the multisourcing approach* and the split of activities between the group center and the business entities. Therewith we follow the approach suggested by Peters (1984) that "strategy follows structure" since capabilities are the primary products of strategy [63,64]. Those capabilities are in a business group for example the proximity to customers derived from the decentralized organization that enables more efficient (sourcing) decisions based on the availability

of needed information [32]. This proposition is also in-line with the corporate strategic management styles defined by Goold and Campbell (1987) as well as the proposed role of a corporate IT function (group center) in a federal IT organization suggestion by Hodgkinson (1996) in terms of the strategic guidance style [35,38]. Furthermore, it supports the suggestion by Whittington et al. (1999) that the formulation of a strategy and its implementation should be closely interlinked [65]. Our proposed model represents this by a tight collaboration between the group center and the business entities in developing the strategy. Figure 5 illustrates the split of activities. The group center focuses on the implementation and execution support as well as on strategic monitoring and steering activities of the multisourcing approach. The development of the multisourcing approach should be accomplished jointly between the group center and the business entities following the suggestion of Whittington et al. (1999) [65]. Besides the development we suggest that the supplier pre-selection as well as the definition of the collaboration process with the suppliers is accomplished jointly between the group center and the business entities. The business entities are responsible for the execution of the multisourcing approach. They focus on operational aspects, like issuing RFPs and signing MBSAs for local adjustments of the contractual framework as well as MPSAs for individual projects. In addition, business entities measure operational performance of multisourcing suppliers and steer them via service-level-agreements (SLAs) and operating-level-agreements (OALs). In order to accomplish a high degree of acceptance and involvement within the business group we suggest that some activities have to be realized jointly. However, we also suggest that the major coordination of the joined activities remains in the group center in order to ensure effectiveness and efficiency.

Nevertheless, this research study also possesses some limitations. One major limitation of this study is that we have only investigated organization A. Although we interviewed thirteen experts, had access to key documents and validated our propositions in a workshop with sourcing experts as well as during follow-up

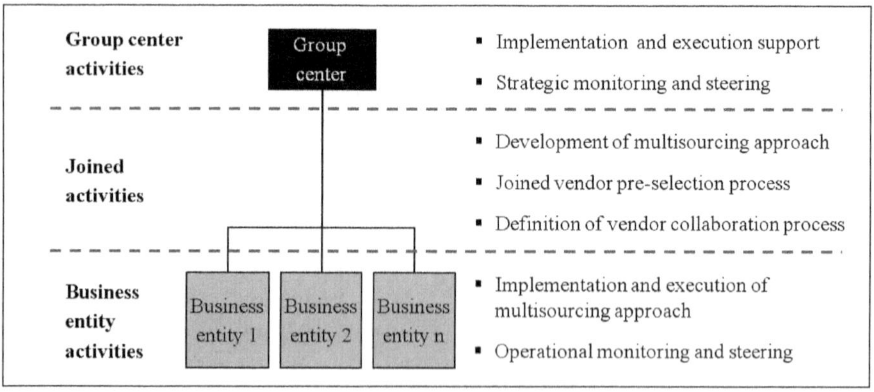

Fig. 5. Suggested split of activities

discussions, a broader sample would help to validate the findings further. Therefore, a multiple case study is planned and will be accomplished over the course of the next months. Another limitation is that the derived propositions are based on the organizational specifics of organization A. Even though the propositions have been generalized to business groups – that are frequently characterized by a federal organizational model – they might not apply to all business groups since the definitions for the term business group diverge.

7 Conclusion and Further Research

Multisourcing has been identified as an emerging key strategy in today‘s IT outsourcing endeavors [2,3,4,5,6,7,8]. However, existing literature provides only limited insights [8] and linear expansion of dyadic IT outsourcing relationships is insufficient to comprehend the nuances of multisourcing [3]. Notably, current literature lacks depth in terms of implementing multisourcing. With this article, we provide an in-depth single case study of a worldwide leading financial services provider and its journey towards multisourcing. Based on a detailed case analysis, we aim to answer the research question:

[RQ] Which mechanisms support the implementation of multisourcing in a business group?

This research study contributes to the body of knowledge in three ways. First, it illustrates and analyzes an extreme and unique case of global multisourcing at a leading financial services provider in a business group context; second, it reveals mechanisms that support the implementation of multisourcing in a business group; and, third, it suggests propositions on governance and sourcing strategy related aspects. In particular, we have observed that the organizational setup of a business group – with the numerous business entities and the federal governance model – determines the multisourcing strategy and we therefore support that "strategy follows structure" in this context. Based on the specifics of a business group we suggest a certain split of activities between the group center and the business entities when implementing multisourcing. Besides the theoretical contribution, this research is also expected to help organizations facing similar challenges.

We seek future research on multisourcing to test the derived propositions. For example, one might study the point of time when multisourcing governance is defined and agreed upon. First expert interviews have shown that a vast number of companies define and agree too late on governance and therefore are likely to fail in their multisourcing endeavors. The question in terms of *how* to implement a sourcing decision [15] requires further research. The present single case study builds the fundament for a multiple case study that we plan to accomplish during the next months in order to investigate governance and management related aspects that are important while implementing multisourcing.

References

1. Mayo, M., Lang, T., Aitchison, D.: The TPI Index - An Informed View of the State of the Global Commercial Outsourcing Market, Fourth Quarter and Full-year of 2009. Technology Partners International, Inc., Houstan (2010)

2. Hakkenberg, M., Himmelreich, H., Ketterer, H., Woelders, F.: Shared KPIs in Multivendor IT Outsourcing. In: BCG (ed.) IT Advantage. The Boston Consulting Group, Boston (2011)
3. Bapna, R., Barua, A., Mani, D., Mehra, A.: Cooperation, Coordination, and Governance in Multisourcing: An Agenda for Analytical and Empirical Research. Information Systems Research 21(4), 785–795 (2010)
4. Cohen, L.R., Young, A.: Multisourcing: Moving Beyond Outsourcing to Achive Growth and Agility. Harvard Business School Press, Bosten (2006)
5. Levina, N., Su, N.: Global Multisourcing Strategy: The Emergence of a Supplier Portfolio in Services Offshoring. Decision Sciences 39(3), 541–570 (2008)
6. Janischowsky, B., Schonenbach, R.: Getting Multisourcing Right! Sovereign Publications, London (2009)
7. Oshri, I., Kotlarsky, J., Rottman, J.W., Willcocks, L.P.: Global sourcing: recent trends and issues. Information Technology and People 22(3), 192–200 (2009)
8. Su, N., Levina, N.: Global Multisourcing Strategy: Integrating Learning from Manufacturing into IT Service Outsourcing. IEEE Transactions on Engineering Management (2011) (forthcoming)
9. Porter, M.E.: Competitive Advantage. Free Press, New York (1985)
10. McMillan, J.: Managing Suppliers: Incentive Systems in Japanese and U.S. Industry. California Management Review 32(4), 38–55 (1990)
11. Richardson, J.: Parallel Sourcing and Supplier Performance in the Japanese Automobile Industry. Strategic Management Journal 14(5), 339–350 (1993)
12. Cross, J.: IT Outsourcing: British Petroleum's Competitive Approach. Harvard Business Review 73(3), 94–102 (1995)
13. Lacity, M.C., Willcocks, L.P.: An Empirical Investigation of Information Technology Sourcing Practices: Lessons from Experience. MIS Quarterly 22(3), 363–408 (1998)
14. Jayatilaka, B.: IT Sourcing a Dynamic Phenomena: Forming an Institutional Theory Perspective. In: Hirschheim, R.A., Heinzl, A., Dibbern, J. (eds.) Information Systems Outsourcing: Enduring Themes, New Perspectives, and Global Challenges, 2nd edn. Springer, Heidelberg (2006)
15. Dibbern, J., Goles, T., Hirschheim, R., Jayatilaka, B.: Information Systems Outsourcing: A Survey and Analysis of the Literature. The DATA BASE for Advances in Information Systems 35(4), 6–102 (2004)
16. Granovetter, M.S.: Business Groups. In: Smelser, N.J., Swedberg, R. (eds.) The Handbook of Economic Sociology. Princton University Press, Princton (1994)
17. Granovetter, M.S.: Coase revisited: Business groups in the modern economy. Industrial and Corporate Change 4(1), 93–130 (1995)
18. Zorn, T., Campbell, N.: Improving the Writing of Literature Reviews Through a Literature Integration Exercise. Business Communication Quarterly 69(2), 172–183 (2006)
19. Charles, R.N.: Multisourcing: Moving Beyond Outsourcing to Achieve Growth and Agility. Journal of Applied Management and Entrepreneurship 11(4), 101 (2006)
20. Treleven, M., Schweikhart, S.B.: A Risk/Benefit Analysis of Sourcing Strategies: Single vs. Multiple Sourcing. Journal of Operations Management 7(4), 93–114 (1988)
21. Cullen, S., Seddon, P.B., Willcocks, L.P.: IT outsourcing configuration: Research into defining and designing outsourcing arrangements. Journal of Strategic Information Systems 14, 357–387 (2005)
22. Carmel, E., Agarwal, R.: The Maturation of Offshore Sourcing of Information Technology Work. MIS Quarterly Executive 1(2), 65–78 (2002)

23. Gallivan, M.J., Oh, W.: Analyzing IT Outsourcing Relationships as Alliances among Multiple Clients and Vendors. In: Proceedings of the 32nd Hawaii International Conference on System Sciences, Hawaii (1999)
24. Currie, W.L.: Using multiple suppliers to mitigate risks of IT outsourcing in two UK companies: ICI and Wessex Water. Journal of Information Technology 13(3), 169–180 (1998)
25. Currie, W.L., Willcocks, L.P.: Analysing four types of IT sourcing decisions in the context of scale, client/supplier interdependency and risk mitigation. Information Systems Journal 8(2), 119–143 (1998)
26. Oshri, I.: Offshoring Strategies: Evolving Captive Center Models. The MIT Press, Cambridge (2011)
27. Leff, N.H.: Industrial Organization and Entrepreneurship in Developing-Countries - Economic Groups. Economic Development and Cultural Change 26(4), 661–675 (1978)
28. Smangs, M.: The Nature of the Business Group: A Social Network Perspective. Organization 13(6), 889–909 (2006)
29. Nicodano, G.: Corporate groups, dual-class shares and the value of voting rights. Journal of Banking and Finance 22(9), 1117–1137 (1998)
30. Guillen, M.F.: Business Groups in Emerging Economies: A Resource-Based View. The Academy of Management Journal 43(3), 362–380 (2000)
31. Gerlach, M.L.: Alliance Capitalism. The Social Organization of Japanese Business. University of California Press, Berkeley (1992)
32. Peters, T.J., Waterman, R.H.: In search of excellence: lessons from America's best-run companies. Harper Business Essentials, New York (2004)
33. Obermeier, G.: Shareholder Value-Oriented Management in the Light of Gutenberg's Theories. In: Albach, H., Brockhoff, K., Eymann, E., Jungen, P., Steven, M., Luhner, A. (eds.) Theory of the Firm: Erich Gutenberg's Foundations and Further Developments. Springer, Berlin (2000)
34. Janssen, M., Joha, A.: Motives for establishing shared service centers in public administration. International Journal of Information Management 6(2), 102–115 (2006)
35. Goold, M., Campbell, A.: Strategies and styles: The role of the centre in managing diversified corporations. Blackwell, Oxford (1987)
36. Zmud, R.W., Boynton, A.C., Jacobs, G.C.: The information economy: A new perspective for effective information systems management. DATABASE 18(1), 17–23 (1986)
37. Weill, P., Ross, J.W.: IT Governance: How top performers manage IT decision rights for superior results. Harvard Business Press, Boston (2004)
38. Hodgkinson, S.L.: The Role of the Corporate IT Function in the Federal IT Organization. In: Earl, M.J. (ed.) Information Management: The Organizational Dimension. Oxford University Press, Oxford (1996)
39. Sambamurthy, V., Zmud, R.W.: Arrangements for Information Technology Governance: A Theory of Multiple Contingencies. MIS Quarterly 23(2), 261–291 (1999)
40. Weill, P.: Dont Just Lead, Govern: How Top-Performing Firms Govern IT. MIS Quarterly Executive 8(1), 1–21 (2004)
41. Handy, C.: Balancing corporate power: A new federalist paper. Harvard Business Review 70(6), 59–72 (1992)
42. Lacity, M.C., Willcocks, L.P.: Global Information Technology Outsourcing: In Search of Business Advantage. Wiley, Chichester (2001)

43. Clark, T.D., Zmud, R.W., McCray, G.E.: The outsourcing of information services: transforming the nature of business in the information industry. Journal of Information Technology 10(4), 221–237 (1995)
44. McFarlan, F.W., Nolan, R.L.: How to Manage an IT Outsourcing Alliance. Sloan Management Review 36(2), 9–23 (1995)
45. Davis, K.J.: IT Outsourcing Relationships: An Exploratory Study of Interorganizational Control Mechanism. Harvard University, Boston (1996)
46. Peterson, R.R.: Information Strategies and Tactics for Information Technology Governance. In: Van Grembergen, W. (ed.) Strategies for Information Technology Governance. Idea Group Publishing, Hershey (2004)
47. Weill, P., Ross, J.W.: A Matrixed Approach to Designing IT Governance. MIT Sloan Management Review 46(2), 25–34 (2005)
48. Yin, R.K.: Case Study Research: Design and Methods. Sage, London (2003)
49. Benbasat, I., Goldstein, D.K., Mead, M.: The Case Research Strategy in Studies of Information-Systems. MIS Quarterly 11(3), 369–386 (1987)
50. Palvia, P., Pinjani, P., Sibley, E.H.: A profile of information systems research published in Information and Management. Information and Management 44(1), 1–11 (2007)
51. Eisenhardt, K.M.: Building Theories from Case-Study Research. Academy of Management Review 14(4), 532–550 (1989)
52. Eisenhardt, K.M.: Better Stories and Better Constructs - the Case for Rigor and Comparative Logic. Academy of Management Review 16(3), 620–627 (1991)
53. Eisenhardt, K.M., Graebner, M.E.: Theory building from cases: Opportunities and challenges. Academy of Management Journal 50(1), 25–32 (2007)
54. Golden-Biddle, K., Locke, K.: Composing qualitative research. Sage, Thousand Oaks (2007)
55. Glaser, B.G., Strauss, A.L.: The Discovery of Grounded Theory: Strategies for Qualitative Research. Aldine Publishing Company, Chicago (1967)
56. Corbin, J.M., Strauss, A.L.: Grounded Theory Research: Procedures, Canons and Evaluative Criteria. Qualitative Sociology 13(1), 3–21 (1990)
57. Brusoni, S., Prencipe, A.: Making design rules: A multidomain perspective. Organization Science 17(2), 179–189 (2006)
58. Denzin, N.: The research act: A theoretical introduction to sociological methods. Transaction Publishers, Piscataway (2009)
59. Michell, V., Fitzgerald, G.: The IT outsourcing market-place: vendors and their selection. Journal of Information Technology 12(3), 223–237 (1997)
60. Willcocks, L.P., Lacity, M.C., Kern, T.: Risk mitigation in IT outsourcing strategy revisited. The Journal of Strategic Information Systems 8(3), 285–314 (1999)
61. Karamouzis, F.: How to Use a Vendor Evaluation Model to Standardize IT Services Provider Selections. Gartner Research, Stamford (2008)
62. Bergeron, B.P.: Essentials of shared services. Wiley, Hoboken (2003)
63. Peters, T.J.: Strategy follows structure: Developing Distinctive Skills. California Management Review 26(3), 114–128 (1984)
64. Grant, R.M.: Contemporary Strategy Analysis, 7th edn. John Wiley and Sons, Chichester (2009)
65. Whittington, R., Pettigrew, A., Peck, S., Fenton, E., Conyon, M.: Change and Complementarities in the New Competitive Landscape: A European Panel Study, 1992-1996. Organization Science 10(5), 583–600 (1999)

Assuring Compliance in IT Subcontracting and Cloud Computing

Gerhard F. Knolmayer and Petra Asprion

Institute of Information Systems, University of Bern
Engehaldenstrasse 8, CH 3012 Bern, Switzerland
{gerhard.knolmayer,petra.asprion}@iwi.unibe.ch

Abstract. Companies and their business processes are subject to many regulations. Today's business processes are widely supported by IT systems. Therefore these systems play an important role in assuring compliance. The need to assure compliance can influence IT outsourcing decisions. We summarize some frameworks that give recommendations on assuring compliance of outsourced activities.

For a service provider with many globally acting customers similar audit activities of many auditors would be time-consuming and expensive. To avoid these costs, the American Institute of Certified Public Accountants (AICPA) suggested that an auditor may provide a SAS 70 Audit Report Type II which confirms the existence and effectiveness of internal controls. Recently, the AICPA replaced the SAS 70 with the attestation standard SSAE 16. Based on frameworks and guidelines we discuss compliance issues in special cases of outsourcing relationships such as Subcontracting and Cloud Computing.

Keywords: Outsourcing, Compliance, Frameworks, Audit, Subcontracting, Cloud Computing.

1 Introduction

Companies and their business processes are subject to many regulations. For instance, Lickel [1] claims that from 1981 to 2006 more than 118,000 regulations have been introduced in the United States. Hurley [2] states that organizations spend an average of 34 percent of their IT resources on activities devoted to satisfying compliance for multiple regulations.

Compliance requirements may be based both on external regulations and on internal policies and rules. In recent years misbehavior of companies and their managers resulted in new, restrictive law (e.g., the Sarbanes-Oxley Act (SOX)) and the world-wide problems recently created by the financial industry will lead to tightened regulations (e.g., Basel III replacing Basel II). The board of directors has the final responsibility for Corporate Governance and, therefore, also for IT Governance and Sourcing Governance (cf. [3]). The associated activities will typically be delegated, e.g., to legal and compliance departments and internal control groups. Several frameworks, guidelines, and audit standards are concerned with governance issues.

J. Kotlarsky, L.P. Willcocks, and I. Oshri (Eds.): Global Sourcing 2011, LNBIP 91, pp. 21–45, 2011.

Ensuring compliance for outsourced manufacturing operations is discussed, e.g., for the pharmaceutical industry [4][5]. Market research shows that reporting associated with HR transactions and processes is one of the most heavily outsourced tasks although more than half of all outsourced HR transactions involve regulatory and compliance services [6]. The Economist Intelligence Unit [7] stated that 44% of companies answering its survey in 2005 did not outsource any compliance-relevant IT activities. On the other hand, 29% of the respondents indicated that they outsourced more than 10% of these tasks. More than 80% of the respondents surveyed in Germany agreed that compliance issues are relevant in outsourcing decisions [8]. Poor governance has been identified as a main reason leading to insufficient results of outsourcing relationships [9]. Thus, governance and compliance issues are highly relevant in outsourcing relationships and in decisions about outsourcing and should therefore attract more interest of the IT community. Steps in this direction are made, e.g., in [10][11][12][13][14].

In the remainder of this paper we assume that a company has outsourced a part of its compliance-relevant IT tasks. After describing frameworks and "standards" developed to govern the assurance of compliance in outsourcing relationships we analyze two special outsourcing situations and their impact on assuring compliance: Service chains resulting from subcontracting and Cloud Computing. We finally discuss industry economic aspects of new and tightened regulations.

2 The Role of IT Systems in Assuring Compliance

Today's business processes are widely supported by IT systems. Therefore these systems play an important role in assuring compliance with regulations and business rules.

Many IT systems, and in particular powerful ERP systems, can provide some evidence about the compliance of the underlying or supported business processes [15]. The observance of most compliance requirements can be audited by referring to IT controls. The types and numbers of active IT controls can often be chosen during system implementation or in subsequent improvement activities.

The widely recognized IT Governance framework COBIT [16] distinguishes between IT General Controls and IT Application Controls. General Controls relate to the environment within which application systems are developed, maintained, and operated, and which are therefore applicable to all IT systems used in a company. Application Controls are a set of automated, embedded controls in an application; in particular, powerful ERP systems provide a large number of embedded application controls. Data delivered by Application Controls can be used in assuring the compliance of the underlying business processes as long as the trustworthiness of the IT system is assured by the General Controls. Recently, specialized Governance, Risk Management, and Compliance (GRC) systems appeared in the market to provide controls beyond those offered by ERP systems; examples are enhanced or new options for defining Access Controls, Process Controls, and Risk Management Processes.

Adjusting IT systems to new regulations means that additional IT General and/or Application Controls have to be implemented. This may have wide implications for IT staff and IT costs (cf. [17][18][19]). In extreme cases the costs of tightened country-specific regulations can lead to abandoning activities and services in these countries.

3 Assuring Compliance of Outsourced Tasks

When deciding between in-house and external fulfillment of IT tasks, companies may be restricted by regulations which forbid all forms of outsourcing, outsourcing to foreign Service Organizations (offshoring, nearshoring), or outsourcing which would imply a data transfer to a certain set of foreign countries.

With respect to the SOX requirements the Public Company Accounting Oversight Board (which was founded as a consequence of introducing the SOX), stated in its Auditing Standard No 2 that the "... use of a Service Organization does not reduce management's responsibility to maintain effective internal control over financial reporting" [20]; this standard has been updated but the citation is still the prevalent opinion.

Several roles have to be distinguished in the process of assuring compliance of outsourced tasks. These roles are typically described as follows:

- The *User Entity* uses a Service Organization. It has direct relationships with a Service Organization and a User Auditor who audits its financial statements.
- The *User Auditor* audits and reports on the financial statements of the User Entity. He is in a direct relationship with the User Entity.
- The *Service Organization* is a third-party organization (or a segment of it) that provides IT services to User Entities. We assume that these services are relevant to financial reporting of the User Entities. The policies and procedures designed, implemented, and maintained by the Service Organization may be covered by a Service Auditor's report. The Service Organization has a direct relationship with its customers (the User Entities) and its Service Auditor.
- The *Service Auditor* is an auditor who, at the request of the Service Organization, provides an assurance report on the controls of a Service Organization. He has a direct relationship with the Service Organization, whose controls are subject of his assurance or audit statement.

The International Standard on Auditing (ISA) 402, titled "Audit Considerations Relating to Entities Using Service Organizations," determines that the User Auditor is responsible for auditing the whole system, thus also for outsourced parts of the system. If the User Entity receives compliance-relevant services from a Service Organization, the User Auditor should obtain an sufficient understanding of the significance of the services provided by the Service Organization and their effect on the User Entity's internal control. The results are relevant for the identification and assessment of risks related to material misstatements (cf. [21]).

The User Auditor has several options to judge whether the outsourced tasks are fulfilled in a compliant way. He may

- obtain a sufficient understanding of the services provided by the Service Organization and the effect on the User Entity's internal control to achieve a basis for assessing risks of material misstatements,
- contact the Service Organization via the User Entity to obtain specific information,
- visit the Service Organization and perform procedures to provide the necessary information about the relevant controls at the Service Organization,
- use another auditor for performing the above mentioned procedures, and
- obtain a contemporary report from a Service Auditor with professional competence and independence from the Service Organization ([cf. [22]).

The last option seems to be most relevant in business practice (cf. [23]). Professional auditing organizations have defined different types of documents for reporting results of audits at Service Organizations (cf. Section 4.3). Figure 1 shows legal and communication relationships which result from outsourcing compliance-relevant tasks and also the sequence in which these tasks may be executed (cf. [12]). Furthermore we assume that Internal Audit functions exist in both the User Entity and the Service Organization. The audit scope will usually be communicated via the User Entity but could also be communicated directly by the User Auditor. The Service Organization will typically receive different requirements from their customers and try to define a union of these sets in the mandate of the Service Auditor. Thus, the scope of the audit is determined by the auditee. The types of reports mentioned in Figure 1 and their differences are discussed in Section 4.3. The information flowing on arcs ④, ⑤, and ⑥ is identical if the User Entity has no specific requirements beyond those covered in the common mandate. Direct communication between the User Auditor and the Service Auditor may be the exception but is allowed.

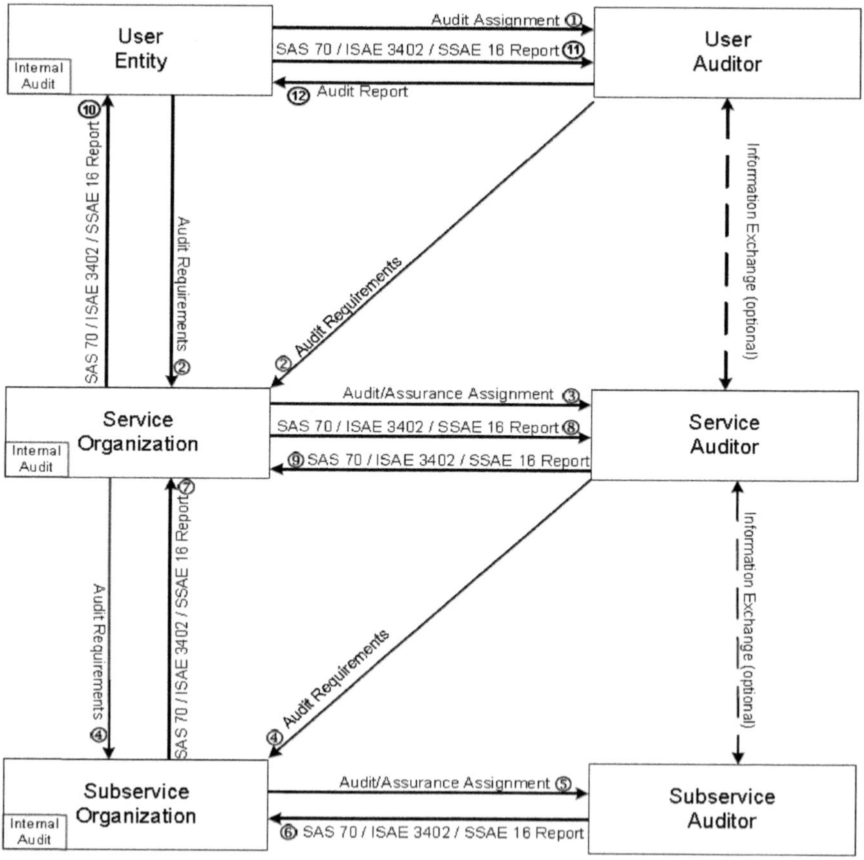

Fig. 1. Compliance-related Communication between User Entities, Service Organizations, and their Auditors

If the User Auditor refers to the report of a Service Auditor, he has to evaluate the professional competence and independence of the auditor and the adequacy of standards applied when issuing the report [22].

It is often argued that one of the advantages of outsourcing results from the arrangement that the User Entity defines *what* to achieve and the Service Organization is allowed to decide *how* it will achieve these requirements. Such an arrangement allows the Service Organization to rely on its expertise and on processes realized for other customers, resulting in economies of scale. However, if compliance-relevant tasks are outsourced, the Service Organization may have to realize certain (e.g., company- or industry-specific) process steps without being free to choose its favorite way of performing the task. Such obligations have to be defined in the outsourcing contract and if new or tightened regulations can only be fulfilled by changing IT processes, this may result in cost-intense contractual supplements and work.

Outsourcing contracts typically contain audit clauses [23] and sometimes also "compliance with law" clauses [18]. The latter clause, however, typically does not imply that the Service Organization has to cover the costs of changing IT systems to respect regulatory changes because the extent of these changes cannot be anticipated and the Service Organization would have to calculate a high risk premium to accept such a clause.

4 Relevant Frameworks, Guidelines, and Standards

Control and monitoring frameworks are considered as a critical element for a healthy outsourcing governance structure [9]. Some regulations, e.g. SOX, explicitly demand the application and declaration of appropriate frameworks. In this section we give a brief overview of selected frameworks that are relevant for assuring compliance especially in IT outsourcing scenarios.

Many frameworks cover compliance-relevant controls and procedures but two emerged as fundamental and have been adopted by many companies: The "Internal Control - Integrated Framework" (COSO report), defined in 1992 by the Committee of Sponsoring Organizations of the Treadway Commission [24], and the "Control Objectives for Information and related Technologies" (COBIT), first published in 1995 and currently at release 4.1, developed and published by the Information Systems Audit and Control Association (ISACA) and its IT Governance Institute (ITGI) [16].

The importance of the COSO report increased significantly due to the provisions of the SOX and similar legislation in other countries. It is a generic framework focusing on controls for financial related processes without considering the implications for IT processes. COBIT is a generic framework based on an IT related process model which has been mapped to the elements of the COSO report. In addition, for important regulations, such as SOX or Basel II, specific COBIT-based guidelines exist [25][26]. Other IT process frameworks or standards such as the IT Infrastructure Library (ITIL) or the ISO/IEC 27000-series may also be useful in fulfilling compliance requirements. For example, ISO/IEC 27002 helps to define *what* should be done and ITIL focuses on *how* service management should be practiced [27]. Both ITIL and ISO/IEC 27002 can be understood as more operational complements to COBIT. We therefore describe IT outsourcing relevant elements of COBIT. However, in practical cases the frameworks may not provide enough guidance to design and implement governance structures [13].

4.1 COBIT

One benefit of COBIT is the mapping to COSO and, thus, the link to the business control requirements. COBIT encompasses 34 IT processes and 318 control objectives. Each control objective defines the result to be achieved and provides a set of high-level requirements to be considered by management for effective control. ISACA [28] selects 4 of the 34 COBIT processes which are closely related to IT outsourcing; they are described in the following.

"**DS2 - Manage Third-party Services**" focuses on the management of the customer/supplier relationship. DS2 control is achieved by identifying and categorizing supplier services, identifying and mitigating supplier risk, and by monitoring and measuring supplier performance. In more detail, four control objectives should be achieved:

"DS2.1 - Identification of All Supplier Relationships": Identify and categorize all supplier services, to maintain formal documentation of technical and organizational relationships, incl. roles, responsibilities, goals, deliverables, and credentials of representatives of these suppliers.

"DS2.2 - Supplier Relationship Management": Formalize the supplier relationship management process for each supplier (e.g., through SLA).

"DS2.3 - Supplier Risk Management": Identify and mitigate risks relating to suppliers' abilities to continue effective service delivery in a secure and efficient manner on a continual basis.

"DS2.4 - Supplier Performance Monitoring": Establish a process to monitor service delivery to ensure that the supplier is meeting current business requirements and continuing to adhere to the contract agreements and SLA.

"DS1 - Define and Manage Service Levels" addresses Service Level Agreements (SLA), both for in-house and outsourced environments. The following control objectives are relevant:

"DS1.3 - Service level agreements": Define and agree to SLA for critical IT services (e.g., customer commitments, service support requirements, quantitative and qualitative metrics for measuring the services, funding and commercial arrangements).

"DS1.4 - Operating level agreements": These agreements define how the services will be technically delivered to support the SLA (e.g., specification of technical processes).

"DS1.5 - Monitoring and reporting of service level achievements": Monitor and report performance criteria.

"DS1.6 - Review of service level agreements and contracts": Review SLA and underpinning contracts with internal and external service providers to ensure that they are effective and that changes in requirements have been taken into account.

"ME2 - Monitor and Evaluate Internal Control" focuses on monitoring and evaluating internal control activities. In our context the following control objectives are important:

"ME2.5 - Assurance of internal control": Obtain, as needed, further assurance of the completeness and effectiveness of internal controls through third-party reviews.

"ME2.6 - Internal control at third parties": Assess the status of external service providers' internal controls. Confirm that external service providers comply with legal and regulatory requirements and contractual obligations.

The fourth process selected by ISACA [28] is titled

"ME3 - Ensure Compliance with External Requirements"; control objectives such as *"ME3.3 - Evaluation of compliance with regulatory requirements"* are relevant as well for internal and external service provision and are therefore not considered here.

COBIT also defines a maturity model: Each COBIT process can be characterized by a maturity level between 0 (non-existent) and 5 (optimized). The maturity models allow to define to-be maturity levels, to measure as-is values, and to determine gaps between them. Figure 2 shows a graphical representation of these gaps which indicates a potential for improving controls.

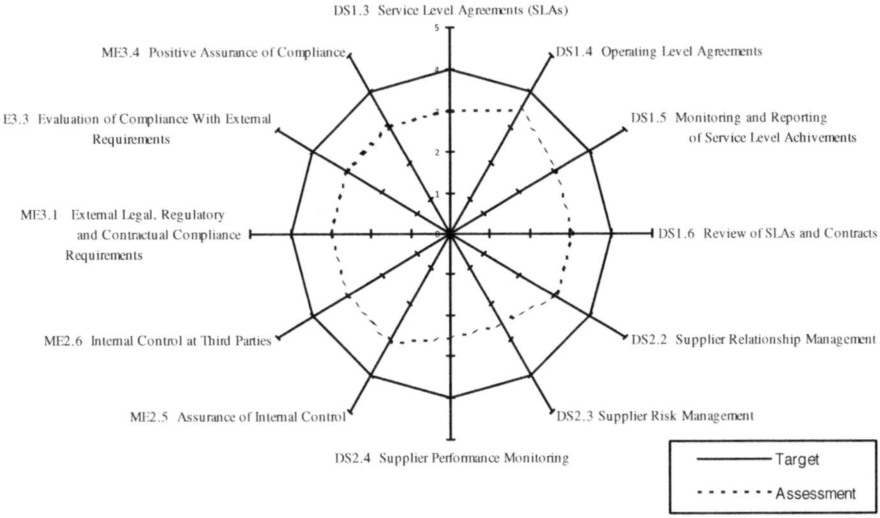

Fig. 2. Kiviat Graph for Maturity of Achieving IT Outsourcing Control Objectives [28]

4.2 BITS Framework for Managing Technology Risk for Service Provider Relationships

Less well-known than COBIT is the BITS Framework for Managing Technology Risk for IT Service Providers Relationships. The framework is developed by the IT Service Providers Working Group, a US-based financial service industry consortium. In BITS, the User Entity is named Receiver Company and the Service Organization is called Service Provider. The Receiver Company should evaluate its governance structure to determine the effect of coordinating with and overseeing a Service Provider, including identification of any relevant regulatory requirements. We summarize some of the recommendations [29]:

- The Service Provider should have a documented process in place to ensure accountability and compliance with the goals and objectives of the Receiver Company. The Service Provider's governance program should be audited regularly and the results should be monitored and signed by its senior executives. Also, the Service Provider should ensure that federal and state regulations are met and managed as they apply to their customers.
- It should also be verified that a specific group or individual at the Service Provider is responsible for monitoring the company's compliance with the objectives of the Receiver Company and with all applicable federal and state regulations. Testing should validate regulatory compliance and all test results should be reported to the Receiver Company's compliance group or to an appropriate individual.
- The Service Provider should have a process in place to identify and assess new control exposures resulting from a change. His test objectives and conclusions should be verified. The change-control records, the test results, and the audit results should be reviewed.
- Procedures for maintaining system integrity and recovery, for data retention, for data backup, and offsite storage should be validated.
- With respect to off- or nearshoring, BITS recommends that the Receiver Company should evaluate its governance structure to determine the effect of coordinating with and overseeing a Service Provider located outside of the United States, including identifying any relevant regulatory requirements.
- Statements documenting compliance with applicable government regulations are required.

BITS developed a Shared Assessment Program which provides Receiver Companies and their Service Providers a means for meeting internal and external compliance and audit requirements. Based on ISO 27001, twelve domains of information security management provide the foundation for two tools which are designed to document the Service Provider's management of information security controls. The document about„ Agreed Upon Procedures" (AUP) provides objectives and consistent procedures that can be performed during an onsite assessment. The AUP document should be completed by either an assessment firm or an audit firm and the results should be made accessible to the Service Provider who may share these reports with his clients.

BITS also developed a Standardized Information Gathering (SIG) Questionnaire. When SIG and AUP are completed, recipients have evidence whether or not the required controls exist and, if so, whether they are able to identify risks, comply with regulatory requirements, and reduce inconsistencies in evaluating the information they receive from their Service Providers [29][30].

In summary, BITS looks at the outsourcing relationship from the viewpoint of User Entities and emphasizes the responsibilities of Service Organizations.

4.3 AICPA Standards Related to Outsourcing

4.3.1 SAS 70

The AICPA developed and published the Statement on Auditing Standards (SAS) No. 70, Service Organizations, already in 1992 and codified it as AU 324 [31]. There are two types of SAS 70 audits: A Type I audit simply states that policies and procedures exist, although it was not audited whether the organization adheres to them. For asserting compliance, a SAS 70 Report Type II is more relevant, covering also whether the controls were operating with adequate effectiveness to provide reasonable assurance that the control objectives were achieved. Such a report confirms that a Service Organization has been through an in-depth audit of their control objectives and control activities, which often include controls over IT systems technology and related processes. In analogy to COSO reports, SAS 70 Audit Reports experienced a renaissance because SOX increased the importance of evaluating the effectiveness of internal control over financial reporting.

The usefulness of SAS 70 Audit Reports is restricted because there is no well defined set of control objectives or control activities that Service Organizations must achieve [29]; the report makes statements solely about issues formulated by the management of the Service Organization [32].

A Type II SAS 70 Audit Report may be quite lengthy and cover a broad spectrum of issues. For instance, some years ago NaviSite, a Service Organization, published the structure of its SAS 70 Report on its Web site [http://www.navisite.com/], explaining 35 items in the following areas:

- Physical Security
- Logical Authentication and Access
- Security Monitoring
- Systems Implementation
- Systems Enhancements and Maintenance
- Problem Management, and
- System Backup.

A SAS 70 report is intended as an auditor-to-auditor communication, designed to provide User Auditors with detailed information about controls implemented at a Service Organization. The User Auditor receives detailed information to determine how the Service Organization's system generates information and how the Service Organization interacts with the User Entity's financial reporting system. The report is not intended as a certification or a marketing instrument addressing the general public, but a Web search shows that quite a few companies use it in this way.

The User Auditor will examine a SAS 70 Report with respect to the following aspects (cf. [33]):

- Is it dated during the User Entity's fiscal year under audit, preferably close to the end of the fiscal year?
- Does it address all control objectives that are critical to the User Entity's financial statements? If the report does not have the right scope, the User Auditor may still have to perform evaluations and testing at the Service Organization.
- Does it identify specific controls that the Service Organization expects the User Organization to perform? For example, the Service Organization may not have control over access to information systems within the User Entity that might impact the services provided. In such a case, the SAS 70 Report might state that the Service Organization expects the User Entity to control access to those information systems. The User Entity should review these expectations and consider their impact on its organization.

The SAS 70 has been established already in 1992. In the meantime its appropriateness with respect to technical and organizational innovations has been critically discussed (cf. [12][34]).

4.3.2 ISAE 3402, SSAE 16, and ISA 402

The International Auditing and Assurance Standards Board (IAASB) is responsible for establishing auditing and assurance standards within the International Federation of Accountants (IFAC). 125 IFAC member countries consider adopting new IAASB standards in accordance. The IIASB and the Auditing Standards Board (ASB) of the AICPA recently replaced the well established but aging SAS 70 by a Service Auditor Standard and a User Auditor Standard. It seems that these standards were provided rather surprisingly; in March 2010 the Gartner Group [35] assumed that SAS 70 may need 2 to 5 years to mainstream adoption and forecast that it is highly unlikely that an accounting or regulatory body will issue a new standard to replace SAS 70.

For Service Auditors two similar attestation standards have been defined:

- The "International Standard on Assurance Engagements No. 3402" (ISAE 3402), titled "Assurance Reports on Controls at a Service Organization" and accepted by the IIASB, and,
- in the US, the "Statement on Standards for Attestation Engagements 16" (SSAE 16), titled "Reporting on Controls at a Service Organization", adopted by the ASB.

The new standards for Service Auditors have similarities with and differences to SAS 70; Tables 1 and 2 present a compressed summary, based on [36][37][38], and [39].

Table 1. Main similarities between SAS 70, SSAE 16, and ISAE 3402 (cf. [36][37][38][39])

<table>
<tr><th></th><th>SAS 70</th><th>SSAE 16</th><th>ISAE 3402</th></tr>
<tr><td rowspan="2">Description of Controls and/or Systems</td><td colspan="3">The Service Auditor's report must contain a description of control objectives and related controls, including complementary user controls.</td></tr>
<tr><td colspan="3">The Service Auditor's report must contain aspects of the Service Organization's control environment, risk assessment process, information and communications systems, control activities, and monitoring controls (COSO Internal Control Framework).</td></tr>
<tr><td rowspan="2">Service Auditor's Reports</td><td colspan="3">Type I and Type II reports can be issued by Service Auditors and services provided by subservice organizations may be included (inclusive method) or excluded (carve-out method).</td></tr>
<tr><td colspan="3">Service auditor reports
▪ are not applicable to examinations of controls over matters other than financial reporting,
▪ do not represent a "certification" of any kind and should be used primarily as an auditor-to-auditor communication tool,
▪ are restricted for the Service Organization, User Entities, and User Auditors.</td></tr>
</table>

Table 2. Main differences between SAS 70, SSAE 16, and ISAE 3402 (cf. [36][37][38][39])

<table>
<tr><th></th><th>SAS 70</th><th>SSAE 16</th><th>ISAE 3402</th></tr>
<tr><td>Nature of the Standard</td><td>AICPA Audit Standard</td><td>AICPA Attestation Standard</td><td>International Assurance Standard</td></tr>
<tr><td rowspan="2">Written Assertions</td><td>A written assertion by management is not required.</td><td colspan="2">A written assertion by management is required and must include the suitable criteria used for its assessment.</td></tr>
<tr><td>For Service Organizations using subservice organizations and if the inclusive method is used, the audit report does not require an assertion by a subservice organization.</td><td colspan="2">For Service Organizations that use subservice organizations and the inclusive method, the audit report must include a written assertion by the subservice organization. The written assertions have to contain the following descriptions:<ul><li>The design and implementation of the relevant systems</li><li>The design of the controls to achieve the control objectives</li><li>A statement that the controls operated effectively to achieve the control objectives.</li></ul></td></tr>
<tr><td>Description of Controls and/or Systems</td><td>The Service Organization must provide a description of controls.</td><td colspan="2">The Service Organization must provide a description of its systems and controls as designed and implemented. Important elements are:<ul><li>The types of services provided,</li><li>the procedures by which the services are provided,</li><li>the related accounting records,</li><li>the process used to prepare reports,</li><li>the specified control objectives and activities designed to achieve these objectives.</li></ul></td></tr>
<tr><td>Service Auditor's Reports of Type II</td><td>The opinion on fair presentation of the system and suitability of design is as of a point in time.</td><td colspan="2">The auditor´s opinions (and management assertions) on fairness of presentation, suitability of design, and operating effectiveness of the controls refer to the entire reporting period covered (and not only for a point of time).</td></tr>
<tr><td>Intentional Acts by Service Organization Personnel</td><td colspan="2">Requires an assessment of the risk and impact on the report.</td><td>Assessment of the risk and impact on the report are not required.</td></tr>
<tr><td>Sampling Deviations</td><td colspan="2">All deviations should be considered consistently.</td><td>Under certain circumstances deviations can be treated as anomalies.</td></tr>
<tr><td>Internal Audit</td><td>Permits the use of the Internal Audit function but does not require disclosure of the work performed by the Internal Audit function or testing performed on that work by the Service Auditor.</td><td>Explicitly discusses the use of the Internal Audit function and requires the Service Auditor to describe the work performed by the Internal Audit function and procedures used to test that work.</td><td>Does not specifically discuss the use of the Internal Audit function, but separate "audits" performed by Internal Audit that are relevant to the Service Auditor's activities can be relied upon.</td></tr>
</table>

Table 2. (*continued*) Main differences between SAS 70, SSAE 16, and ISAE 3402

	SAS 70	SSAE 16	ISAE 3402
Subsequent Events	Must disclose subsequent events that occurred after the period covered by the Service Auditor's report but before the date of the Service Auditor's report.	Must disclose events that take place (1) after the period of the audit but before the date of the Service Auditor's report (2) following the date of the Service Auditor's report.	Must disclose only events that take place after the period of the audit but before the date of the Service Auditor's report.
	Requires disclosure of subsequent events that would have a significant effect on User Organizations.	Requires disclosure of subsequent events if User Organizations would otherwise be misled.	Requires disclosure of subsequent events that have a significant effect on the report.

Ernst & Young [40] expect that the new management sign-off may require additional activities of Service Organizations, e.g., more adequate descriptions of the processes and controls they operate for User Entities, more adequate risk analysis of those processes, so management can attest whether the controls address these risks sufficiently, and additional effort for management to assess whether the controls operated effectively.

Bierce and Kenerson [41] argue that the change from SAS 70 to ISAE 3402 / SSAE 16 reports reduces the professional liability of auditors from high-value, high-risk audits to an attest function. In such a function, the auditor does not examine all material processes and functions, but merely relies upon the Service Organization's assertion that its control system works. The SSAE 16 report removes a layer of comfort for User Entities since Service Auditors will be less critical than in a SAS 70 report. From this point of view it seems that the AICPA has changed the procedures to become more auditor-friendly.

The AICPA is also developing a new Service Organization Controls (SOC) guide, Reporting on Controls at a Service Provider Relevant to Security, Availability, Processing Integrity, Confidentiality, or Privacy, that addresses reporting on a Service Organization's controls over subject matter other than financial reporting. The publication of this guide is expected for 2011 and the associated report will be far broader than those discussed in this section.

4.4 Managing Assurance, Security and Trust for Services (MASTER)

In this large EU Project a set of methodologies and tools was developed to facilitate the implementation of quantifiable indicators aimed at assessing the level of control of IT systems underlying these business processes through continuous control monitoring. MASTER wants to improve audits and reports as follows:

- Instead of yearly manual audit procedures, MASTER aims at ongoing real-time security information throughout the entire year.
- MASTER recommends an automated approach that assesses the level of compliance and security of business processes through the analysis of communications and provides detailed indicators that deliver a level of information concerning control weaknesses far beyond those gained by manual audit procedures.
- MASTER aims to provide additional information to Service Auditors who should be able to do their work more efficiently and with less audit fees.
- The staff of the Service Organization will have less effort in preparing information requested by the Service Auditor [42].

MASTER reflects technical properties of the IT systems in more detail than other frameworks and standards, e.g., assuming that the target IT systems are based on a Service-oriented Architecture. Protection Level Agreements are proposed to state the level of assurance clearly. Three compliance and security indicators are suggested:

- The Key Assurance Indicator measures the level of compliance of business process with regards to the traces of events accessing the business process.
- The Key Security Indicator measures the level of correctness of the control process protecting the business process.
- The Key Security Indicator measures the level of coverage of the control process protecting the business process [42][43][44].

4.5 Framework for Outsourced Global Software Development

Recently, the Sherwood Applied Business Security Architecture (SABSA), based on a 6x6 matrix, was combined with elements from COSO, ISO 20000, and ISO 27001 to develop a Risk and Compliance Management Framework for outsourced global software development [45]. The framework distinguishes between Risk Management at business level, operational level, and project level, and is divided in four phases:

- Strategic Phase, owned by the User Entity,
- Implementation Phase, owned by the Service Organization,
- Change and Configuration Management Phase, shared by both organizations,
- and Monitoring and Auditing Phase, owned by the User Entity (cf. [45]).

5 Assuring Compliance in Subcontracting Relationships

Subcontracting is a highly relevant phenomenon, among others because of specialization and manpower shortages, but often neglected in outsourcing research. Outsourcing contracts may specify whether the Service Organization has the right to outsource the full task or parts of it to a "Subservice Organization", a subcontractor. Such a transfer results in a chain of service providers. If a Subservice Organization is involved, one has to distinguish whether or not the delegated parts of a task are compliance-relevant.

In case of compliance-relevant subcontracting, the AICPA distinguishes between the Carve-Out and the Inclusive Method. It is recommended to

- explore the compliance intentions of subcontractors,
- determine what type of controls reports they issue,
- discuss the type of "description" they will issue to Service Auditors,
- identify whether the "carve-out" or the "inclusive" method will be used,
- consider how this will influence the compliance efforts of the Service Organization, and determine the needs of the User Entities (cf. [41]).

(1) The Carve-Out Method

The Subservice Organization's relevant control objectives and controls are excluded from the scope of the Service Auditor's engagement. The Service Organization states that the Subservice Organization's control objectives and related controls are omitted from the description and that the control objectives in the report include only the objectives the Service Organization's controls are intended to achieve.

It is surprising that AICPA [46] interprets that a disclosure of the identity of the Subservice Organization is not required. AICPA even states that the name of the Subservice Organization may (!) be included in the description given to the Service Auditor, if the identity of the Subservice Organization is relevant to User Entities.

The Carve-out Method may not seem plausible if the report is intended for only one User Entity. However, SAS 70 and ISAE 3402 / SSAE 16 reports typically address several User Entities and User Auditors and outsourcing to a Subservice Organization may only be realized for a subset of the Service Organization's customers. In this case, information about a subcontractor could be confusing in a report which addresses all User Entities and, thus, also those not involved in subcontracting.

Carve-out does not mean that the auditor can neglect the controls at a Subservice Organization, but that there should be controls in place to monitor the effectiveness of the controls at the Subservice Organization. The most typical way to address this is to obtain a SAS 70 resp. ISAE 3402 / SSAE 16 report from the Subservice Organization.

If the User Auditor plans to use a report which excludes the services provided by a Subservice Organization and those services are relevant to the audit of the User Entity's financial statements, the User Auditor has to apply the requirements of ISA 402 to the services provided by the Subservice Organization [22]. Thus, the User Auditor may be obligated to attest the compliance of a subcontractor directly. This may be difficult if he is unfamiliar with the controls of the Tier 1 Service Organization.

Most Service Auditors use the Carve-Out Method when Subservice Organizations are compliance relevant and their reports disclaims the role of the Subservice Organization. It is easier for the Service Auditor to avoid coordination with another Service Organization; in a blog the Carve-Out Method has even been characterized as a "cop-out" [47].

(2) The Inclusive Method

When applying the Inclusive Method, the relevant controls of the Subservice Organization are included in the description and in the scope of engagement of the Service Auditor. The set of control objectives includes all objectives a User Auditor would expect both the Service Organization and the Subservice Organization to achieve. To accomplish this, the Service Organization should coordinate the preparation and presentation of the description of controls with its Subservice Organization. The management of the Subservice Organization also has to provide a written description.

Figure 3 shows a situation in which some compliance-relevant parts of a task are assigned to a subcontractor. The Figure assumes that the Service Auditor applies the Carve-out Method and that both the Service Organization and the subcontractor provide SAS 70, ISAE 3402, or SSAE 16 reports. The Service Auditor needs the report from the Subservice Auditor before he can finish his own report. Of course, the information delivered along arrows ⑥, ⑦, and ⑧ is not identical to the information provided at arrow ⑨ although the same type of report is delivered. The Service Auditor will include information received via ⑧ as a (probably small) part of the information delivered in his report via ⑨. The information transported via arrows ⑨, ⑩, and ⑪ is identical if no company-specific requirements that are not covered in the common mandate of the Service Auditor exist.

Waiting for a report from another Service Organization is infeasible if two Service Organizations mutually fulfill compliance-relevant tasks. In this case only the Inclusive Method seems to be applicable.

6 Assuring Compliance in Cloud Computing

Today, Cloud Computing [48][49][50] is one of the most popular buzzwords in IT Management. It can be regarded as a special form of outsourcing and the present hype around it makes it necessary to discuss the related compliance issues.

The National Institute of Standards and Technologies defines Cloud Computing as a model for enabling ubiquitous, convenient, on-demand and network access to a shared pool of configurable computing resources (e.g., networks, servers, storage, application and services) that can be rapidly provisioned and released with minimal management effort or service provider interaction [51].

With respect to deployment options four types of Cloud Computing are distinguished [51]:

Private Cloud: The cloud infrastructure is operated solely for an organization. It may be managed by the organization or a third party and may exist on premise or off premise.

Community Cloud: The cloud infrastructure is shared by several organizations and supports a specific community that has shared concerns (e.g., mission, policy, and compliance considerations). It may be managed by the organizations or a third party and may exist on or off premise.

Public Cloud: The cloud infrastructure is made available to the general public or a large industry group and is owned by an organization selling cloud services.

Hybrid Cloud: The cloud infrastructure is a composition of two or more clouds (private, community, or public) that remain unique entities but are bound together by standardized or proprietary technology that enables data and application portability (e.g., load-balancing between clouds).

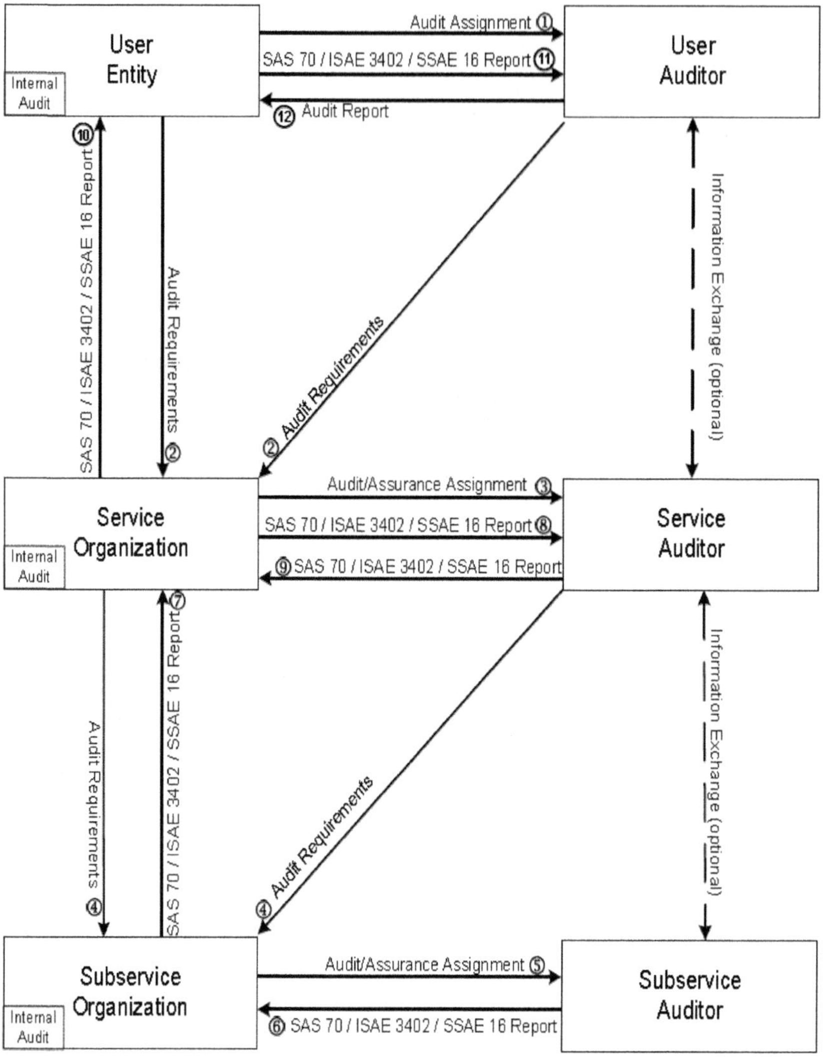

Fig. 3. Outsourcing of compliance-relevant Tasks to a Subcontractor

Private clouds may be established internally or externally. However, in the context of this paper only externally managed private clouds are of interest.

With respect to the subcontracting issues discussed in Section 5 one should keep in mind that Cloud Service Providers may use a network of partners to augment their cloud services [52][53]. Contracts should define whether a Cloud Provider may use subservice providers.

In the contract for using Amazon's Web Services the responsibility of the User Entity is accentuated. In particular, Article 4.1 (b) defines that the user is solely responsible for compliance of his content with the Acceptable Use Policy, the other policies, and the law [54].

Opinions of the effects of Cloud Computing on assuring compliance differ. IDC reports that 255 respondents of a survey regard security and compliance issues as top challenge for moving both to public and private clouds [55]. Also Gens [56] puts "Regulatory Issues" and "Legislative Issues" on top of his list of problems associated with Cloud Computing. The Cloud Security Alliance [57] sees "compliance and audit" as one of 13 domains in which security issues need to be addressed and gives several recommendations. Some Public Clouds do not accept audits by external User Auditors. A key problem of Cloud Computing is that it is not underpinned with the formalities of a traditional outsourcing relationship [3]. IDC predicts that issues such as security, compliance, SLAs, and data location will not be solved in 2011 [58].

In contrast, Mell and Grance [59] envision a "Simplification of Compliance Analysis" through Cloud Computing; it is also argued that outsourcing storage and archival systems to external clouds allows to discard managing these systems according to compliance requirements [60]. The book by Mather et al. [61] on Cloud Security and Privacy contains a chapter on "Audit and Compliance;" however, the recommendations given are very similar to those for traditional outsourcing. The awareness of compliance issues related to Cloud Computing is documented by the existence of a CloudAudit Group and its A6 (Automated Audit, Assertion, Assessment, and Assurance API) Working Group (http://groups.google.com/group/CloudAudit).

One of the main obstacles for broad acceptance of Cloud Services are security concerns. The User Entity has, among others, to deal with the way the provider runs its organization, the architecture of the provider's systems, and its organizational culture and policies [62]. Some risks associated with Cloud Computing are availability and confidentiality, location where data actually reside, disaster recovery management, and compliance to regulations and laws in different countries because the physical location dictates jurisdiction and legal obligation [62].

In some types of Cloud Computing the employees may receive services directly from the cloud and bypass the User Entity's IT system. Thus, Cloud Computing may make internal controls less powerful and its indicators less meaningful. Data which is relevant to assure compliance may not be stored in one place and may be difficult to retrieve and compile. Furthermore, it should be guaranteed that authorities demanding data do not receive more data than necessary. And it is inadmissible that some providers of cloud services reserve the right to withhold information from authorities (cf. [62]).

Public clouds are not well-suited for supporting compliance-relevant processes. It is argued that only the "carve-out" method is feasible in this case [41]. In all other types of clouds some of the main advantages of Cloud Computing, in particular global resource sharing, disappear. Private enclaves could make it easier to enforce compliance issues because the auditor has only to deal with the part of the cloud related to client data or processes rather than with the entire cloud [63]. Certified auditors could provide attestations to make User Entities more confident in Cloud Computing providers [64].

Thus far no cloud-specific frameworks or standards exist and most IT-related regulations have not been formulated with Cloud Computing in mind. From the viewpoint of Cloud providers, supporting individual customer audits seems to be particularly challenging - from a resource perspective, from a confidentiality perspective given the high degree of shared infrastructure, and from a data collection perspective given the virtual nature of many cloud environments [61]. Maintaining separate compliance efforts for different user environments is regarded as not sustainable. Service Organizations are urged to implement a strong internal control monitoring function coupled with a robust external audit process. User Entities have to define their control requirements, understand the internal control monitoring processes of the Service Organization, analyze external audit reports, and execute their responsibilities as partners of the Service Organization [61].

It is argued that SAS 70, SSAE 16, and ISAE 304 reports do not dive deep enough to attest a cloud as compliant. ISACA [62] suggests a major cloud-specific governance initiative in which a broad set of stakeholders should be involved. Some regulatory requirements specify controls that are difficult or impossible to achieve in certain types of Cloud Computing [57]. User Entities receiving cloud services should develop processes to collect and store compliance evidence including audit logs, activity reports, copies of system configurations, change management reports, and other test procedure output. The Cloud Provider may have to provide much of this information and could deliver at least a SAS 70 resp. SSAE 16 or ISAE 304 Type II report (cf. [65]); this, however, does not show that the provider is compliant but only that security controls are in place [66]. In addition, an ISO 27001 certification of security management or the demonstration of alignment with ISO 27002 practices is suggested [57]. Furthermore, if a Cloud Provider is certified as, e.g., PCI DSS compliant, this does not necessarily mean that its customers are also PCI DSS compliant because, say, the Cloud Provider may not review the logs on a daily basis [67].

The contracts with Cloud Computing Providers should specify which control frameworks have to be used and the tasks that have to be fulfilled in supporting external audits of the Cloud Provider. Typical governance activities must include special considerations when dealing with cloud technology and its providers; a security officer of the User Entity should be involved in all governance processes if a company plans to move to Cloud Computing [62]. Not only the User Entity and the Cloud Provider but also the Cloud itself may become an audit object; for instance, the auditor may have to test the secure tunnel between provider and client periodically [68].

Brandic et al. [69] devised an approach for compliance management in Clouds, named Compliant Cloud Computing (C3). They propose new languages for specifying compliance requirements concerning security, privacy, and trust by leveraging domain specific languages and compliance level agreements. They also suggest a Compliant Cloud Computing (C3) approach responsible for the deployment of certifiable and auditable applications and for enactment and enforcement of compliance requirements.

7 Conclusions and Outlook

7.1 Conclusions

In this paper we looked at outsourced IT Systems that are relevant for assuring the compliance of business processes of User Entities. The responsibility for being compliant always remains in the User Entity. Several widely recognized but also some almost unknown frameworks and guidelines exist which suggest certain actions by internal and/or external auditors. Typically the actions are triggered by the User Entity and the results provided by the Service Organization or its Auditor.

In 2010, the well-established SAS 70 reports were replaced by other AICPA recommendations that change the report perspective from "auditing" to "attestation". The new ISAE 3402 / SSAE 16 reports may be more convenient for auditors because the increased management responsibility and the obligatory management sign-off will strengthen the motivation of managers to fulfil the compliance requirements.

We also discussed the assurance of compliance in Cloud Computing, as a special form of outsourcing, and came to the conclusion that compliance issues are even more important in decisions about Cloud Computing than in traditional outsourcing decisions. In particular, at the present state of the art Public Clouds seem inappropriate for outsourcing compliance-relevant tasks. Special frameworks and guidelines are expected to govern a transfer of compliance-relevant tasks to the Cloud.

7.2 Outlook

SAS 70, SSAE 16, and ISAE 304 reports are applicable only to examine controls over financial data; for instance, controls over privacy of customer-related information or about realizing Good Manufacturing Practices [4] are not considered by these standards. However, there may be a demand for assuring controls beyond those on financial data [70]. To address these demands, the management of the User Entity may ask the Service Organization for an independent auditor's statement on the effectiveness of its controls over, e.g., the privacy of the information processed for User Entities. The AICPA is expected to publish a recommendation with respect to such far broader attestation objects in 2011 [71].

Given the tendency to increased regulation, the question arises whether this phenomenon favors outsourcing of compliance-relevant tasks to avoid the complications associated with providing assurance or whether these tasks are considered as so critical that they may hinder outsourcing or even result in backsourcing. This question is typically discussed with respect to the SOX but, of course, also relevant for other far-reaching regulations. Some statements that favor the concept of outsourcing may be seen as indicators for regulation-induced outsourcing: "In a world of changing regulations, employers are increasingly looking to Service Organizations to help ensure they meet all applicable mandates. Expect more contracts, especially mid-market ones, to tack on compliance as part of the service delivery ... As long as employers are unwilling or unable to invest internally in their compliance programs, providers will continue to advance their processes and technologies to support clients' needs" [6].

Lanz and Tie [72] argue that many factors influence companies to outsource IT, but few are as pressing as the requirements of the SOX. Compliance with these provisions requires computing resources that a growing number of company executives feel are best obtained from vendors with superior systems and skilled personnel. But they also mention that some managers evaluate the risks of outsourcing some IT tasks may be too high, resulting in a financial and organizational catastrophe. Lepeak

[73] compiles arguments why a Service Organization may be in a better position to fulfill compliance requirements but also mentions that many Service Organizations struggled to establish compliance capabilities.

A more skeptical position is taken by Hall and Liedtka [74]: „... IT outsourcing should not be a default response to SOX. To the extent that many large-scale IT contracts are irreversible and the full implications of SOX are still uncertain, we recommend that firms maintain IT assets in-house until they are certain that the outsourcing response is appropriate. Similarly, preexisting IT outsourcing contracts may no longer be optimal in light of SOX and thus should be reevaluated.

Establishing enhanced internal control and the means to perform frequent assessments are challenges IT departments may not be equipped to handle in the short term. However, top management must realize that vendors with the same desperate need for qualified personnel are also struggling to meet the demands of SOX.“

In a survey conducted by the previous Meta Group, 21% of the respondents answered that they would enlarge their outsourcing activities after the introduction of the SOX, but 19% replied that they would outsource less [74]. We assume that this difference is not statistically significant. Similar results were obtained in a German survey in which 19% of the respondents saw compliance issues as argument against outsourcing and 27% as argument favoring outsourcing. 24% assessed compliance issues as a phenomenon which may as well favor as hinder outsourcing and only 30% saw no impact on outsourcing behavior [8].

Different viewpoints also exist with respect to global sourcing. Some Indian outsourcing providers said that their SOX-related business was growing at more than 50 percent a year; other companies claimed that SOX compliance hurt their business as U.S. companies took longer to decide which parts of their operations they could run abroad while staying in compliance with the new law [75].

Thus, empirical studies on these controversial perspectives would be very interesting but, as for many other subtle outsourcing issues, reliable empirical data seems to be very hard to obtain.

References

1. Lickel, C.M.: Introduction. IBM Systems Journal 46, 202 (2007)
2. Hurley, J.: The Struggle to Manage Security Compliance for Multiple Regulations (2004), https://www4.symantec.com/Vrt/offer?a_id=24482
3. Kendrick, R.: Outsourcing IT: A Governance Guide. IT Governance Publishing, Cambridgeshire (2009)
4. Linna, A., Korhonen, M., Mannermaa, J.-P., Airaksinen, M., Juppo, A.M.: Developing a tool for the preparation of GMP audit of pharmaceutical contract manufacturer. European Journal of Pharmaceutics and Biopharmaceutics 69, 786–792 (2007)
5. Swider, M.G.: FDA Recommendations to Industry Regarding Outsourcing. How to ensure compliance in the outsourcing environment. The BioPharm International Guide 33, 6–9 (2009), http://biopharminternational.findpharma.com/biopharm/Outsourcing+Articles/FDAs-Recommendations-to-Industry-Regarding-Outsour/ArticleStandard/Article/detail/590354

6. Vales, K.A.: Compliance Outsourcing Gaining New Ground in HRO Contracts. HRO Today 7 (2008), http://www.hrotoday.com/content/1965/compliance-outsourcing-gaining-new-ground-hro-contracts
7. Economist Intelligence Unit: The role of IT in compliance (2005), http://www.fairfactories.org/pdf/ITandCompliance.pdf
8. Amberg, M., Mossanen, K., Kramolisch, W., Biermann, S., Lehr, L.: Compliance im IT-Outsourcing: Theoretische und empirische Ermittlung von Einfluss nehmenden Compliance-Faktoren, Nürnberg, http://www.accenture.com/SiteCollectionDocuments/Local_Germany/PDF/ComplianceimITOutsourcing.pdf
9. Oshri, I., Kotlarsky, J., Willcocks, L.P.: The Handbook of Global Outsourcing and Offshoring. Palgrave Macmillan, Houndmills (2009)
10. Beulen, E.: Governance in IT Outsourcing Partnerships. In: Van Grembergen, W. (ed.) Strategies for Information Technology Governance, pp. 310–344. IDEA Group, Hershey (2004)
11. Beulen, E., Ribbers, P.: Control in outsourcing relationships: governance in action. In: Proceedings of the 40th Hawaii International Conference on System Sciences. IEEE Computer Society, Los Alamitos (2007)
12. Knolmayer, G.F.: Compliance-Nachweise bei Outsourcing von IT-Aufgaben. Wirtschaftsinformatik 49 (Special Issue), S98–S105 (2007)
13. de Jong, F., van Hillegersberg, J., van Eck, P., van der Kolk, F., Jorissen, R.: Governance of Offshore IT Outsourcing at Shell Global Functions IT-BAM Development and Application of a Governance Framework to Improve Outsourcing Relationships. In: Oshri, I., Kotlarsky, J. (eds.) Global Sourcing of Information Technology and Business Processes. LNBIP, vol. 55, pp. 119–150. Springer, Heidelberg (2010)
14. Beulen, E., Ribbers, P., Roos, J.: Managing IT Outsourcing, 2nd edn. Routledge, London (2011)
15. Asprion, P., Knolmayer, G.F.: Compliance und ERP-Systeme: Eine bivalente Beziehung. Zeitschrift für Controlling & Management 53(Special Issue 3), 40–47 (2009)
16. ITGI COBIT 4.1, Rolling Meadows: ITGI (2007), http://www.isaca.org/Knowledge-Center/cobit/Pages/Downloads.aspx
17. Schneider, G.P., Bruton, C.M.: New Regulations that Impact Information Systems Employees. In: Proceedings of the Academy of Legal, Ethical and Regulatory Issues, vol. 8, pp. 193–196. Allied Academies, Candler (2004)
18. White, A.: Impact new laws and reg existing IT systems, Bird&Bird (2004), http://www.twobirds.com/English/News/Articles/Pages/impact_new_laws_and_reg_existing_IT_systems.aspx
19. Nace, M.: Basel III Requirements and Their Bottom-Line Impact on IT & Business Integration (2010), http://portal.integrella.com/basel-iii-requirements-and-business-integration
20. PCAOB: Auditing Standard No. 2 - An Audit of Internal Control Over Financial Reporting Performed in Conjunction with An Audit of Financial Statements (2004), http://www.auditcommittee-institute.ch/docs/20040309_PCAOB_Approved_Auditing_Standard_No.2.pdf

21. AICPA: Statement on Auditing Standards, Audit Considerations Relating to an Entity Using a Service Organization (2010), http://www.aicpa.org/Research/Standards/AuditAttest/ASB/DownloadableDocuments/Clarified%20SAS%20Service%20Organizations_Effective%20Date%20Change_Clean.pdf
22. IFAC: International Standard on Auditing 402, Audit Considerations relating to an Entity using a Service Organization. In: Handbook of International Quality Control, Auditing, Review, Other Assurance, and Related Services Pronouncements, 2010th edn., pp. 345–367. Part I (2010), http://web.ifac.org/media/publications/e/2010-handbook-of-internatio/2010-handbook-of-internatio-3.pdf
23. Beulen, E., Ribbers, P.: Governance of Complex IT Outsourcing Partnerships. In: Rivard, S., Aubert, B.A. (eds.) Information Technology Outsourcing, pp. 224–243. Sharpe, Amonk (2008)
24. AICPA: Internal Control - Integrated Framework. AICPA, New York (1992)
25. ITGI: IT Control Objectives for Sarbanes-Oxley: The Role of IT in the Design and Implementation of Internal Control Over Financial Reporting. 2nd edn. ITGI, Rolling Meadows (2006)
26. ITGI: IT Control Objectives for Basel II: The Importance of Governance and Risk Management for Compliance. ITGI, Rolling Meadows (2007)
27. ITGI: Aligning CobiT 4.1, ITIL V3 and ISO/IEC 27002 for Business Benefit. A Management Briefing from ITGI and OGC (2008), http://www.isaca.org/Knowledge-Center/Research/Documents/Aligning-COBIT,ITILV3,ISO27002-Bus-Benefit-12Nov08-Research.pdf
28. ISACA: Outsourced IT Environments Audit/Assurance Program. ISACA, Rolling Meadows (2009)
29. BITS Financial Services Roundtable: BITS Framework for Managing Technology Risk for IT Service Provider Relationships, Revised Version (2010), http://www.bits.org/downloads/Publications%20Page/FrameworkFeb2010.pdf
30. BITS, The Santa Fe Group, BSI: An Integrated Approach: ISO 27001 and BITS Shared Assessments Program. A Perspective of BSI Management Systems and the Shared Assessments Program (2008), http://www.sharedassessments.org/media/pdf-ISOWP2008.pdf
31. AICPA: Service Organizations: Applying SAS No. 70, as Amended, With Conforming Changes as of May 1, 2006. AICPA, New York (2006)
32. Bednarz, A.: Offsite security complicates compliance. NetworkWorld Executive Guide 22, 30–31 (2005), http://seclists.org/isn/2005/Mar/113
33. Gazzaway, T.: SAS 70: New life for an old audit standard. Financial Executive (2004), http://www.allbusiness.com/human-resources/workforce-management-hiring/143004-1.html
34. AGA: SAS 70 Reports: Are They Useful and Can They Be Improved? AGA CPAG Research Series: Report No. 15 (2008), http://www.agacgfm.org/research/downloads/CPAG15.pdf
35. Caldwell, F.: Hype Cycle for Regulations and Related Standards, 2010. Gartner RAS Core Research Note G00175154 (2010), http://www.gartner.com/DisplayDocument?ref=clientFriendlyUrl&id=1331647

36. ISACA: New Service Auditor Standard: A User Entity Perspective. ISACA White Paper (2010), http://www.isaca.org/Knowledge-Center/Research/Documents/New-Serv-Audit-Std-Wht-Paper-7July2010-Research.pdf
37. PWC: New level of trust and transparency. A perspective on the transition from SAS 70 to SSAE 16 and ISAE 3402. PricewaterhouseCoopers (US), (2010), http://www.pwc.com/en_US/us/third-party-assurance/assets/ssae16.pdf
38. A-lign: SAS 70/SSAE 16/ISAE 3402 Comparison, (2010), http://www.aligncpa.com/userfiles/files/SSAE16-SAS70-ISAE3402%20Comparison.pdf
39. Sinha, A., Jaiswal, A., Gupta, R., Chaurasiya, V.K.: SAS 70 to SSAE16 / ISAE 3402: An Insight into Outsourcing Security and Process Controls, and Significance of New Service Audit Standards. In: Internet Session Summer 2011 Global Conference on Business and Finance (2011), http://www.theibfr.com/INTERNET/CR03161106-PRESENTATION-ankita.pdf
40. Ernst, Young: New gold standard to change third party assurance. Internal Auditing & Business Risk magazine (2010), http://www.ey.com/Publication/vwLUAssets/Internal_Auditing_and_Business_Risk_magazine_-_February_2010_-_ISAE_3402_and_internal_audit/$FILE/EY_Internal_auditing_and_business_risk_magazine_-_February_2010.pdf
41. Bierce, W.B., Kenerson, M.L.: Belt and Suspenders, and From SOX to SOC's: Changes in Service Audit Standards on the Service Organization's Risk Management, Security and Process Controls (2010), http://www.outsourcing-law.com/tag/aicpa/
42. MASTER: D3.1.2: MASTER Methodology Handbook v2 (Compliance with Outsourcing between Trust Domains), FP7-216917 (2010), http://www.master-fp7.eu/index.php?option=com_docman&task=doc_download&gid=94&Itemid=60
43. Lotz, V., Pigout, E., Fischer, M., Kossmann, D., Massacci, F., Pretschner, A.: Towards Systematic Achievement of Compliance in Service-Oriented Architectures: The MASTER Approach. Wirtschaftsinformatik 50, 383–391 (2008)
44. Pasic, A., Bareño, J., Gallego-Nicasio, B., Torres, R., Fernandez, D.: Trust and compliance management models in emerging outsourcing environments. In: Cellary, W., Estevez, E. (eds.) Software Services for e-World. IFIPAICT, vol. 341, pp. 237–248. Springer, Heidelberg (2010)
45. Magnusson, C., Chou, S.-C.: Risk and Compliance Management Framework for Outsourced Global Software Development. In: Proceedings 2010 International Conference on Global Software Engineering, pp. 228–233. IEEE Computer Society, Los Alamitos (2010)
46. AICPA: AU Section 9324: Service Organizations: Auditing Interpretations of Section 324 (2002), http://www.aicpa.org/Research/Standards/AuditAttest/DownloadableDocuments/AU-00324_9.pdf
47. Linford, N.: Subservice Organizations and the Carve-out or Inclusive Method (2010), http://linfordco.com/2010/03/subservice-organizations-and-the-carve-out-or-inclusive-method/
48. Rhoton, J.: Cloud Computing Explained, 2nd edn. Recursive Press (2010)

49. Velte, A.T., Velte, T.J., Elsenpeter, R.: Cloud Computing: A Practical Approach. McGraw-Hill, New York (2010)
50. Willcocks, L., Venters, W., Whitley, E.: Cloud and the Future of Business: From Costs to Innovation, Part One: Promise. Accenture (2011), http://outsourcingunit.org/publications/cloudPromise.pdf
51. Mell, P., Grance, T.: The NIST Definition of Cloud Computing (Draft). Special Publication 800-145 (2011), http://csrc.nist.gov/publications/drafts/800-145/Draft-SP-800-145_cloud-definition.pdf
52. Hietala, J., Willoughby, M.: Managing Compliance and Security for Cloud Computing. Cutter IT Journal 22, 44–50 (2009)
53. Bowen, J.A.: Legal Issues in Cloud Computing. In: Buyya, R., Broberg, J., Goscinski, A. (eds.) Cloud Computing: Principles and Paradigms, pp. 593–613. Wiley, Hoboken (2011)
54. Amazon Web Services: AWS Customer Agreement (2011-02-08), http://aws.amazon.com/agreement/
55. Bunn, F.: Confidence in the Cloud. Symantec (2010), http://www.worldhostingdays.com/downloads/2011/mF1e.pdf
56. Gens, F.: Cloud Computing in the Enterprise, http://csis.pace.edu/~marchese/CS865/Cloud%20Computing%20in%20the%20Enterprise2.ppt
57. Cloud Security Alliance: Security Guidance for Critical Areas of Focus in Cloud Computing V2.1 (2009), https://cloudsecurityalliance.org/csaguide.pdf
58. IDC: Cloud Adoption Will Have Major Impact on European Software Market in 2011, According to IDC (2011), http://www.idc.com/getdoc.jsp?containerId=prDK22728011
59. Mell, P., Grance, T.: Effectively and Securely Using the Cloud Computing Paradigm, NIST, Information Technology Laboratory (2009), http://csrc.nist.gov/groups/SNS/cloud-computing/cloud-computing-v26.ppt
60. Sakka, M.A., Defude, B., Tellez, J.: Document provenance in the cloud: Constraints and challenges. In: Aagesen, F.A., Knapskog, S.J. (eds.) EUNICE 2010. LNCS, vol. 6164, pp. 107–117. Springer, Heidelberg (2010)
61. Mather, T., Kumaraswamy, S., Latif, S.: Cloud Security and Privacy. An Enterprise Perspective on Risks and Compliance. O'Reilly Media, Sebastopol (2009)
62. ISACA: Cloud Computing: Business Benefits With Security, Governance and Assurance Perspectives. ISACA Emerging Technology White Paper (2009), http://www.isaca.org/Knowledge-Center/Research/Documents/Cloud-Computing-28Oct09-Research.pdf
63. Khan, K.M., Malluhi, Q.M.: Establishing Trust in Cloud Computing. IT Professional 12(5), 20–27 (2010)
64. Price, S.G.: The 21st Century Version of SAS 70.....SSAE 16, http://www.aligncpa.com/userfiles/files/The%2021st%20Century%20Version%20of%20SAS%2070.pdf
65. Krutz, R.L., Vines, R.D.: Cloud Security. A Comprehensive Guide to Secure Cloud Computing. Wiley, Indianapolis (2010)
66. Brandl, D.: Don't cloud your compliance data. Control Engineering 58, 23 (2010) http://www.controleng.com/index.php?id=483&cHash=081010&tx_ttnews[tt_news]=8780

67. Savage, M.: PCI DSS compliant cloud providers: No PCI panacea (2011), http://searchcloudsecurity.techtarget.com/news/2240033583/PCI-DSS-compliant-cloud-providers-No-PCI-panacea?asrc=EM_NLN_13525892&track=NL-102&ad=821278
68. Rai, S., Chukwuma, P.: Security in a Cloud. Internal Auditor 66, 21–23 (2009)
69. Brandic, I., Dustdar, S., Anstett, T., Schumm, D., Leymann, F., Konrad, R.: Compliant Cloud Computing (C3): Architecture and Language Support for User-driven Compliance Management in Cloud. In: 3rd International Conference on Cloud Computing, pp. 244–251. IEEE Computer Society, Los Alamitos (2010)
70. McCallum, A.: How to Conduct an Audit of an Outsourcing Provider. BioPharm International, Supplement, 40–46 (2008)
71. AICPA: Service Organizations Controls, Managing Risks by Obtaining a Service Auditor's Report (2010), http://www.aicpa.org/InterestAreas/InformationTechnology/Resources/TrustServices/DownloadableDocuments/10957-378%20SOC%20Whitepaper.pdf
72. Lanz, J., Tie, R.: Advise Businesses on External IT Resources. Journal of Accountancy 197(6), 55–62 (2004), http://www.journalofaccountancy.com/Issues/2004/Jun/AdviseBusinessesOnExternalItResources.htm
73. Lepeak, S.: United States: The Impact of Regulatory Compliance Mandates on Business Process and IT Outsourcing (2005), http://www.mondaq.com/unitedstates/article.asp?articleid=34676
74. Hall, J.A., Liedtka, S.L.: The Sarbanes-Oxley Act: Implications For Large-Scale IT Outsourcing. Communications of the ACM 50(3), 95–100 (2007)
75. Bellman, E.: A cost of Sarbanes-Oxley: Outsourcing to India. Pittsburgh Post-Gazette 2005-07-14, http://www.post-gazette.com/pg/05195/537848.stm

Governance Mechanisms as Substitutes and Complements – A Dynamic Perspective on the Interplay between Contractual and Relational Governance

Thomas L. Huber, Thomas A. Fischer, and Jens Dibbern

University of Bern, Institute of Information Systems
Engehaldenstrasse 8, CH-3012 Bern
{thomas.huber,thomas.fischer,jens.dibbern}@iwi.unibe.ch

Abstract. In recent years scholars have discussed the relationship between contractual and relational governance in information systems (IS) outsourcing. Findings regarding this relationship are still mixed. Some hint at a substitutional relationship, others at a complementary relationship. Moreover novel investigations favor another argument: relational and contractual governance mechanisms can simultaneously be complements and substitutes.

If governance mechanisms can be both, substitutes and complements, the question arises whether the relationship between different types of governance mechanisms is the outcome of distinct processes of interaction. To answer this question we conducted an exploratory, multiple-case study of five IS outsourcing projects at a leading global bank. We identified four archetypical interaction processes (archetypes): Three archetypes yield complementary relationships, one yields a substitutional relationship. Based on these findings, we searched for patterns in the occurrence of the archetypes as well as for their underlying reasons.

Our analysis revealed three salient patterns in the occurrence of the archetypes, each representing a sequence of archetypes: In the first two patterns sequenced archetypes reinforced each other leading to either a "success" (pattern 1) or "failure path" (pattern 2). Pattern 3 - the "interrupted path" - demonstrates how a success path is broken and turned into a failure path induced by an external stimulating event.

Our major contribution is a shift in perspective. We show that the relationship between governance mechanisms is not static but dynamic. Dynamic interactions between governance mechanisms facilitate or corroborate perceived quality of IS outsourcing governance. Our findings pave the way towards a process-theoretic view on IS outsourcing governance.

Keywords: Relational Governance, Contractual Governance, Complements, Substitutes, IS Outsourcing, IS Offshoring.

1 Introduction

Despite a long lasting information systems (IS) outsourcing history, many global outsourcing projects fail to achieve expected results (e. g. cost reduction). Especially,

J. Kotlarsky, L.P. Willcocks, and I. Oshri (Eds.): Global Sourcing 2011, LNBIP 91, pp. 46–65, 2011.

the choice of control and governance mechanisms is supposed to be decisive, as governance and control costs are often higher than initially estimated [1]. Contractual and relational governance have been identified as the two main determinants for IS outsourcing success [2].

From a managerial point of view the question arises how different types of governance mechanisms - such as contractual and relational governance - should be combined. To answer this question it is, first of all, important to understand how contractual and relational governance relate to each other. In recent years scholars have discussed the relationship of contractual and relational governance in IS outsourcing. For a long time the substitutional view of governance mechanisms was dominant, predicting that complex contracts are an opposing alternative to unwritten agreements based on trust [3]. Empirical results, however, challenged this view and rather supported the competing perspective, implicating that relational and contractual governance are complements [4,5]. However, results of novel investigations [6-8] favour another argument: Relational and contractual governance mechanisms can simultaneously be complements *and* substitutes. Given these inconsistencies we performed a study analyzing the interaction between contractual and relational governance over time. In a first step, we found out that the relationship (substitutional or complementary) between contractual and relational governance is the outcome of four archetypical processes of interaction between contractual and relational governance. Based on these findings the following research question arose. *Are there patterns in the occurrence of these archetypes, and if yes, how can the occurrence of these patterns be explained?*

Our results show that there are three salient patterns in the occurrence of the archetypes, whereas each pattern represents a sequence of archetypes: Pattern 1 - called the *"success path"* - occurs, if the quality of the performed governance mechanisms is high. Pattern 2 - the *"failure path"* - appears in case the quality of the performed governance mechanisms is low. Pattern 3 - the *"interrupted path"* - demonstrates how a success path is broken and turned into a failure path induced by an external stimulating event.

In answering the research question we close a current research gap and create a basic understanding on *how* contractual and relational governance dynamically interact and furthermore how this interaction results in dynamically changing relationships between contractual and relational governance over time. In addition we trace back the occurrence of the above-mentioned patterns to governance quality and external stimulating events. For that purpose, we conducted an exploratory, multiple-case study of five IS outsourcing projects at a leading global bank.

2 Literature Analysis

2.1 Contractual and Relational Governance

An outsourcing contract is a central component of each outsourcing engagement to manage the relationship between client and vendor. Usually, the contract contains overall objectives of the partnership as well as certain obligations for both client and vendor. Several contractual elements which are likely to appear in a contract are service levels or other performance indicators as well as corresponding measurement methodologies [5]. These written obligations make up the formal contract. The management based on this formal contract can be understood as contractual governance. In other words, *contractual governance* is "the use of a formalized, legally-binding agreement or a contract to govern the interfirm partnership" [9, p. 898].

In contrast to contractual governance the mechanisms underlying *relational governance* are usually unwritten [2]. They build on the ability of social processes to establish obligations, promises and expectations [4]. Relational norms on the one hand form the basis for relational governance and are on the other hand reinforced by its application. In this context former research has identified trust and commitment as the two most important relational norms [5]. Therefore a well-attuned relational governance is *indicated through* high levels of trust and commitment and *manifests in* informal interaction between client and vendor employees (e.g. in meetings or phone calls), informal information sharing and open communication [4,5,2]. In the following, we refer to contractual governance in the sense of formal mechanisms and equate relational governance with informal mechanisms.

2.2 Complementarity versus Substitution between Contractual and Relational Governance

From a theoretical viewpoint there are two major perspectives on the relationship of contractual and relational governance: the complementary and the substitutional view. Referring to the concepts of dualism and duality[1], this chapter points out their major differences and traces them back to the agency-structure problem.

The substitutional view characterizes contractual and relational governance as dualism, meaning that contractual and relational mechanisms are separate concepts that differ in terms of their base (power vs. shared values) as well as in their mechanism to align conflicting goals (suppression vs. consensus) [12]. This conceptualization of contractual and relational governance as dualism radiates on their relationship: *contractual and relational governance are seen as substitutes implying that contractual governance is detrimental for relational governance, while relational governance reduces the need for contractual regulations* [13]. As an example the substitutional view argues that in situations of weak relational norms complex contracts are needed to mitigate opportunism, while in situations of a good relationship opportunism is less likely to occur and thus contracts are seen as unnecessary or at worst counter-productive [4].

The complementary view characterizes contractual and relational governance as duality, hence it rather points to their similarities and mutual dependency, while not neglecting their conceptual distinction. Consequently, the former separation of contractual and relational governance is removed in favour of an emphasis on their functional equivalence, as they are seen as "equivalent functional alternatives which simultaneously and parallel to each other absorb uncertainty and reduce complexity" [12, p. 204]. This is not a marginal issue, because it implies that anticipation of an actor's behaviour is not based on either structure (contractual) or agency (relational), but on both at the same time. Consequence of this dualistic conceptualization is the complementary relationship between contractual and relational governance. It purports

---

[1] Although subtle, the difference between dualism and duality is important [10]. While dualism refers to "the division of an object under study into separate and opposed paired elements", duality refers to their interdependence without discarding their conceptual distinction [11, p. 545].

that contractual and relational elements enable each other and that the level of control exercised through contractual agreements positively affects relational norms and vice versa [10]. As an example, the complementary view argues that precise contractual stipulations might foster trust by creating reliable mutual expectations.

Given these conflicting views, the question arises, which of the views has experienced stronger empirical support. While Poppo and Zenger [4] found evidence for a complementary relationship, other studies substantiate the substitutional view [14,15]. Moreover, recent studies found out that relational and contractual governance are not either complements or substitutes, but that their relationship is contingent and therefore can be both substitutes and complements [6,8]. More specifically, Tiwana [8] shows that the relationship between governance mechanisms is contingent upon the type of the mechanisms: While, informal control mechanisms strengthen the influence of formal behavior control mechanisms (complementarity), they weaken the influence of formal outcome control mechanisms (substitution). In contrast, Klein-Woolthuis et al. [6] point out that the (initial) intention with which a contract is drawn determines the relationship between contractual and relational governance, therefore, it depends on the intention whether they are either complements or substitutes.

Hence, theoretical as well as empirical findings draw a contradictory picture on the relationship between contractual and relational governance. However, as governance mechanisms can be both substitutes and complements, we made the supposition that the relationship between different types of governance mechanisms is the outcome of interaction processes between these mechanisms. To this end we conducted an exploratory empirical study, which is taken up next.

3 Research Design

3.1 Methodology

This research takes an exploratory multiple-case study approach. This approach seemed to be particularly appropriate, as our study strives for answering a "how" question [16], and it deals with "operational links needing to be traced over time" [17, p. 6]. Furthermore, the events that need to be linked defy control of the researcher and they are rather contemporary than part of the "dead" past [17]. Since this study is concerned with the exploration of interaction processes between contractual and relational governance in IS outsourcing arrangements, the unit of analysis is the relationship between client and vendor. In order to allow for generalization we followed replication logic and conducted five case studies in the German financial services industry. The explorative nature of this study implies that the processes and relationships would have been difficult to access in a quantitative manner only, therefore we rely on qualitative data to gain an in-depth understanding of the interaction processes described above. This data was mainly gathered in semi-structured interviews but in order to improve validity of our findings [18] we triangulated them with a review of the underlying contracts.

3.2 Data Collection and Analysis

To stay in line with the research objectives and the multiple case study design we pursued a purposeful sampling strategy [19,20]. Striving for literal replication we chose similar cases, hence each case was expected to show similar results [17]. Therefore each case was required to fulfill the following criteria: 1) only projects with approximately the same size, (2) that are delivered by vendors of approximately the same size and 3) only outsourcing projects with a minimum duration of three months since the project went live. The first criteria was chosen in order to improve comparability of the findings, because it was found to be an important antecedent for the choice of governance mechanisms [21,22]. A minimum duration was chosen because literature suggests that substitutional and complementary effects of governance mechanisms unfold over a specific period of time [23] - the value of three months was decided on because after that time period an outsourcing arrangement has "progressed to a reasonable maturity" [24]. In order to control for potential bias of organizational [25] as well as departmental culture [26], we chose the same department of a single client organization for all outsourcing relationships - the HR department of a German-based financial services provider (GLOBAL BANK).

A total number of 21 interviews was conducted (see Table 1 for a short overview). To reflect the unit of analysis in data collection each analyzed relationship consisted of at least two expert interviews: a client employee involved in managing the partnership with the vendor and a respective counterpart from the vendor. On client side experts from senior and operational level were interviewed, enabling us to capture interactions between relational and contractual governance, as responsibilities for those mechanisms are typically situated on different levels of the hierarchy. The interviews were held either face-to-face or by telephone. All interviews were tape-recorded and transcribed. In sum, the interview protocols resulted in more than 91500 words of qualitative data.

Table 1. The Analyzed IS Outsourcing Cases

Case Name	Project Description	Interview Partner
TALENT	ALPHA delivers an online application for managing employee's talent and performance.	Client: C14, C15 Vendor: V6
GRAD-RECRUIT	BETA delivers an online application for managing the graduate recruiting process.	Client: C6, C7, C8 Vendor: V2
RECRUIT	GAMMA delivers an online workflow management application for the entire recruitment process.	Client: C11, C12, C13 Vendor: V5
PAYROLL	DELTA processes the payroll for GLOBAL BANK's Indian operations.	Client: C1, C2, C3, C4, C5 Vendor: V1
HR-OPS	EPSILON delivers HR back-office processes for GLOBAL BANK's Indian operations	Client: C9, C10 Vendor: V3, V4

The data was analyzed in the following way: As a first step, the interview transcripts were coded and revealed four archetypical processes of interaction between contractual and relational governance. Following this coding, as a second step, each piece of data was carefully analyzed by the first and second author to find patterns in the occurrence of the archetypes. After three salient patterns were identified the first and the second author, as a final step, explored the data to find factors explaining the occurrence of these salient patterns.

4 First Step: Discovering Archetypes

Our analysis *yielded four archetypical processes of interaction between contractual and relational governance explaining* a complementary or substitutional relationship respectively. Based on the four archetypes, we can explain *how* the interplay between contractual and relational governance result in their complementarity or substitution. Three of the identified processes explain a complementary, while the fourth explains a substitutional relationship. The following chapter outlines these four archetypes (see Table 2 for an overview of the archetypes).[2]

Table 2. Overview of Archetypes

Archetype		Explained Relationship
A1	*Contractual Governance as Enabler for Relational Governance*	comp-lementarity
	Contract-based mechanisms provoke relational governance by prescribing social interaction.	
	Reverse: Deficient contractual governance hampers the evolvement of social exchange and thus the build-up of a satisfying relational governance.	
A2	*Relational Governance as Enabler for Contractual Completeness*	comp-lementarity
	A well-attuned relational governance gives access to knowledge which would otherwise be hard to get and which is subsequently used to refine the contract (improving the contractual completeness).	

[2] For a more detailed description of the four archetypical processes of interaction and how they were derived, please see [27].

Table 2. (*continued*)

	Reverse: A deficient relational governance hampers informal knowledge transfer and consequently causes an undesired incompleteness of the contract.	
A3	*Contractual Governance as Safety Net*	comp-lementarity
	The awareness that the contract contains the relevant stipulations mitigates the perceived relational risk. As a consequence relational governance can develop freely.	
	Reverse: Disbelieve in the protecting role of the contract increases perceived relational risk and consequently distrust hampers the free development of relational governance.	
A4	*Relational Governance as Amplifier for Contractual Openness*	substitution
	A well-attuned relational governance devalues the need for safeguarding and revalues the need for flexibility. As a consequence the need for detailed and strict contractual stipulations is reduced.	
	Reverse: Decreasing relational governance revalues the need for safeguarding while devaluing need for flexibility and consequently the contract is refined.	

Archetype 1 - Contractual Governance as Enabler for Relational Governance

The first pattern of interaction between contractual and relational governance is characterized by contract-based mechanisms provoking relational governance by prescribing social interaction. Therefore this pattern describes a complementary relationship: Contractual governance mechanisms like regular meetings and calls, are an important driver to form relational governance, as they route people to social interaction. In turn, this social exchange leads to shared norms and expectations as well as mutual trust, what again promotes continuous informal communication and information exchange or put another way it promotes relational governance. In this sense *contractual governance enables relational governance*. The reverse relation was also identified. Hereby a deficient contractual governance hampers the evolvement of social exchange and thus the build-up of a satisfying relational governance.

Archetype 2 - Relational Governance as Enabler for Contractual Completeness
In the second pattern of interaction between contractual and relational governance a well attuned relational governance is prerequisite to refine an existing contract. This archetype describes how relational governance complements contractual governance by means of laying the foundation for a refinement of the contract: relational governance and the strong social ties associated with it give access to knowledge which would otherwise be hard to access [28] and which is subsequently used to refine contractual clauses. This archetype differs from the widely accepted view that relational aspects, such as mutual trust facilitate initial contract negotiations because trusting parties are more willing to compromise [e.g. 29] as it points out that relational governance is not merely a remedy for a deficient willingness, but for a deficient (initial) capability to contract sufficiently complete. In this sense *relational governance enables contractual completeness.* Again, the reverse effect was also observed: a bad relational governance was the cause for an undesired incompleteness of the contract.

Archetype 3 - Contractual Governance as Safety Net
While in the first two archetypes presented here one type of governance mechanisms *directly* stimulated the occurrence of the other, archetype 3 describes another more *indirect* constellation. The awareness that the contract contains the relevant stipulations mitigates the perceived relational risk. As a consequence relational governance can develop freely. Hence, contractual governance complements relational governance.

This interaction between contractual and relational governance can be illustrated with a metaphor - the one of a tightrope artist. As long as everything is fine, the safety net is not needed, otherwise the artist always knows that he is protected from falling if he makes a mistake. Otherwise a want of confidence regarding the rope would hinder the artist to act free of fear (A3 reverse). Transferred to the context of contractual and relational governance it seems that a contract may take the role of a safety net. That is, individuals know that there is something to rely on, when the other contracting party is not acting like agreed and expected. In this sense *contractual governance acts as a safety net for relational governance.*

Archetype 4 - Relational Governance as Amplifier for Contractual Openness
Contrary to the archetypes described above archetype 4 describes how contractual and relational governance become substitutes. As a deep relationship seems to devalue the importance of safeguarding (satisfied with a high degree of contractual completeness) and revalue the importance of flexibility, a bad relational governance increases the need for detailed and strict contractual stipulation. That is to say a well attuned relational governance reduces the need for detailed and strict contractual stipulations. In this sense, *relational governance amplifies contractual openness.* The reverse effect was also observed that is decreasing relational governance resulted in a refinement of the contract.

Summing up all archetypes
Archetypes A1, A2 and A3 share the characteristic that one type of governance mechanism is not simply the precursor for the oppositional mechanism rather

practicing one governance mechanism establishes the basis for additionally exercising the other governance mechanism (complementarity). While sharing this characteristic the three archetypes differ in their mode of operation: A1 explains how contractual clauses stipulate social interaction fertilizing relational governance. A2 shows how strong social ties give access to knowledge which would otherwise be hard to access and which is utilized to refine contractual clauses. The third archetype (A3) demonstrates how one mechanism (contractual governance) is protecting the application of the other one by reducing perceived relational risk. This is contrary to the fourth archetype (A4), where relational governance is not taking on a protecting role regarding the use of contractual governance. Instead, relational governance reduces the need for a strong contract.

Though there are slight overlaps, the archetypes demonstrate essential differences that exist in the interaction between contractual and relational governance. As an example both A2 and A4 deal with the impact of relational governance on contractual completeness. However, the *opposite directions* both archetypes describe makes the important difference: while in A2 a well attuned relational governance enables a contract with a higher degree of contractual completeness (complementarity), in A4 quite the opposite is observable: a well attuned relational governance reduces the desire for a complete contract. A1 and A3 also exhibit refined but important distinctions. Both archetypes explain how contractual governance enables relational governance (complementarity), but they differ in their mode of operation. That is, *contractual stipulation of social interaction and as a consequence evolution of relational norms* on the one hand (A1) and *a contractual governance assuming the role of safety net reducing perceived relational risk and enabling relational governance to develop freely* (A3) on the other hand.

Starting point for our second step of analysis, was the following remarkable finding: apart from one exception[3], all archetypes occur in each of the analyzed IS outsourcing cases. This finding implies that the relationship between contractual and relational governance is not static but subject to change in course of time. Furthermore, when one and the same case exhibits a multitude of differential interaction processes (explaining both substitution and complementarity) the question arises whether there are patterns (i.e. paths or sequences) in the occurrence of the archetypes, and if yes, how these patterns can be explained. In doing so, the *aim of the second step is to draw a rich picture on the dynamic interplay and the changing relationship between governance mechanisms.*

For that purpose, we analyzed the data again to find out, if archetypes occur in a certain order and what factors influence the appearance of these archetypes generally.

5 Second Step: Illustration of Patterns

Analyzing the appearance of archetypes within different IS outsourcing cases, we found out that the archetypical processes sometimes emerge in a sequence.

For a better understanding, which archetypes could occur in a sequence, we refer to Fig. 1. The figure indicates that to generate a sequence, an archetype starting with

[3] A4 did not appear in the PAYROLL case.

relational governance (RG) has to follow on an archetype ending with relational governance (possible sequences: A1—A2, A1—A4, A3—A2, A3—A4, A1—A2—A3, A1—A2—A1 and so on). Otherwise, an archetype ending with contractual governance (CG) can be followed by an archetype starting with contractual governance of course.

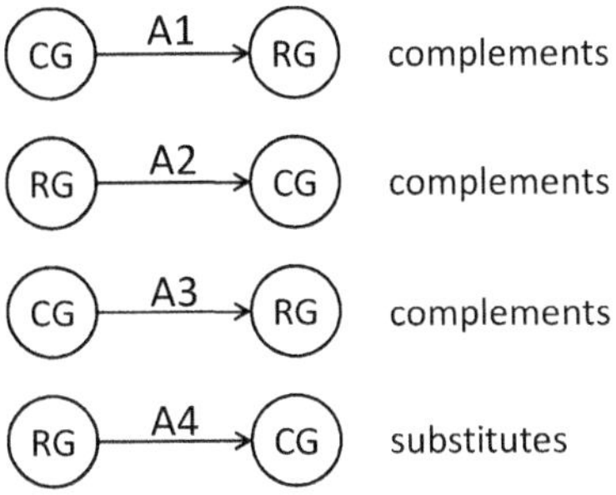

Fig. 1. The Archetypes as Building Blocks for Sequences

We characterize a *"path"* as a sequence of archetypes. When analyzing archetypes in a sequence two basic patterns occurred: on the one hand sequences of archetypes complementing each other in such a way that governance quality is increasing continuously. This basic pattern is called *success path* and is nothing but a sequence of "non-reverse archetypes". On the other hand sequences of archetypes complementing each other in such a way that governance quality is decreasing, that is a sequence of "reverse archetypes" are called *failure path*. Both success and failure path seem to be self-enforcing in that way that if one archetype (e.g. A1) occurs, another archetype (e.g. A2) will be triggered.

The following paragraph will give exemplary illustrations for both success and failure path. That means the specific concatenated archetypes presented here are merely *one possible option* to link archetypes together to form a success or a failure path. Afterwards we show, how certain external stimulating events within the analyzed IS outsourcing projects led to an interruption of these sequences.

5.1.1 Exemplary Illustration of a Success Path

This chapter describes the success path, as a sequence of A1, A2 and A3. Following the logic of archetype A1, contractual governance mechanisms like contractually defined meetings and calls, are an important driver to form relational governance, as they route people to social interaction leading to shared norms and expectations as well as mutual trust, what again is the fundament for relational governance. This archetype is often followed by archetype A2 that is a good relational governance complements contractual governance by means of laying the foundation for a refinement of the contract.

In the PAYROLL case, scoping meetings between GLOBAL BANK and DELTA were contracted. These meetings took place and people started to interact with each other. Based on this social interaction a trustful and open working atmosphere developed, indicating archetype A1. Moreover, within these meetings necessary requirements, policies and processes were discussed and finally a "Note of Understanding" was signed off at the end of the transition phase. V1 outlined this positive sequence of archetypes as follows:

> "We have a scoping meeting with GLOBAL BANK. Based on this scoping meeting at that time we created the understanding note, like we understood it". (V1)

The "Note of Understanding" became an addendum to the contract and therefore part of the contractual governance. Hence, the contract became more complete, what is the expected effect of archetype A2. Interview partner V1 feels very comfortable with this new contract, because the contents are "mutually exchanged and agreed upon" (V1). This is the reason, why she does not have to consult the contract again and again. Nevertheless, the perceived relational risk is reduced, by knowing that there is a contract, which covers most of the relevant factors. Moreover, she believes in the contract, by saying:

> "I don´t think there is any scope for misunderstanding … [because everything] … is very well captured formally … I think there are no such places for misunderstandings on either side" (V1).

As described within archetype A3, a good relational governance can develop freely, based on the awareness that there is a contract, which covers points that are deemed relevant, e.g. because otherwise they would be a potential source of misunderstanding. Interestingly, in this case relational governance, reflected by trust and commitment, increased. Finally, V1 concludes:

> "In a nutshell I would say the relationship between us is going very strong." (V1)

The last described interrelation between contractual and relational governance adds archetype A3 to the occurrence of A1 followed by A2, what leads to the success path A1—A2—A3.

To illustrate, how *success paths* take place, we gave an example of a concatenation of A1, A2 and A3. In this case, the contract acted as a starting point. Based on contractual defined meetings a good relational governance developed. In turn, the good social ties enabled a refinement of the contract. Subsequently, participants of this refinement phase reported to be satisfied with the contents covered by the contract. As a result they were enabled to draw on relational governance, as they could really rely on the contract, without having to consult it permanently. Hence, this path exhibits an upward movement regarding the quality level, starting with a contract that enables better relational governance, which in turn allows to advance the contract, which again allows the enhancement of relational governance. We therefore call this basic pattern a "success path". Fig. 2 illustrates the above described success path ("+" symbols mark a "good" executed governance mechanism).

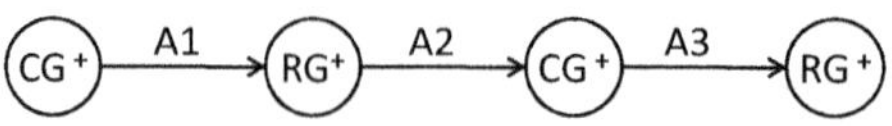

Fig. 2. Success Path

5.1.2 Exemplary Illustration of a Failure Path

While the preceding paragraph pointed out how a sequence of archetypes might result in a success path, the RECRUIT case is adequate to illustrate the reverse basic pattern - a failure path. The following section will give an example for this basic pattern consisting of two archetypes in a sequence, namely A3 Reverse and A2 Reverse.

A3 describes how a contract complements relational governance as the contract enables relational governance to develop freely. The contract succeeds in doing that when the parties involved know or assume that the relevant contractual stipulations are in place - as a consequence perceived relational risk is reduced (A3). Conversely, when the parties involved do not know or assume whether the relevant contractual stipulations are at hand the contract cannot play a safeguarding role and as a consequence relational governance is not supported (A3 Reverse). This pattern can be observed in the RECRUIT case in which disbelieve in the safeguarding role of the contract and distrust within the relationship are intertwined. The application owner on client-side (C13) delivers evidence for this interaction. She explains that she is not aware of whether the vendor has received and acknowledged distinct security policies and whether they are part of the contract. In addition the contract did not clearly define the criticality of the different services. As a consequence, she is not able to rely on the contract. Interestingly, the relationship between client and vendor in this case is characterized by distrust - indicating a *bad relational governance*.

Interestingly, as soon as relational governance mechanism were identified as not feasible, GLOBAL BANK's managers started to complain about the degree of contractual completeness, while it was deemed adequate as long as the relationship was fine.

> "The contract doesn't cover too much... It is very superficial and therefore it is difficult to manage day-to-day business based on this contract." (C13)

As a consequence GLOBAL BANK conceived a desire for a higher degree of contractual completeness and this desire was accomplished subsequently, when GLOBAL BANK enforced an addendum to the contract in the shape of an operational level agreement (OLA), which in detail regulates day-to-day interaction by explicitly defining criticality of services and the security policies the vendor has to comply with:

> "This caused us to create this OLA, which describes how the collaboration should take place." (C13)

However, the process of contract refinement is described as costly and time-consuming and above all not even the result in terms of contractual completeness is satisfactory. One reason for this can be traced back to the "difficult relationship" (C13) between client and vendor that makes it not only difficult to compromise, but also to share the necessary knowledge to refine a contract. As an example GLOBAL BANK analyzed the entire e-mail traffic between its employees and vendor employees in order to determine in detail whether the vendor has received the abovementioned security policies, because GLOBAL BANK did not trust the information on this topic provided by the vendor. However, even after refining the contract the parties still complained about its quality and traced this problem back to the insufficient sharing of knowledge between GLOBAL BANK and the vendor:

> "We never really got to the stage that the relationship was such that we ... could be consulted of about that issues." (V5)

Thus, in this case a bad relational governance was the cause for an exceptional costly and time-consuming contracting process and the inability to refine the contract adequately (A2 Reverse).

To illustrate, how a *failure path* takes place, we gave an example of a concatenation of A3 Reverse and A2 Reverse. Starting with the perception of an undesired incomplete contract the involved parties were less able to execute relational governance, because they did not feel to be sufficiently protected by the contract (A3 Reverse). This triggers the desire for a higher degree of contractual completeness. However, the bad relational governance inhibits sharing of the relevant knowledge for an adequate refinement of the contract - which makes the contracting process costly, while the resulting contract remains lacking in terms of completeness (A2 Reverse). Hence, this path exhibits a downward movement, starting with the perception that the contract cannot safeguard contractual governance, which therefore decreases in the aftermath, which in turn inhibits the contract to become sufficiently complete and makes the contracting process exceptionally costly. We therefore call this basic pattern a "failure path". Fig. 3 illustrates the above described failure path ("-" symbols mark a "bad" executed governance mechanism).

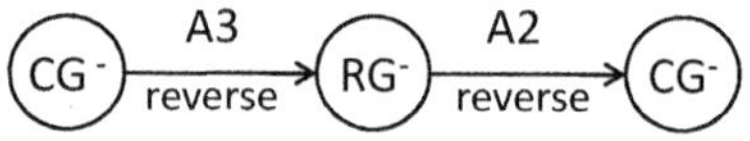

Fig. 3. Failure Path

5.1.3 Comparison of Success and Failure Path

Comparing success and failure path, it comes apparent that they differ in quality of executed governance mechanisms. A governance mechanism is labeled as high or poor quality when interviewees report to *perceive* governance quality as high or poor (see Appendix A for exemplary quotes).

A success path seems to start with a well executed governance mechanism like a good, e.g. comprehensive and detailed, contract like in the PAYROLL case. Anyway, if the first governance mechanism is performed in a good quality, the enabled governance mechanism is also of good quality. Hence, the overall level of governance quality is higher than before. Over time these gradual processes of adapting governance mechanisms lead to an improvement in that way that when the subsequent archetype is triggered (e.g. A2), the quality level increases again. This increase in quality of the performed governance mechanisms over time is illustrated in Fig. 4. This shows that a success path is a gradual upward movement towards a higher level of governance quality.

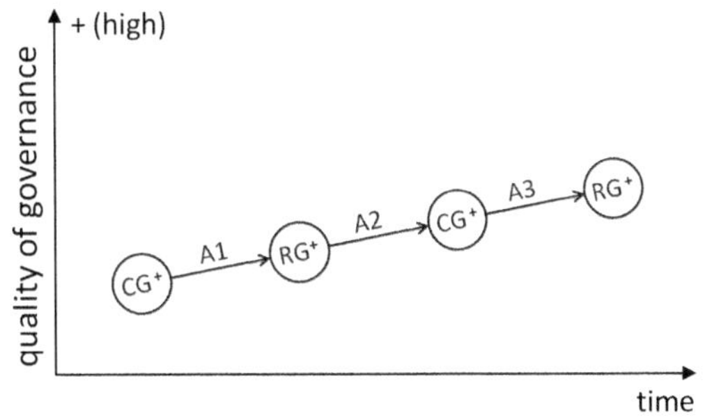

Fig. 4. Success Path as Upward Movement

The opposite effect is typical for a failure path. Hereby the concatenation of archetypes goes from a bad executed governance mechanism to another bad performed governance mechanism. Hence, the failure path is a movement towards a lower level of governance quality (see Fig. 5) as the consequence of gradually adapting governance mechanisms.

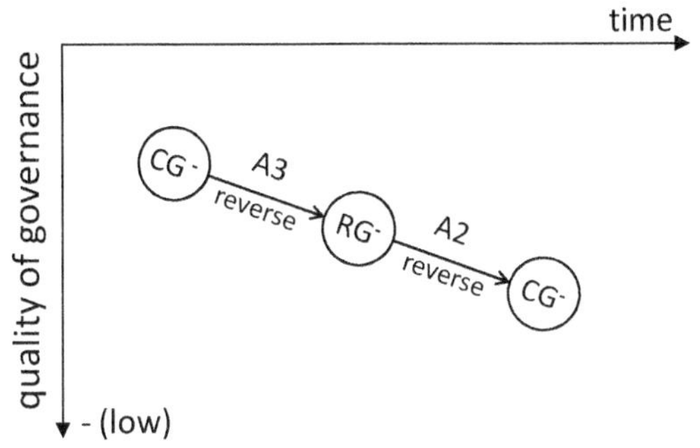

Fig. 5. Failure Path as Downward Movement

5.1.4 Exemplary Illustration of an Interrupted Path

Recapitulating the abovementioned, a success path depends on an interaction of relational and contractual governance, being both of good quality. As the opposite, a failure path is founded on poorly executed governance mechanisms. When analyzing the cases a third pattern occurred - an interrupted path.

This third pattern draws on both the success path and the failure path and deals with an exciting question: Is it possible to leave a path or is a partnership "trapped" to follow either a success or a failure path? The RECRUIT case clears up this question as it exhibits a switch from a success to a failure path and supplies evidence for the reasons to switch a path.

As mentioned before the RECRUIT case can be described as following a failure path when an incomplete contract fails to take on a safeguarding role for relational governance (A3 Reverse) and the bad relationship undermines the knowledge exchange necessary for an adequate refinement of the contract (A2 Reverse).

Notably however in the RECRUIT case is that the partnership between client and vendor was not from the beginning on a failure path but that it started with a success path. In a first step the involved parties contractually defined regular meetings and calls, hence social interaction was contractually prescribed, which provoked relational governance (A1). In a second step the well-attuned relational governance gave the parties access to knowledge that was subsequently utilized to refine the contract (A2). Or put another way: The partnership between client and vendor in the RECRUIT case was on a success path.

However, a stimulating event caused this partnership to lose the success path and instead follow the failure path. To understand how this stimulating event affected the partnership to switch from success to failure one has to flash back to the bidding process: Before GLOBAL BANK outsourced their recruiting application it organized a request for proposal process. In this process two vendors were at choice: GAMMA and COMPETITOR. GLOBAL BANK opted for GAMMA as the software solution promised a better fit to the requirements of GLOBAL BANK. After the project went live interviewees reported an overall satisfaction on business as well as on relational level (as a result of the success path followed). A few months later GAMMA was taken over by COMPETITOR, the company GLOBAL BANK initially opted against. After this takeover two events happened: First, some "vendor-employees we [GLOBAL BANK] cooperated previously with, were laid off" (C13). Second COMPETITOR decided to abandon GAMMA's recruiting software - the very piece of software which was the reason why GLOBAL BANK initially decided for GAMMA. Both events stimulated the above mentioned change in the perception of the contract that is the contract was considered to be sufficiently complete as long as the relationship was fine, but right after the takeover the involved parties started complaining about the insufficient degree of contractual completeness that inhibits a well-attuned relational governance to evolve (A3 Reverse) - in other words the events relocated the involved parties from a success path to the starting point of a failure path (see Fig. 6 for an illustration). More specifically the external event seems to fundamentally change the perceived quality of governance mechanisms (in this case, the appropriateness of the contract) and triggers the client to adapt his governance strategy.

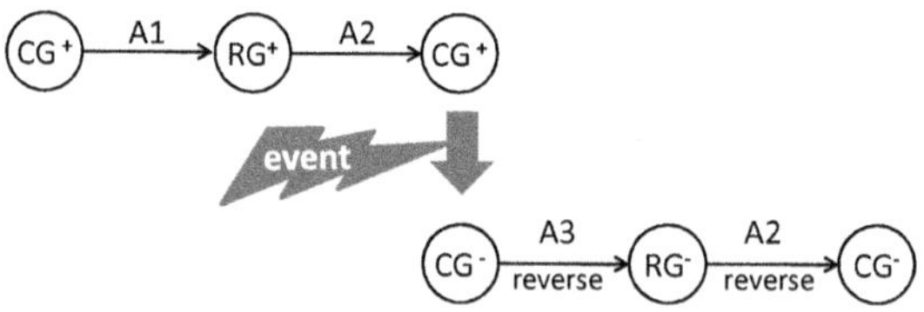

Fig. 6. Interrupted Path

Notably, we did not find any other example for leaving one path and entering the other. This suggests the assumption that the unique stimulating event (the takeover) was responsible for switching between the sequences. In addition, the fact that this switch was not the result of an action from inside the partnership but from turbulence that was rather carried into the partnership from outside was salient. We therefore conclude that sequence switches are induced from *external stimulating events that cause turbulence in the partnership.*

6 Discussion

6.1 Conclusion

This study was motivated by the question, whether the relationship between different types of governance mechanisms is the outcome of distinct processes of interaction. We identified four archetypical interaction processes (archetypes): Three archetypes yield complementary relationships, one yields a substitutional relationship. Based on these findings, we searched for patterns in the occurrence of the archetypes as well as for their underlying reasons.

Our analysis revealed three salient patterns in the occurrence of the archetypes, each representing a sequence of archetypes (see Fig. 7 for illustration): In the first two patterns sequenced archetypes reinforced each other leading to either a "success" (pattern 1) or "failure path" (pattern 2). Pattern 3 - the "interrupted path" - demonstrates how a success path is broken and turned into a failure path induced by an external stimulating event. Both success and failure path are self-enforcing. One archetype triggers the next archetype to occur, thus representing directed movements. While the success path describes an upward movement towards a higher level of governance quality, the failure path describes a downward movement towards a lower level of governance quality. Furthermore, as both success and failure paths are virtually self-enforcing there seems to be a notable tendency to persist on one of these two paths. The interrupted path affirms this tendency, as its occurrence requires an external stimulating event.

However, this is not to say that outsourcing projects are set on a success or failure path from inception. This would imply that the project team simply glides along a path unless interrupted by an exogenous factor and that management can not do anything about it. Instead the findings can be interpreted as change processes that are driven by different change motors [30]. Following Van de Ven and Poole [30], the paths can be interpreted as periods of relative stability in which governance mechanisms seem to be chosen in a process of competitive selection towards an increased alignment ("Fit") with the situation (in the notion of Van de Ven and Poole "evolutionary motor"). These periods of relative stability are *driven or facilitated by interactions between the governance mechanisms,* as these interactions and their self-enforcing nature form persisting paths (success and failure path). These paths are interrupted when external events change the perceived quality of governance mechanisms and trigger a client to reformulate his or her governance strategy. As a consequence a rather revolutionary period takes place that is characterized by fundamental changes ("teleological motor"). When reformulating the governance strategy interactions between governance mechanisms seem to be of minor importance, while (rational) goal setting and plan formulation gain center stage. However, while a new governance strategy is being implemented it seems that a project (slowly) returns to a path and therefore interactions again gain in importance increasingly.

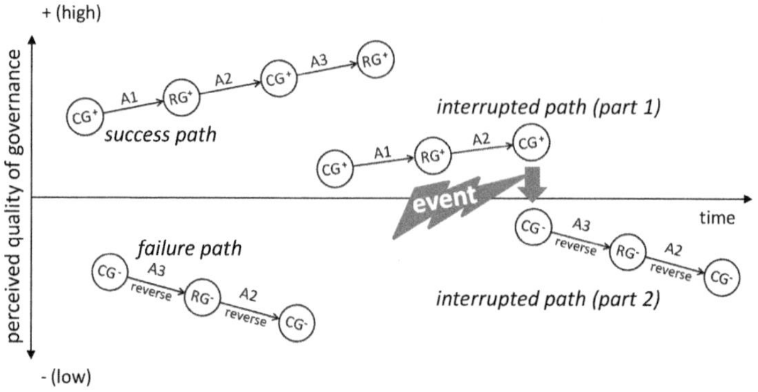

Fig. 7. Identified Sequences of Archetypes

6.2 Theoretical Implications

Our study offers a number of theoretical contributions. First of all, it enables a shift in perspective. Our findings contradict both substitutional and complementary view as these advocate an exclusive relationship, meaning that contractual and relational governance are depicted as *either* substitutes *or* complements [14,15,31]. In contrast our study rather suggests that the relationship between contractual and relational governance is the outcome of their interaction. As sequences of archetypical interaction processes occurred in each of the analyzed cases and as the involved archetypes yield either a substitutional or a complementary relationship, the relationship between contractual and relational governance is not stable over time - it is dynamic.

Moreover, our findings form a point of departure from studies which framed the relationship between contractual and relational governance as contingent upon various factors: On the one hand these studies purport that the type of governance mechanism [8] is decisive for a complementary or substitutional relationship. On the other hand the intention with which the contract is drawn, determines their temporal stable relationship [6]. However, this study's results draw a more complex picture on the relationship between contractual and relational governance: Contractual and relational governance may complement each other at an early date (e.g. A1, A2), but substitute each other at a later date (A4) and vice versa. Hence, the *relationship between contractual and relational governance is subject to change in course of time*. This does not only exceed research that took a static view, it even extends previous work that took a dynamic view, insofar, as not only the degree of contractual, respectively relational governance, may change over time [23] but also their relationship.

Although a dynamic perspective draws a very complex picture of the relationship between governance mechanisms, the salient basic patterns demonstrate that this complex picture is not devoid of regularities. These basic patterns highlight two important implications. First, their is a "dark side" of complementarity: Goo et al. [5, p. 122] argue that "the combined power of formal contracts and relational governance may be much higher ... than either governance choice in isolation". While the success path confirms this statement, the failure path - which might very well be a concatenation of *complementary* processes - sharply contradicts it. Therefore, the success and the failure path point to the fact *that complementarity works in both ways* - it might have positive consequences, but it might also result in downward movement towards a lower level of governance quality. This is the "dark side" of complementarity and it is reason enough to be suspicious of praises of the "combined power" of governance mechanisms.

Second, research on governance of IS outsourcing projects has rarely considered the (perceived) quality of governance mechanisms, instead the pure existence of distinct contractual clauses or distinct relational aspects was investigated [e.g. 5]. However, a contract might consist of a huge number of clauses and still be perceived as inadequate or incomplete, or put another way the perceived quality of the contract is low. This is not a marginal issue, because our findings indicate that the perceived quality of governance mechanisms is an important predictor for the path to be taken (success or failure path).

Finally, our findings might have the explanatory power to unify contradictory empirical results: while some researchers found evidence for a complementary relationship [e.g. 4] and others for a substitutional relationship [e.g. 15] this study highlights the importance of a dynamic perspective, as the very same types of governance mechanisms could be both complements and substitutes - at different points of time. Therefore, former contradictory empirical findings could be the result of neglecting the role of time.

6.3 Limitations and Implications for Future Research

There are several limitations to take into account. First, the study findings are based on a single-site multiple case study. This may influence the results, as there is a potential bias in the answers of the interview partners, e. g. based on the culture of the bank. Although a single-site case study enables comparability between the analyzed cases, we are aware that generalization of our findings or the transferability to other outsourcing relationships should be empirically substantiated by future research. Hence, we call for replication studies that use multiple sites in different industries in order to test or extend the archetypes and sequences presented in this study. A second limitation, which should be subject to subsequent research efforts, are missing quantitative measures. These should be developed to further investigate related effects caused by or in regard of different archetypes. Furthermore, this study could be the starting point to examine the interplay of archetypes by taking a confirmatory research approach. For that purpose we would recommend the study to be guided by path-dependence theory [32], as the relationships we discovered (paths, stimulating events) resemble major explanatory approaches of this theory. Finally, while our data revealed several "success paths" (of which we only presented one example), the "failure path" and the "interrupted path" were only observed once in our data. The reader may intuitively expect that other projects exists, which for example are ill-conceived from the beginning and therefore "doomed" to failure. Nevertheless, in the limited number of cases investigated in this study, we did not find such a discrete "failure path". Therefore we call for further research to examine whether other paths exist. Such a study could also investigate which management interventions have the potential to break failure paths and to (re)direct a project to a success path.

Acknowledgements. The authors are very grateful to the two anonymous reviewers of the 5th Global Sourcing Workshop 2011 for their insightful comments and invaluable suggestions that greatly helped improve the quality of the paper. Moreover, the authors are also thankful to participants at the 5th Global Sourcing Workshop 2011 for providing valuable suggestions that also helped improve our paper.

References

1. Dibbern, J., Winkler, J., Heinzl, A.: Explaining Variations in Client Extra Costs Between Software Projects Offshored to India. Mis Quarterly 32(2), 333–366 (2008)
2. Lacity, M., Khan, S., Willcocks, L.: A review of the IT outsourcing literature: Insights for practice. Journal of Strategic Information Systems 18(3), 130–146 (2009)
3. MaCaulay, S.: Non-Contractural Relations in Business: A Prelimnary Study. American Sociological Review 28(1), 55–67 (1963)
4. Poppo, L., Zenger, T.: Do formal contracts and relational governance function as substitutes or complements? Strategic Management Journal 23, 707–725 (2002)
5. Goo, J., Kishore, R., Rao, H., Nam, K.: The Role of Service Level Agreement in relational Management of Information Technology Outsourcing: An Empirical Study. Mis Quarterly 33(1), 119–145 (2009)
6. Klein-Woolthuis, R., Hillebrand, B., Nooteboom, B.: Trust, contract and relationship development. Organization Studies 26(6), 813 (2005)
7. Mellewigt, T., Madhok, A., Weibel, A.: Trust and formal contracts in interorganizational relationships—substitutes and complements. Managerial and Decision Economics 28(8), 833–847 (2007)
8. Tiwana, A.: Systems Development Ambidexterity: Explaining the Complementary and Substitutive Roles of Formal and Informal Controls. Journal of Management Information Systems 27(2), 87–126 (2010)
9. Lee, Y., Cavusgil, S.: Enhancing alliance performance: The effects of contractual-based versus relational-based governance. Journal of Business Research 59(8), 896–905 (2006)
10. Möllering, G.: The trust/control duality. International sociology 20(3), 283 (2005)
11. Jackson, W.: Dualism, duality and the complexity of economic institutions. International Journal of Social Economics 26(4), 545–558 (1999)
12. Reed, M.I.: Organization, Trust and Control: A Realist Analysis. Organization Studies, vol. 22(2), p. 201. Walter de Gruyter GmbH & Co. KG (2001)
13. Bachmann, R.: Trust, power and control in trans-organizational relations. Organization Studies 22(2), 337–365 (2001)
14. Larson, A.: Network Dyads in Entrepreneurial Settings: A Study of the Governance of Exchange Relationships. Administrative Science Quarterly 37(1), 76–104 (1992)
15. Ring, P.S., Van de Ven, A.H.: Developmental processes of cooperative interorganizational relationships. Academy of Management Review 19(1), 90 (1994)
16. Miles, M., Huberman, A.: Qualitative data analysis: An expanded sourcebook. SAGE publications, Inc., Thousand Oaks (1994)
17. Yin, R.: Case study research, Thousand Oaks, California (2003)
18. Benbasat, I., Goldstein, D.K., Mead, M.: The Case Research Strategy in Studies of Information Systems. Management Information Systems Quarterly 11(3), 369 (1987)
19. Eisenhardt, K.M.: Building theories from case study research. Academy of Management Review 14(4), 532 (1989)

20. Patton, M.Q.: Qualitative Research and Evaluation Methods, 3rd edn. Sage Publications, Thousand Oaks (2002)
21. Van de Ven, A.H., Delbecq, A.L., Koenig, R.: Determinants of Coordination Modes within Organizations. American Sociological Review 41(2), 322 (1976)
22. Kirsch, L.: Portfolios of control modes and IS project management. Information Systems Research 8(3), 215 (1997)
23. Inkpen, A.C., Currall, S.C.: The Coevolution of Trust, Control, and Learning in Joint Ventures. Organization Science 15(5), 586–599 (2004)
24. Rustagi, S., King, W., Kirsch, L.: Predictors of formal control usage in IT outsourcing partnerships. Information Systems Research 19(2), 126 (2008)
25. Hofstede, G.: Cultures and Organizations. Software of the mind. McGraw-Hill, London (1991)
26. Wilkins, A., Ouchi, W.: Efficient cultures: Exploring the relationship between culture and organizational performance. Administrative Science Quarterly 28(3), 468–481 (1983)
27. Fischer, T.A., Huber, T.L., Dibbern, J.: Contractual And Relational Governance As Substitutes And Complements - Explaining The Development Of Different Relationships. In: ECIS Proceedings 2011 (2011)
28. Nonaka, I., von Krogh, G.: Perspective—Tacit Knowledge and Knowledge Conversion: Controversy and Advancement in Organizational Knowledge Creation Theory. Organization Science 20(3), 635–652 (2009)
29. Kale, P., Singh, H., Perlmutter, H.: Learning and Protection of Proprietary Assets in Strategic Alliances: Building Relational Capital. Strategic Management Journal 21, 217 (2000)
30. Van de Ven, A.H., Poole, M.S.: Explaining development and change in organizations. The Academy of Management Review 20(3), 510–540 (1995)
31. Poppo, L., Zenger, T.: Do formal contracts and relational governance function as substitutes or complements? Strategic Management Journal 23(8), 707–725 (2002)
32. Sydow, J., Schreyögg, G., Koch, J.: Organizational path dependence: Opening the black box. The Academy of Management Review (AMR) 34(4), 689–709 (2009)

Maturing IT Outsourcing Relationships: A Transaction Costs Perspective

Erik Beulen

Tilburg University/EquaTerra,
P.O. Box 90153, NL-5000 LE Tilburg, The Netherlands
+31 613430398
erik.beulen@uvt.nl

Abstract. Outsourcing of information technology truly started in the early nineties. This market has grown substantially since that time. A substantial part of this market is application management. This publication provides lessons learned based on six case studies. Three historic case studies describe outsourcing engagements in the 1990s, and three recent case studies describe outsourcing engagements in the 2000s. By comparing the two, the transformation of service providers into service integrators becomes clear. This transformation resulted in substantial reductions in the total cost of ownership by investing in retained organization, resulting in an increase of the coordination costs, improved performance and more predictable cost patterns, which in turn resulted in a decrease of the production costs.

Keywords: application management, offshore outsourcing, output obligations, outsourcing, service integrator and transaction costs theory.

1 Introduction

IT outsourcing is handing over the responsibilities for the execution of IT services to an outside service provider [[26], [24] and [40]]. Excluded from the scope of this definition are public-private partnerships [[13]] and other joint venture-type of engagements [[28] and [46]], as these relationships are sourcing relationships, not outsourcing relationships. Offshore outsourcing is a specific type of IT outsourcing. In offshore outsourcing, the execution of the IT services is located in low-cost countries [[9], [10] and [34]]. Cost is not the only driver for offshore outsourcing; the availability of IT professionals is also important [[6]]. The level of proficiency and the number of available IT professionals in countries such as Brazil, Russia, India and China (BRIC countries) and countries such as the Argentina, Hungary, Mexico, Philippines, Poland or South Africa is very high [[19], [35] and [36]]. The increasing global demand for IT services can only be met by leveraging these developing countries.

Application management includes maintaining the application, bug fixing and improving and adjusting the application by the implementation of change requests, i.e., application development [[30] and [36]]. Application management is

J. Kotlarsky, L.P. Willcocks, and I. Oshri (Eds.): Global Sourcing 2011, LNBIP 91, pp. 66–79, 2011.

different from infrastructure management, such as server, desktop or network management, which requires less interaction with the client and vicinity to the locations of the client than application management [[7]]. Application management includes two types of applications. The first type is the standard software package such as Enterprise Resource Planning (ERP) software, Management Information Systems (MIS) or Database Management software: Commercial Off The Shelf (COTS) software. These standard applications are implemented and frequently modified to meet the specific requirements of a client. Application management also includes a second type of software development: dedicated software developed for the unique specifications of a particular client. This dedicated software is 100.

2 Transaction Cost Theory[1]

Implementing new business models, such as outsourcing application management, has implications for companies strategies. One important question we have already encountered is whether one should produce a certain good or service oneself or buy it from an external supplier. In part, this depends on the efficiency of the transaction involved. According to transaction cost theory [[12], [43] and [45]] companies engaging in exchanges with external companies incur several kinds of costs, collectively called coordination costs. Transaction cost theory can also be applied to outsourcing information technology services [[1], [2] and [3]]. Also included in transaction costs are a) operations risk costs, which arise from the possibility that ones partner may misrepresent the situation, withhold information or underperform, and b) opportunism risk costs [[11]], referring to partners wanting to renegotiate after the other side has already made certain investments, or simply because there are few alternatives (i.e., switching costs) [[38] and [39]]. For some application management, these costs are higher than for other IT services, as application management requires, above all, the transfer of tacit knowledge. But companies will always weigh production costs against coordination costs, that is, the advantages of internal management (also called the hierarchy), against those of external procurement governed by a market mechanism.

Two aspects of inter-business relationships play a role in application management: transaction aspects, such as uncertainty, exchange frequency, the specificity and complexity of the products and services delivered [[44] and [23]], and behaviour aspects [[43]], in particular, bounded rationality and opportunism. There are three aspects to transactions that exert a powerful influence over the decision whether to insource or outsource: asset specificity, product complexity and transaction frequency. The asset specificity of a transaction refers to the degree to which it is supported by assets that are specific to this transaction alone and that cannot be used otherwise or elsewhere without incurring a significant reduction in their value. For instance, if you need trained personnel for the transaction, this is called human capital specificity [[14]]. Application management

[1] This section is based on Beulen et al., 2011: pages 188-190.

is a very asset-specific service, as general technical knowledge of an application and/or application portfolio has to be supplemented by specific knowledge of the concerning applications in an outsourcing engagement.

Commodity products are simple and often standardized. Buyers choose on the basis of their price, and markets offer a way to compare these [[31]]. Complex products, as application management, however, involve a significant exchange of information. Even standard ERP application packages such as Microsoft, Oracle or SAP require a high degree of customization based on specific requirements of clients [[29]]. Therefore, the exchange of information in application management engagements is less easily achieved on markets because it increases the transaction costs. As product complexity rises, buyers tend to prefer single-supplier relationships that are more hierarchical.

Finally, even though some circumstances may point toward a preference for insourcing a certain transaction, setting up transactions hierarchically involves significant organization costs. Such investments are only recouped if the volume or frequency of the transactions is high enough. If they are low, the goods or services are still better procured from a market [[14]]. Outsourcing application management usually involves a high volume of transactions, such as incidents and change requests; however, the nature of the incidents and change requests is broad: different modules of the in-scope applications require different knowledge and experience from IT professionals. Companies facing outsourcing decisions for application management must attempt to strike a balance between these conflicting arguments.

Behavioral assumptions also impact outsourcing decisions for application management. Human beings try to make decisions rationally, with a view to optimizing the outcome and turning it to our advantage. The problem is that there are often too many variables for us to take them all in. Many questions are simply too complex to answer, even when we have all the information needed. This is referred to as bounded rationality: the fact that human beings intend to behave rationally but are simply incapable of doing so to more than a limited degree. This challenge is all the more daunting in complex or uncertain situations, such as the outsourcing of application management. With so many specifications unknown, it is very difficult to reach a decision and set it forth in a contract, for example, future information requirements of the business. The coordination costs of transactions may thus become very high in situations when bounded rationality and complexity or uncertainty reinforce each other.

Another human trait is that, regrettably, not all of us are equally honest. Some people try to exploit situations to their own advantage by making what has rather euphemistically been called self-disbelieved statements [[43]]. Since one can never entirely rule out the possibility that ones partner is less than fully honest, many transactions involve inspections, contracts and the like, even when the partner involved is considered perfectly trustworthy. In application management, examples include testing new functionality or monitoring the performance of resolving incident tickets. The occurrence of opportunism may therefore increase transaction costs. This is especially important if there are few potential suppliers, as in most application management engagements. Those suppliers will then care less about their reputations since there are few alternatives to which their clients might turn if they are not satisfied. Under such circumstances, which we call small numbers exchange, the possibility of opportunism is very likely to make transaction costs rise.

3 Responsibilities in Application Management

The coordination responsibilities are detailed in the IS function framework [[16], [17], [41] and [42]]. In offshore outsourcing engagements, project management capabilities also could be considered. In literature project management, capabilities are not considered specific for the IS function, but rather they are seen as organizational capabilities [[17] and [42]]. Nevertheless, offshore outsourcing engagements increase the need for including project management capabilities in IS functions. They give the client organization more control over the delivery of their services [[5]]. The specific coordination responsibilities in application management that will be taken into account in the analyses are a) define the requirements of the client organization, and b) control the performance.

Mature suppliers will proactively bring innovation to their clients by facilitating workshops with the Chief Information Officer, information managers and business representatives: the technology push. This provides input for the definition of the client organization requirements. For control of performance, the applied service management tooling is subject to discussion: supplier tooling or client tooling. Client tooling supports an integral reporting on performance across all domains and its associated suppliers. Both responsibilities in application management are considered coordination costs in terms of the transaction cost theory. By outsourcing application management, the costs associated with these responsibilities will go up. The suppliers service portfolio impacts the definition of requirements and results in additional coordination effort in the client organization. The coordination costs related to the control of performance are substantially higher in outsourcing. Managing a supplier requires extra effort compared to managing an internal department.

In addition, the service delivery and the coordination of performance are taken into account. The execution of service delivery and the coordination of performance in outsourcing engagements is always the responsibility of the supplier. Although, in immature outsourcing engagements, there can be involvement by representatives of the client company. As part of the service delivery, the supplier will also execute root cause analysis in case the service levels are not met. Root cause analysis determines the cause of the disruption and who was responsible for the disruption ex ante analysis as part of the ITIL process problem management. The coordination of performance is included in managing the day-to-day operation, including monitoring and enabling proactive actions. This includes ticket allocation and managing change requests; both responsibilities are production costs in terms of the transaction cost theory. By outsourcing application management, the costs associated with these responsibilities will decrease through economies of scale, standardization (in other words, a service catalogue), leveraging process maturity and geographical spread (enabling offshore outsourcing). The production costs related to the coordination of performance are substantially lower in outsourcing by using an industrialized approach supported by tooling.

4 Market Developments

Outsourcing of information technology truly began in the early nineties. Eastman Kodak and General Dynamics were early adopters [[24] and [20]]. This market has grown substantially since that time. The current application management market (enterprise application outsourcing) according to Gartner is 279 billion USD. The expected Calculated Annual Growth Rate for 2009 - 2014 is 3.8.

In addition to the increase in size, there is also a clear shift towards output based and managed services. In the nineties, suppliers provided qualified resources to offer IT services managed by clients. From 2000 onwards, output obligations, including service credit arrangements, were introduced [[4]]. Since 2005, multi-supplier sourcing [[33] and [27]]) and leveraging delivery centers in developing countries [[34]] has come into fashion [[25]]. This required end-to-end managed services contracts and for suppliers to transform into service integrators. Over time, the responsibilities of the providers are increasing. The remaining responsibilities of the client are limited to managing the service integrator, including coordinating the IT requirements of the organization. This minimizes the coordination costs for the client. Today, service integrators have end-to-end responsibility for managed services based on Service Level Agreements to provide the IT services and Operating Level Agreements to facilitate contract management of the underlying suppliers who are responsible for parts of the IT service provisioning [[18]]. These underlying service providers also have, as the service integrator, Service Level Agreements with the client for providing IT services. The Operating Level Agreements reflect the governance for managing an end-to-end managed service.

5 Research Approach

Outsourcing engagement and the management of outsourcing engagements has changed over the last few decades. The current research approach is to compare outsourcing engagements from the late nineties with recent outsourcing engagements from 2003 onwards. All analyzed case studies include large client companies and mature suppliers. The interviews for these historic case studies took place between 1997 and 1999, while the interviews for the three recent case studies took place between 2004 and 2008. The interview scripts of all interviews were analyzed to understand the changing responsibilities in contract management in IT outsourcing. We chose a qualitative research method of multiple respondents covering the perspective of both parties as an appropriate method for exploring contract management practices in IT outsourcing. The understanding of contract management in IT outsourcing depends on the knowledge of reality as socially constructed by the individual human actors [[37]]. The author interviewed representatives of both the client and supplier organization (see Table 1). In addition to the interviews, desk research is included in this research analysis. Including historic and recent case studies along with multiple perspectives provided a rich picture in this otherwise often messy and iterative process [[32]]. The findings presented here are further based on information drawn from the corporate documents of the companies involved: requests for proposal, meeting minutes, contracts, and service level agreements. Information available in the public domain, such as annual reports and newspaper clippings, was also included in this research. This process of cross-validating the documentary data with the topics emerging from interviews and the authors observations allowed for within method data triangulation and increased interpretive validity [[22]]. This approach was also adopted to bridge the notions of generalizability of the results.

6 Analyzed Case Studies

There are three historic and three recent case studies analyzed to understand the transformations that have occurred in contract management in IT outsourcing. The services for each analyzed historic case study were delivered out of a single European delivery center by a single supplier. The contractual provisions of these analyzed case studies were best-effort based and only to a limited degree were there service levels detailed in the contract. The recent case studies include output-based obligations and clearly defined service levels for multiple suppliers. The contracts of the fourth and fifth case study also included penalties. All recent contracts include an end-to-end service delivery responsibility. The service provisioning of each analyzed recent case study were per supplier delivered out of multiple delivery centers, such as delivery centers in developing countries, which included, amongst others, delivery centers in India and China.

7 Analysis

The analysis of the case studies includes the four responsibilities in outsourcing engagements. The first responsibility is the definition of the requirements. The maturity of the client information management organizations in the three historic case studies is limited. Also, the involvement of business representatives in the requirements definition was not sufficient in the three historic case studies. The utility company (case study 3) had issues involving communications with their supplier, although this company had implemented the ITIL processes to facilitate this communication. The utility companys IT strategy was ambiguous and includes insufficient guidance for the supplier. Contrarily, the IT strategy of the truck manufacturer (case study 2)was clear. Their IT strategy was endorsed by senior business and IT management. Their IT strategy also enabled communication with the supplier. To enable communication and define the requirements

Table 1. Key characteristics of the analyzed case studies

		Company profile	IT services	Engagement (TCV in US$ - duration - start initial contract)	#inter-views @ client com-pany	#inter-views @ supplier com-pany
Historic case studies	Case study 1	International manufacturer	IT support and software maintenance and support	+10 million US$ / 5 year / 1997	2	2
	Case study 2	International truck manufacturer	Infrastructure management and application management	+30 million US$ / 5 year / 1992 (renewed)	2	2
	Case study 3	Utility company	IT support and software maintenance and support	+25 million US$ / 5 year / 1996	2	2
Recent case studies	Case study 4	International CPG company	ERP services	Confidential / 3 year / 2003	1	3
	Case study 5	Global natural resources company	Customization of ERP software	Confidential / 2 year / 2007	4	3
	Case study 6	International chemicals and coatings company	Application Management	+30 million / 3 year / 2003 (renewed)	2	1

better, the utility company (case study 3) retained a team of technical specialist in house. This team was an overlap of the supplier team. This inefficiency did not contribute to the effectiveness and cost effectiveness in this application management engagement. The requirements of the international manufacturer (case study 1) were different per business unit. This impacted the effectiveness of the definition of requirements. Representative involvement was too limited, resulting in rework for the supplier.

The client organizations in the recent case studies are more mature in defining requirements. The change control board of the international CPG company (case study 4) includes business representatives ensuring a proper definition of these requirements. In the global natural resources company (case study 5), it became clear that part-time participation by business representatives in the design of the implementation of the ERP software impacted the effectiveness of the definition of the requirements. Therefore, this company added a senior project manager to the project team to ensure improvement in the definition of the requirements. The international chemicals and coatings company (case study 6) had embedded information management in the business unit. This organizational design enabled the definition of the requirements ,as the information management and business representatives were in a single organizational unit. In addition, the information management reported to the corporate Chief Information Officer (functional reporting). By including business representatives in the definition of requirements, they avoided a significant amount of rework. Involving representatives of the business increased the coordination costs and resulted in a decrease of the production costs through a reduction of rework. As production costs in application management are the bulk of the effort, the investment of business representative participation results in a lower Total Cost Ownership for application management.

The second responsibility is the control of performance. Contracts are the basis for performance control. The contract and contract structure of the historic case studies were immature. The contracts were best-effort based and most of the contracts lacked a proper Service Level Agreement. The international manufacturer (case study 1) had a very pre-elementary underpinning Service Level Agreement with only a few performance indicators. The contract structure of the international truck manufacturing (case study 2) was fairly mature; however, it was not actively used by the client and supplier to control performance. In addition, the utility company (case study 3) had issues with the availability of the contract manager. Their contract manager simply had too limited time available for managing this contract, limited to about 10.

This is different for all recent case studies. The international CPG company (case study 4) had a single contract that included a service catalogue with the supplier and internal contracts with their operating companies. This reduced the coordination costs for managing the outsourcing engagement: A single contract versus a large number of contracts by operating company impacted the effectiveness of the coordination positively. This single contract also covered cooperation between the involved suppliers: the ERP software vendor, application maintenance supplier, hardware vendor and the functional support supplier. It also included the reporting of actual performance to the international CPG company. Alignment across the involved suppliers reduced the costs of controlling the performance significantly. As an entry criteria, the involved application maintenance supplier and the functional support supplier had to provide evidence of certification of their service delivery processes. This highly contributed to the effectiveness of controlling performance. Initially, the global natural resources company (case study 5) had issues with performance control. The performance reports provided insufficient detail. By improving the quality and the level of detail, the global natural resources company was able to correct in time the lack of progress in project implementation. The supplier also added a senior SAP QA resource to the team; the concept of sneak previews was implemented and additional physical meetings scheduled. The international CPG company (case study 4) and international chemicals and coatings company (case study 6) had implemented a proper governance structure covering the strategic, tactical and operational levels. The focus in performance control by ITIL processes was on monitoring the agreed improvement of the service provision. Supplier ISO certification contributed to the clients ability to control performance for the international CPG company and the international chemicals and coatings company. As improvement was the top priority for the international chemicals and coating company (case study 6), the contracts did not include penalty clauses.

By including governance improvement and actual performance reporting, the quality of the service delivery can be improved and the total cost of ownership reduced. Improving governance requires an additional effort from both the client and the supplier organizations. They have to participate in meetings and follow up on the agreed actions. Improving reporting requires investments in service management tooling and in processes, such as ITIL and/or COBIT, and in certification such as ISO. These investments will increase the coordination costs; however, these additional coordination costs will be offset by a reduction in costs and improving the quality of service delivery: the production costs. A proper governance and detailed reporting mandate enables a proactive management of the engagement.

The third responsibility is the service delivery, including the root cause analysis. As a general observation, the client organizations of the historic case studies were partly involved in performing the service delivery. For example, the international manufacturer in case study 1 employs about 30 IT professionals, supplemented by a large number of contractors. This resulted in a shared responsibility for the service delivery. The absence of a uniform and agreed upon conceptual framework between client and supplier organization causes problems. In addition, the responsibility for the service delivery was a shared responsibility between the international truck manufacturer and the supplier. The client contract manager was not only responsible for managing the contract, he was also responsible for performing the service delivery. In performing the service delivery, the utility company (case study 3) leveraged ITIL and service management tooling. Despite the shared responsibility for the service delivery, ITIL and the service management tooling contributed to the effectiveness and cost levels. All of the recent case studies investigated leveraged ITIL and service management tooling to perform the service delivery. There were also very clear role descriptions at the supplier end. For example, at the international CPG company (case study 4), the supplier organization implemented the role of customer operations director. The customer operations director was fully responsible for the service delivery and reporting to the contract manager of the client organization. There were no responsibilities left for the client company.

This split in responsibilities at the supplier organization is similar to the split observed at the international chemical and coatings company (case study 6), who appointed a service delivery manager. In addition, there was a service manager dedicated to maintaining the relationship with client company. The supplier organization of the international CPG company (case study 4) created a similar role: account executive. The supplier for the natural resources company (case study 5) was fully responsible for the implementation of the ERP software and no shared delivery responsibilities were involved. None of the suppliers in the historic case studies performed root cause analysis. With respect to the recent case studies, root cause analysis was an explicit responsibility for the suppliers. It was also a prerequisite to achieve the committed continuous improvement in performing the services, as detailed in the contracts for the international CPG company (case study 4) and the international chemicals and coatings company (case study 6). The outcome of any root cause analysis is an improvement plan that results in future improvements in the service delivery. For example, the average resolution time and the number of incident tickets were two performance indicators specified in the contract for the international chemicals and coatings company (case study 6).

By making service delivery the sole province of the supplier, coordination costs will be reduced. Production costs will be reduced, as well, as the supplier can maximize the leverage of its processes and tooling. By implementing root cause analysis, coordination costs will increase. However, this investment will also reduce production costs. The future service delivery will be more cost effective as improvement plans are implemented. The net effect of implementing root cause analysis is a decrease in the Total Costs of Ownership.

The fourth responsibility is the coordination of performance. As with the third responsibility, there is significant involvement by the information managers and contact managers of the three historical case study client organizations. This impacts the effectiveness performance coordination and increases coordination costs. In the recent case studies, this responsibility was within the domain of the supplier. However, there were issues found in the recent case studies that need to be discussed. Coordination costs related to performance coordination for all three outsourcing engagement increased because of leveraging (multiple) offshore location(s) (for all three case studies, India; and for case study 6, India, China and Argentina) and multiple suppliers. Because of this, production costs in all three outsourcing engagements decreased, predominantly through labor arbitrage. The biggest increase for the international company (case study 4) was related to the large number of suppliers: the ERP software vendor, application maintenance supplier, hardware vendor and the functional support supplier. To ensure a proper coordination of performance, in addition to the contracts between the international CPG company and the supplier, Operating Level Agreements (OLAs) were implemented between the involved suppliers. The OLAs describe the responsibilities for the involved suppliers towards one another. The increase of the coordination costs for the international CPG company (case study 5) were significant, as the largest portion of the delivery team was located in India and the remaining part of the delivery team was located in Europe. To compound the problem, the business representatives were on another continent, and the European regional headquarters was in a different European country. This resulted in additional coordination costs. The international chemicals and coating company (case study 6) had not implemented OLAs. However, the collaboration between the involved suppliers went smoothly, regardless. A typical issue for this supplier was the relatively small size of the teams of IT professionals, as this contract included a large number of different technologies spread over multiple delivery centers across the globe. In response, the supplier appointed technical leads per technology base. A technical lead is the senior professional responsible for performance coordination within their domain.

By making performance coordination a supplier responsibility, the coordination costs are reduced. Furthermore, production costs also will be reduced, as the supplier can maximize the leverage of their offshore locations. By implementing OLAs, the increase of the coordination costs will decrease while leveraging the improved competitiveness in the supplier landscape. The net effect of introducing offshore and multiple suppliers is a decrease in the Total Costs of Ownership.

The impact of the maturing of IT outsourcing relations in application management on the transaction costs are summarized in the below table.

Table 2. Impact of the maturing IT outsourcing relations in application management on transaction costs

responsibilities in outsourcing engagements	**historic case studies**	**recent case studies**	**resulting in**
Definition of requirements	from limited involvement of business representatives	to sufficient involvement of business representatives	avoiding rework
	from immature ITIL processes	to mature ITIL processes including change control boards	ensuring a smooth process
	from immature information management (CIO office)	to mature information management (CIO office)	clear IT strategy
Control of performance	from no service levels agreements	to service level agreements and underpinning operating level agreements	improved governance
	from dedicated service descriptions	to service catalogues	improved ordering of services
	from resolving incidents only	to root cause analysis and improvement plans	continuous improvement
Service Delivery	from shared responsibility	to outsourced responsibility	clear demarcation of responsibilities
	from minimal processes and service management tooling	to detailed processes and a full suite for service management	improved efficiency and effectiveness of the service delivery
	from combined front office roles	to dedicated front office roles such as delivery manager	improved focus for staff in front office roles
Coordination of the performance	from onshore and single delivery center	to nearshore and offshore and multiple delivery center	a decrease of the TCO by leveraging labor arbitrage
	from simple governance structure to	to multi level and multi country governance	a increase of the coordination cost
	from centralized service provisioning	to decentralized service provisioning	decreased production costs and increased coordination costs

8 Conclusions

In application management, the relationships have matured and supplier commitments have increased. Client organizations should invest in implementing demand management and involve business representatives to improve the definition of the requirements. Both client organizations and the supplier organization should invest in implementing a proper governance structure. The supplier should invest in increasing the quality and level of detail of the reporting requirements. These investments in the governance and reporting improve the control of performance. By making these investments in coordination costs, both in terms of the improvement of the definition of the requirements and in the control of the performance, the production costs decrease, as rework will avoided.

By contracting the implementation of root cause analysis resulting in an additional contract commitment for continuous improvement, the coordination costs increase and the production costs decrease for the supplier. The quality of service delivery will increase at substantially lower costs. Finally, in regard to the coordination of performance, there are issues to be addressed, as leveraging labor arbitrage is meant to stay. By including multiple delivery centers in developing countries, the coordination costs increase significantly, and the production costs decrease to an even greater extent. Working with multiple suppliers increases coordination costs, but by increasing the level of competition, reduces production costs. The collaboration between multiple suppliers is supported by the implementation of OLAs. These agreements help decrease the increase in the coordination costs by facilitating collaboration between multiple suppliers. The net effect is more mature IT outsourcing relationships and increased commitments in application management at a reduced Total Cost of Ownership.

These preliminary conclusions must be verified by investigating additional outsourcing engagements in application management. Alternatively, a practitioners survey could provide valuable insights. The participation of both client and supplier representatives is clearly important in this area; it might be interesting to investigate different type of services, such as infrastructure services or business process outsourcing. Will this result in differences, and if so, how can these differences be explained?

References

1. Aubert, B., Rivard, S., Patry, M.: A transaction cost approach to outsourcing behavior: Some empirical evidence. Information and Management 30(2), 51–64 (1996)
2. Aubert, B., Rivard, S., Patry, M.: A transaction cost model of IT outsourcing. Information and Management 41(7), 921–932 (2004)
3. Bahli, B., Rivard, S.: Validating measures of information technology outsourcing risk factors. Omega 33(2), 175–187 (2005)
4. Barthlemy, J.: The hard and soft sides of it outsourcing management. European Management Journal 21(5), 539–548 (2003)
5. Beulen, E.: The management of global sourcing partnerships: Implications for the capabilities and skills of the IS function presented at the Global Sourcing workshop, Val dIsre (March 2007)
6. Beulen, E.: Long-held perceptions of the consequences of IT offshoring will become a reality: Fewer IS jobs in developed countries. Journal of Information Technology 25, 376–377 (2010)
7. Beulen, E., Fenema, P., Currie, W.: From application outsourcing to infrastructure management. European Management Journal 23(2), 133–144 (2005)
8. Beulen, E., Ribbers, P., Roos, J.: Managing IT outsourcing, 2nd edn. Routledge, Oxon (2011)

9. Carmel, E.: Global software teams, collaboration across borders and time zones. Prentice Hall, Englewood Cliffs (1999)
10. Carmel, E., Tjia, P.: Offshoring information technology: Sourcing and outsourcing to a global workforce. Cambridge University Press, Cambridge (2005)
11. Clemons, E., Reddi, S., Row, M.: The impact of information technology on the organization of economic activity: The move to the middle hypothesis. Journal of Management of Information Systems 10(2), 9–35 (1993)
12. Coase, R.: The nature of the firm. Economica 4(16), 386–405 (1937)
13. Cordella, A., Willcocks, L.: Outsourcing, bureaucracy and public value: Reappraising the notion of the contract state. Government Information Quarterly 27(1), 82–88 (2010)
14. Douma, S., Schreuder, H.: Economic approaches to organizations, 2nd edn. Prentice Hall Europe, Hertfordshire (1998)
15. Eisenhardt, K.M.: Building theory from case study research. Academy of Management Review 14(4), 532–550 (1989)
16. Feeny, D., Willcocks, L.: Re-designing the IS function around core capabilities. Long Range Planning 31(3), 354–367 (1998a)
17. Feeny, D., Willcocks, L.: Core IS capabilities for exploiting information technology. MIT Sloan Management Review 39(3), 9–21 (1998b)
18. Goo, J., Kishore, R., Rao, H., Nam, K.: The role of service level agreements in relational management of information technology outsourcing: An empirical study. Management Information Systems Quarterly 33(1), 119–146 (2009)
19. Gray, T.: How to gauge the rush to emerging markets, The New York Times (January 9, 2010)
20. Grover, V., Cheon, M., Teng, J.: A descriptive study on the outsourcing of information systems functions. Information and Management 27(1), 33–44 (1994)
21. Harris, J., Hale, K., Brown, R., Young, A., Morikawa, C.: Forecast: Outsourcing, worldwide, 2000-2014, Gartner research report, ITST-WW-DB-DA03 (September 13, 2010)
22. Jick, T.: Mixing qualitative and quantitative methods, triangulation in action. Administrative Science Quarterly 24, 602–611 (1979)
23. Klein, S.: The configuration of inter-organizational relationships. European Journal of Information Systems 5(2), 75–84 (1996)
24. Lacity, M., Hirschheim, R.: Information systems outsourcing. John Wiley and Sons Ltd., Chichester (1993)
25. Levena, N., Su, N.: Global multisourcing strategy: The emergence of a supplier portfolio in services offshoring. Decision Sciences 39(3), 541–570 (2008)
26. Loh, L., Venkatraman, N.: Determinants of Information Technology outsourcing: A cross-sectional analysis. Journal of Management information systems 9(1), 7–24 (1992)
27. Longwood, J.: The role of the multisourcing service integrator in delivering end-to-end outsourced services, Gartner report, G00200898 (June 21, 2010)
28. McFarlan, W., Nolan, R.: How to manage an IT outsourcing alliance. Sloan Management Review 36(2), 9–24 (1995)
29. Morton, N., Hu, Q.: Implications of the fit between organizational structure and ERP: A structural contingency theory perspective. International journal of information Management 28(5), 391–402 (2008)
30. Murphy, P., Moore, S., Heffner, R., Hammond, J., Vollmer, K., DeGennaro, T.: Application modernization taxonomy clarifies choices and paves a path for progress, Forrester research report (October 17, 2008)

31. Nooteboom, B.: Inter-firm alliances: Analysis and design. Routledge, London (1999)
32. Parkhe, A.: 'Messy' research, methodological predispositions, and theory development in international joint ventures. Academy of Management 18, 227–268 (1993)
33. Patton, S.: Cutting cost with multiple outsourcers. CIO Magazine (January 16, 2007)
34. Rottman, J., Lacity, M.: Proven practices for effectively offshoring IT work. Sloan Management Review 47(3), 56–63 (2006)
35. Shang, S.: China ICT market 2010-2014 forecast and analysis, IDC research report, April, CN8037301S (2010)
36. Shuchat, R.: Worldwide and U.S. application management services 2010-2014 forecast update, IDC research report, November 2010, Doc 225648 (2010)
37. Walsham, G.: The emergence of interpretivism in IS research. Information Systems Research 6, 376–394 (1995)
38. Whitten, D., Wakefield, R.: Measuring switching costs in IT outsourcing services. The Journal of Strategic Information Systems 15(3), 219–248 (2006)
39. Whitten, D., Chakrabarty, S., Wakefield, R.: The strategic choice to continue outsourcing, switching vendors, or backsource: Do switching costs matter? Information and Management 47, 167–175 (2010)
40. Willcocks, L., Fitzgerald, G.: Market as opportunity? Case studies in outsourcing information technology and services. Journal of Strategic Information Systems 2(3), 223–242 (1993)
41. Willcocks, L., Feeny, D.: IT outsourcing and core IS capabilities: Challenges and lessons at Dupont. Information Systems Management 23(1), 49–56 (2006)
42. Willcocks, L., Feeny, D., Olson, N.: Implicating core IS capabilities: Feeny-Willcocks IT governance and management framework revisited. European Management Journal 24(1), 28–37 (2006)
43. Williamson, O.: Markets and hierarchies. Free Press, New York (1975)
44. Williamson, O.: Transaction cost economics: Governance of contractual relations. Journal of Law and Economics 22(2), 233–261 (1979)
45. Williamson, O.: Organizational innovation: the transaction cost approach. In: Ronen, J. (ed.) Entrepreneurship. Lexington Books, Lexington (1983)
46. Ybarra, C., Turk, T.: The evolution of trust in information technology alliances. Journal of High Technology Management Research 20(1), 62–74 (2009)

Examining the Implications of Organizational Structure Changes from a Transaction Cost Perspective

Albert Plugge[1] and Jacques Brook[2]

[1] Faculty of Technology, Policy and Management,
Delft University of Technology, The Netherlands
[2] Faculty of Strategy, Marketing and International Business,
Maastricht School of Management, The Netherlands

Abstract. Firms' rationale to outsource parts of their IT function are mainly based on cost reduction. Many vendors applied a high level of standardization in organizing the delivery of IT services to decrease their cost level. Drawing on the Transaction Cost Economics the objective of our study is to examine how environmental uncertainty and asset specificity affect vendors' functional organizational structure and, in turn, influences ex-post transaction costs. A retrospective view on a case study was investigated from the perspective of a global outsourcing vendor. Our results suggest that the vendor's functional organizational structure can be considered as a mediator in minimizing the ex-post transaction costs. Executives and managers need to be aware that uncertainty and asset specificity may lead to an increase of the coordination costs. Therefore, vendors need to reassess their organizational structure regularly and implement adjustments to control their ex-post transaction costs.

Keywords: Outsourcing, Strategic management, Organizational structure, Transaction cost.

1 Introduction

Nowadays, firms' rationale to outsource parts of their IT function is mainly based on cost reduction [1]. As a result, the growing competition in the vendor market has largely been focused on competitive pricing in IT services propositions. In this context, many vendors adopted a high level of standardization in developing and providing IT services in order to decrease their cost level. Moreover, vendors established offshore centres to benefit from reduced cost and process streamlining [2]. The vendors' adoption of standardized ways of working in IT outsourcing tends to lead to a static view of how to organize IT services over time. As the environment of firms changes frequently, it is key to assess these changes to determine their impact. Consequently, changes in the environment of the client are also relevant for the vendor to assess how these exogenous developments affect their organizational structure. Interestingly, studying the effects of the environment of ITO decisions is still under-researched [3].

On a functional level IT outsourcing vendors establish a specific organizational structure to facilitate the delivery of IT services to their customers. Hence, different

J. Kotlarsky, L.P. Willcocks, and I. Oshri (Eds.): Global Sourcing 2011, LNBIP 91, pp. 80–98, 2011.

dimensions of organizational structures can be addressed that play a role organizing tasks, processes and resources. These dimensions, for example, include the level of formalization, specialization, decision-making and hierarchy of authority [4]. Since environmental developments are likely to change over time vendors have to review their organizational structure and accompanying dimensions regularly. This means that vendors' organizational structure, which is often based on the delivery of standard IT services, may change to meet the client's demand. However, changing the organizational structure may have consequences for the degree of idiosyncrasy to support the delivery of IT services. This refers to the nature of asset specificity [5]. As assets can be transaction-specific they determine the mode of governance (market, hybrid, hierarchal). However, the decision to reconfigure the vendor's organizational structure may affect the cost structure (e.g. financial business case) of the outsourcing agreement over time. The relationship between the vendor's standardized organizational structure and environmental developments results in a serious tension. Drawing on the Transaction Cost Economics (TCE), the objective of our study is to examine how IT delivery characteristics, environmental uncertainty and asset specificity, affect vendors' functional organizational structure. We argue that the vendor's functional organizational structure can be used as a mediator to minimize the ex-post transaction cost. This research theme has strong strategic relevance, as the vendor's decision-making to participate in long-term outsourcing arrangements is influenced by exogenous developments over time, which, in turn, may affect their cost structure. This means that IT delivery characteristics *environmental uncertainty* and *asset specificity* can be considered as important determinants of strategic decision-making.

This paper is organized as follows. Section 2 presents the theoretical framework of transaction cost and organizational structure. Section 3 explains the research approach. Subsequently, the case study findings are presented in section 4. We then discuss these findings in section 5. Finally, our conclusions and recommendations are presented in section 6.

2 Literature Review

2.1 TCE

With regard to the field of IT outsourcing, the TCE is applied discussing sourcing decision-making [6] [7], IT operations [8] and costs [9]. Williamson [10] proposes that costs comprise not only production costs, the costs of capital, labor and material, but also transaction costs. This means that firms, and thus decision-makers, have to consider integral costs - production costs plus transaction costs - when considering producing services. The level of transaction costs depends on specific characteristics of the services to be delivered, economic aspects and the way in which the organization is structured. Previous research [11] revealed that firms are able to produce goods or services at lower costs due to economies of scale that can be achieved via mass production efficiencies. Due to this rationale IT outsourcing vendors focus on reducing their average costs by allocating fixed costs over more units of output and by receiving discounts due to bargaining power. Important determining factors that refer to outsourcing transactions concern the uncertainty surrounding the transaction and the specificity of the assets. At any time, there is a level of *uncertainty* surrounding transactions. Lacity and Willcocks [12] describe the relationship between uncertainty of the transaction and the coordination costs. The more uncertainty surrounds a transaction, the higher coordination costs will become for a vendor. Previous research [13] defines uncertainty as the degree of specifiability of intended performance and predictability of the environment within which the contract is to be executed. The extent to which uncertainly reveals itself also relates to the market in which a vendor is acting. For instance, in very dynamic or so-called 'high velocity' markets, changes are unpredictable and become non-linear. Moreover, measuring the extent of uncertainly is important to determine the impact on the transaction including aspects such as quantity, quality and price [14]. Addressing the determinant of uncertainty, two forms can be considered: behavioural uncertainty and environmental uncertainty [15] [16]. For instance, when a client is not willing or able to specify an IT service, this will lead in some extent to uncertainty on the vendor side. This refers to the form of behavioural uncertainty. The second form, environmental uncertainty, refers to a firm's ability to predict future developments [17]. It is impossible to anticipate all future eventualities and to describe them in a contract. This may lead to opportunistic behavior of firms neglecting additional cost such related to negotiation and coordination as a result of changing circumstances [17]. In this paper we focus on the latter form of uncertainty. The second determinant factor that is important refers to *asset specificity*. The degree of customization, specific or non-specific, of the transaction type can be measured by the difference between costs of the asset and the value of its second best use [18]. As asset specificity increases they become increasingly costly to implement [8]. Investments in specific assets will lead to higher transaction costs; therefore a vendor who is investing in specific assets is looking for guarantees from their client. One of the TCE assumptions is the existence of a relationship between asset specificity and the complexity of governance structures. As Dyer [5] stated: 'The standard (transaction cost) reasoning is that as asset specificity increases, more complex governance structures are required to eliminate or attenuate costly bargaining over profits from specialized assets'. When a firm does not possess the required competences for the internal coordination of services, they can develop or acquire them with the acceptance of high transaction costs. This means that a firm has to adjust their existing coordination mechanism. This coordination mechanism can be considered as an organizational structure that a firm applies to produce and transfer a product or service towards their clients.

2.2 Organizational Structure

Formal organizational structure and the roles that people play, including the competences and responsibilities involved have been investigated extensively in organizational literature [19] [20] [21]. An organization is a unit of formal positions, usually occupied by individuals, with explicit objectives, tasks, processes and assets [22] and is related to firm performance [23]. Vendors that rely on the division of labour, as outsourcing vendors do, can only stay in business when they are able to organize their internal transaction of IT services more efficiently than other firms. Existing literature suggests that the nature of organizational structure in industrial versus post-industrial firms can be regarded as mechanistic (inorganic) versus organic [24] [25]. Daft [21] argues that the mechanistic paradigm is effective when environments have a high degree of certainty and organizations are designed to handle handling large volumes (e.g. products or services). Internal forms tend to be vertical, functional and bureaucratic. The organic paradigm, on the other hand, is characterized by an unstable, even chaotic nature of the external environment. Typical features of these types of organizations are teamwork, face-to-face interactions, learning and innovation. Daft [21] studied various organizational dimensions such as the level of formalization, specialization, standardization, hierarchy of authority, and professionalism. Germain [26] focuses on specialization, centralization, and decentralization. Nahm [4] concentrate on the degree of centralization of the decision-making process, formalization of rules and procedures and structural differentiation in their research into environmental uncertainty and organizational form. Among this variety of sub-dimensions for organizational structure, the four commonly discussed are deemed relevant to this study. These sub-dimensions concern the number of layers in hierarchy, the level of horizontal integration, the locus of decision-making, and the level of communication. The *number of layers in hierarchy* is the degree to which an organization has many versus few levels of management [27] [28]. In a more traditional command-and-control model, an expanding hierarchy is necessary as a result of the need to control behaviour. In a commitment model, the management form tends to be flat, relies upon shared goals for control and lateral coordination, influences based on expertise and information rather than position and minimizes status difference. The *level of horizontal integration* is the degree to which departments and workers are functionally specialized versus integrated in their work, skills and training [29] [30]. Firms that are based on production (e.g. products), usually separate functional departments so that work can be carried out in a sequential manner. However, firms that are focusing on the provisioning of services will integrate functionalities of different departments and their employees. The justification for this choice is based on an adequate response to the changing environment and needs of the client organization and therefore it adds value. The *locus of decision-making* is the degree to which decisions are made higher versus lower in the organizational hierarchy [21] [26] [29]. Firms that are operating in an uncertain environment should delegate decisions to the level where employees are able to quickly adapt to changing circumstances and add value to their customers. When organizational uncertainty is high, strategic decision-making authority may be centralized [31] but operational decision-making authority should be decentralized. The lower the locus, the more decentralized decision-making. The sub-dimension, *level of communication*, refers to characteristics like speed, complexity and regularity. In a management model where control is leading, vertical and horizontal communication will be slow, difficult and limited in nature. Organizations that apply a management model based on commitment will find that the level of horizontal communication will increase and the nature of vertical communication will change [29].

2.3 Towards a Research Framework

Although the client-vendor outsourcing relationship is our starting point, the unit of analyses of this research is the vendor organization. Since environmental uncertainty increases over time, vendors involved in outsourcing arrangements will develop strategies to meet their client's business needs. As it is impossible to anticipate all future contingencies, business environmental uncertainty may result in changes in the vendor's organizational structure. The extent to which uncertainty can be demonstrated is also dependent to the market in which a vendor is acting. The more uncertainty surrounds a transaction, the higher the impact on vendors organizational structure will become. This brings us to our first proposition.

Proposition 1: Environmental uncertainty will lead to adjustment in vendor organizational structure.

When vendors provide highly standardized IT services to clients, the degree of asset specificity can be considered as low. As the complexity to coordinate the outsourcing transactions increases, the degree of asset specificity increases, too. However, TCE models have often been criticized that the social context in which transactions are embedded are not taken into account [32]. This refers to topics such as culture, mutual cooperation, and distance. It can be assumed that the degree of idiosyncrasy of the transaction type will affect the organizational structure of a vendor. The degree of asset specificity thus influences the various organizational dimensions as described earlier. This brings us to our second proposition.

Proposition 2: An increase of asset specificity will lead to adjustment in vendor organizational structure.

Throughout the outsourcing arrangement, it can be assumed that the vendor's situation is subject to change that could lead to changes in their supporting organizational structure and accompanying dimensions. As a result of an increase of environmental uncertainty and a higher level of customization, the investments in specific assets will lead to higher transaction costs. In particular, the coordination cost to provide the delivery of IT services towards the client will increase. For example, a vendor has to pay more attention towards monitoring, controlling and managing the IT services internally. As such, it is expected that the adjustment of vendor's organizational structure will result in increased transaction costs. This results in our last proposition.

Proposition 3: Vendors adjustment of their organizational structure will lead to an increase of ex- post transaction costs.

A basic premise of this research is that environmental uncertainty and asset specificity influences the vendor's organizational structure, which in turn may affect the ex-post transaction costs. These ex-post transaction costs refer to the costs of monitoring and enforcing the outsourcing agreements [16]. As prior research is only limited, a straightforward and relatively conceptual framework, as depicted in figure 1, was used for investigating the propositions as mentioned earlier. In order to assess the extent to which vendors have to rearrange their organizational structure, the changing client circumstances need to be known. Our framework identifies the relationships between environmental uncertainty, and the level of asset specificity on the vendor's organizational structure and, subsequently, on ex-post transaction costs.

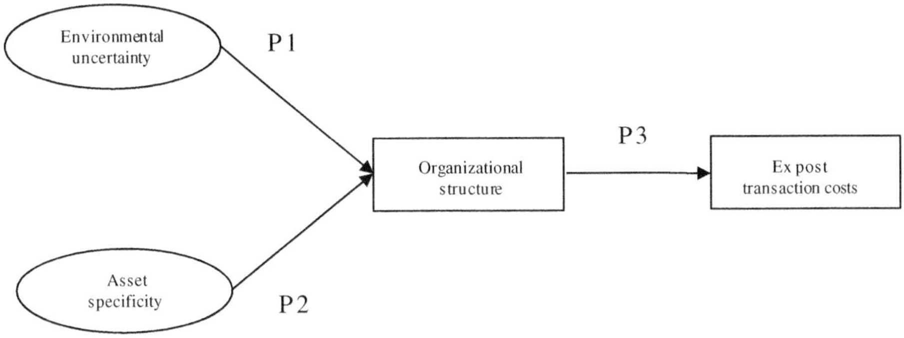

Fig. 1. Conceptual framework

3 Methodology

3.1 Case Study

Studying the literature, we found that empirical research of the influence of environmental uncertainty on vendors' organizational structure is under-researched [33] [34]. Due to the complex nature of outsourcing arrangements, we opted for an exploratory, case-study-based research. This would gain us a deep understanding of the phenomenon under study [35]. Case study research is one of the most common qualitative methods used in the field of Information Systems [36]. Especially, an in-depth understanding of the influence of environmental uncertainty on organizational structure may reveal the consequences that are related to increased vendor's coordination cost. We selected an IT outsourcing vendor that operates globally and acts in a dynamic market (see About this research). We assume that changing client circumstances will influence the organizational structures of the vendor significantly. As a result, we are able to study the impact of environmental uncertainty and asset specificity and their effect on organizational structure and related transaction costs.

3.2 Data Collection

Next, we selected a client case, which can be seen as our unit of observation studied from a retrospective approach. Due to the aspect of researchability, we took the decision to study the vendor with a focus on the Netherlands. We collected data by conducting in-depth interviews with eight vendor staff members, including IT executives, service delivery managers, sales managers and experts positioned across the firm. In this way we apply a cross-section within the organizations that yield to establish a holistic view. All interviewed participants had been engaged in the outsourcing arrangement with the client since the start in 2001. This was to ensure internal consistency within the vendor organization. The varying hierarchical levels of the interviewed staff members prevent that potential limitations of the evolving phenomenon will arise. Interviewees were asked how they perceived the various episodes and the vendor's response (the questions used in the interview are described in Appendix A). Interviews varied from 60 minutes to 120 minutes in duration. Additional information was gathered from annual reports, outsourcing contracts, satisfaction reports and financial information. All the interviews were then transcribed, and the transcripts were sent to the participants to be confirmed. All interviews were carried out during the period June to August of 2008. Also other relevant information such as the contract, organizational structures, satisfaction reports and programme plans were collected.

3.3 Data Analysis

When executing our qualitative research concept maps are used to guide us through the process of data analysis. Since knowledge is fairly nonlinear, concepts can be seen as organized networks. By selecting and organizing relevant information we are able to identify links between concepts, so that we can fathom the data [37]. When executing our qualitative research, Atlas ti v5.2 was used for coding and combing the interview data. Interview data of the eight staff members was translated into concept maps. As a result of the coding process, we were able to create more insight and identify relevant concepts and relationships. The empirical study was clustered around four client episodes. As all different types of episodes during the outsourcing arrangement may have an impact on the vendor we start with an analysis of the extent to which client episodes affect the vendor. As [38] pointed out, the validity of interpretive analysis defies quantification. We will include excerpts (see Appendix B) from the transcribed interviews to support readers to judge for themselves the validity of our research. This process allows us to develop a qualitative, interpretative approach to construct a case study research.

4 Findings

Since we have conducted an empirical study from a retrospective approach, we are able to determine the extent to which environmental uncertainty have affected the vendor organization. We identified a number of critical client episodes, around which our findings have been clustered. Each episode is described with the client development and the vendor's response. Studying these episodes we were able to determine the effect on the vendor's organizational structure.

About this Research

Context of the Global Vendor

Our vendor under study is a leading global company for consulting, systems integration and outsourcing. The company employs more than 90,000 persons, in 80 countries worldwide. The vendor classifies its key capabilities and solutions in the global market as applications outsourcing, infrastructure outsourcing, managed hosting, system integration and consulting. As a global company the vendor supports large client organizations with a global reach. Most of their clients are served directly by the industry vertical business units. These organizations are responsible for integrating all of the company's capabilities to deliver business results and industry process expertise to their clients. The conundrum of being global is that the actual delivery of services needs to take place in local contexts, including concerns related to language, culture and local business practices. Their geographical, -local-, organizations provides understanding of the cultures and markets in which they operate and providing a channel for developing long-term relationships with local clients.

Context of the Client Object of Study

The object of our case study is a global diversified resources company. This global company holds significant positions in major commodity businesses, including aluminum and energy coal. Due to a limited number of competitors the resources market as a whole is static. However, the pressure to deliver the resources globally toward customers is dynamic. Being a global company and distributing the resources to customers all over the world calls for a flexible mindset. Therefore the company needs to be able to adapt to their customers and meet their demands. In 2000 the company decided to outsource a significant part of their IT landscape to various vendors. They divided their IT landscape into three main plots: (1) IT infrastructure and global application maintenance, (2) local application support and (3) networks, data and telecommunications. The company's sourcing strategy is based on a multivendor policy. Our vendor under study was selected for the IT infrastructure plot that constitutes 65% of all IT activities. The seven year, $700 million outsourcing contract included the transfer of the customers IT staff to the vendor under study. In 2007, the contract was extended for a period of three years.

4.1 Episode: Delivery Struggle

After our vendor under study was selected by the client in 2001, a formal transition programme was initiated. Our vendor developed a transition scheme to insource the IT infrastructure as originally managed by the client.

'In general, it is our believe that the transformation phase has the strongest influence on performance. We have the opinion that completing the transition phase successfully; we have created the required starting point for a stable delivery phase. Subsequently, we experienced that a sound performance will be the result'. (Source: a delivery director).

After the completion of the transition programme the formal delivery phase started. Although a thorough and in-depth delivery model was developed and discussed extensively, a major disruption occurred. The vendor applied a leveraged delivery model, meaning that all necessary operational available resources, capabilities and technical assets, were shared with other clients. We observed that the client experienced an increase in lead times of IT services, while the communication between vendor and client was slow due to formal internal procedures as applied by the vendor. Moreover, decision-making on the vendor's side was slow as a result of the multiple layers in the hierarchy. As a result, business departments within the client's organization experienced difficulties in businesses operations such as the processing of customers orders and their confirmation. However, to assure business performance the client demanded dedicated operational support. Consequently, the vendor announced the introduction of a client-oriented team. This client-oriented team offered a dedicated approach in that they are responsible for the delivery of services. The introduction of a client-oriented team contributes to achieving flexible solutions that are proactive and adaptive. As a result, a handover of decision-making was effectuated towards the client-oriented team while shorter internal communication lines were assured. This dedicated customer approach was realized in each geographical customer location.

4.2 Episode: Business Needs for On-demand Support

As the business of the client under study can be characterized as dynamic and demanding, the same dynamic attitude is required from the vendor. However, the client experienced that the vendor was insufficiently meeting client expectations. Our interviews with the vendor's respondents revealed that client employees were dissatisfied about the quality of the service desk when they reported incidents or initiated changes. Long queues and undefined contact persons resulted in negative satisfaction reports. Additionally, when delivery issues occurred the vendor was not able to bring additional resources into action. When employees of business departments of the client experienced disruptions, or even failures, in their IT systems, these problems would result in financial losses. After an assessment, the vendor concluded that the existing service level agreements did not fit with the high business demands of the client. The client stated the need for on-demand support of their vendor. Responding to the identified business need, the client-oriented team developed a new service based on on-demand support. This new service provides sufficient on-site support as additional service agents were introduced in-house to solve the client's incidents. Incidents or problems concern IT applications, for instance, or hardware such as desktops and printers. Only after having solved the problem, the corresponding administration and financial settlement is processed. By developing this new on-demand service, service levels became more differentiated. Moreover, the client is willing to pay for this additional service. This on-demand service offers flexibility, meets client's business needs and contributed positively to client satisfaction.

'The more demanding a client is, the more business uncertainty and organizational structure will affect each other. For instance, by supporting our demanding client it is

crucial to apply a flexible behaviour. That's why our service agents solve the client's issue's first and register the issues later'. (Source: a service delivery manager).

4.3 Episode: Integrating IT Services

Based on the sourcing strategy of the client, three vendors were selected to support the main IT activities. Since the start of the sourcing arrangements, the client experienced that managing the three vendors became more complex. On the one hand, the main object of the sourcing management organization of the client was to deliver end-to-end services towards their business departments and end-users. On the other hand, the vendors all delivered single services that still needed to be integrated by the sourcing management organization of the client. This integration not only required ample effort but also sufficient technical knowledge, which had been outsourced as a result of the sourcing arrangements. This resulted in increasing lead times for delivery to business departments. Therefore, the client informally requested our vendor under study to integrate the various technical services of all three vendors. The vendor agreed to do so and since 2007, our vendor acts as a service integrator, managing their own services as well as those of the other contractors. However, in practice this integration activity has not been formally agreed and included in the contract. As a result, there is a serious tension in the relationship with the client and other vendors. The interviews demonstrate that the client expects to receive an end-to-end service which was not delivered. The cause of this underperformance is that the other vendors will not cooperate with the integrator since they are not formally informed by the client. The interviews with respondents of our vendor under study show a lack of formal agreements and responsibilities. Additionally, as this integration role has not been formally agreed in a contract our vendor does not receive any financial contributions. This item is still a topic of negotiation.

'The subcontractors won't cooperate to integrate the various single services. Their motivation is clear: since there is no contract that mentions the integration aspect, they are also not paid. As we are not paid either, but still deliver an integral service this issue causes a lot of tension in the relationship to both the client and other vendors'. (Source: a sales manager).

4.4 Episode: Client Sourcing Strategy

Executive management of the client's global organization experienced that market dynamism increases over time. In order to respond quickly to the changing customer needs the company also needs to change. As a result of the client adapting their organization to the changing market circumstances, our IT vendor needs to align with their client's organizational structure. The client announced that they developed a new sourcing strategy, changing their IT organization into a federative model. In this approach the central IT department becomes globally responsible for devising policies and related standards. In the federative model each business unit becomes responsible for managing the IT vendors once they have been selected. The vendor responded to this new client sourcing strategy with a sourcing integration model supported by various processes such as service management and contract management. This resulted in two-way communication towards the client. First, communication with the client's centralized IT department is intensified discussing topics like architecture and policies. Secondly, communication was started with decentralized departments to ensure the adequate delivery of day-to-day services. Consequently, the vendor is developing both new assets and strengthening existing assets, managing subcontractors and developing integral process management. Moreover, organizational structures needed to be redesigned to support the services as agreed.

'We noticed that our client developed a new sourcing strategy that will have a very important effect on our business. Their decision change towards a fully decentralized multivendor approach means that each BU becomes responsible for managing multiple vendors. This will cost us money as we globally have to adapt our organizational structure in delivering IT services'. (Source: a senior manager).

5 Discussion

In the previous chapter we presented an overview of four episodes from the perspective of the client and discussed the vendor's response. The relationship between the episodes and the TCE determinants are summarized in table 1. The following sections are clustered around the described determinants. The empirical findings are analyzed focusing on the relationship with the vendor's organizational structure.

Table 1. Relation between episodes and TCE determinants

Episode	Transaction Cost Theory
Delivery struggle	Environmental uncertainty Asset specificity
Business needs for 'on-demand' support	Asset specificity
Integrating IT services	Environmental uncertainty Asset specificity
Client sourcing strategy	Environmental uncertainty Asset specificity

5.1 Environmental Uncertainty

The results of our research provide strong evidence that environmental uncertainty has an impact on the organizational structure as applied by the global vendor. Based on the episodes described in section 4.2, various examples underpin how the organizational structure is affected. Remarkably, at the start of the transition phase we find that the vendor applied a leveraged delivery model. As a result of ample experience of the vendor we expected to find a more customized approach, related to an organizational structure to support the client. Since it is hard to predict future developments, which are even more difficult to describe in contracts, our study shows that the global vendor acts opportunistically by neglecting both the complexity of the client organization and the dynamic market in which the client is acting. Moreover, with regard to the length of the contract period the vendor could foresee that changes in the client environment would occur. This is consistent with transaction cost reasoning of environmental uncertainty. Evidence showed that the extension of the vendor's organizational structure by a client-oriented team was a response to changing client circumstances, in this case environmental uncertainty. This approach ensures the continuity of IT services and sustains the long-term relationship with the client. This finding is congruent with the vendor's business strategy to focus on customer intimacy. We found that the organizational structure of the client-oriented team, including their dimensions, is closely aligned to the client organization in order to facilitate the delivery of IT services. Since the client operates in a dynamic environment, flexibility is a requirement in order to cater for uncertainty on the client side. The vendor's respondents indicate that their organization is now capable of dealing with this demand. The interviews show that the organization is supported by many processes and procedures to deal with projects in a flexible way. To facilitate major projects with a global reach, rapid response teams were additionally introduced that become responsible to execute these projects. This assures direct decision-making and fast communication.

'The client's demand for flexibility is intense. When we want to answer client proposals for new projects, this requires sufficient resources and capabilities form our side. If we can't respond adequately, it becomes a serious problem. Therefore, we introduced 'forecasting' in our Client Focus Team so that we can prepare ourselves and prevent some surprises'. (Source: a programme delivery manager).

Based on the findings of the various episodes evidence was found that the functional organizational structure of the vendor was affected. As a result, the vendor adjusted their organizational structure and accompanying dimensions regularly. This supports our first proposition.

5.2 Asset Specificity

Discussing the second proposition, we found an interesting tension. Our analysis shows that the global vendor started their outsourcing arrangement based on an organizational structure that can be identified as highly standardized, and therefore non-specific. Each IT service, such as IT infrastructure management and data center services, e.g. Hosting, was provided by a separate business unit that was organized in such a way that only mass production of the IT service could be supported. Based on the interviews with vendor representatives we found that the processes to deliver the IT services were standardized, meaning that no exceptions were allowed to accommodate variations in preferences (e.g. other service levels). Referring to this situation, the level of asset specificity can be considered as low, while transactions are relatively frequent. However, all episodes indicated that asset specificity affected the vendor's functional organizational structure to support the delivery of the client's IT services. This can be explained by the introduction of dedicated resources that dispose of specific knowledge to support the client, resulting in an increase of the degree of asset specificity. Moreover, the vendor changed their organizational structure, which required more mutual cooperation between the team member's located onsite, onshore and offshore. This is consistent to transaction cost reasoning that as asset specificity increases, more complex governance structures are required to attenuate costly bargaining over profits from specialized assets [5]. Since asset specificity refers to the degree of customization [10] vendors seek the promise from their clients before actually making the investment [8]. This is consistent with the findings in our case study as the outsourcing arrangement studied is based on a long-term contract period. The tension reveals itself that if the transaction costs are too high, it is more appropriate to conduct the transaction in-house, e.g. client side. Another aspect that influences asset specificity concerns the client's decision to reorganize their sourcing management function by establishing a centralized and a decentralized structure. Additionally, the clients change towards a federative structure requires the alignment of processes between the centralized and decentralized client business units to establish effective governance. Aligning these processes provided input for governance decisions while formalizing the processes implementing those decisions [39]. Examples that were found included the IT investment proposal process, the architecture process, and the service level management process. Based on our interviews with the vendors' respondents we found that implementing a more idiosyncratic organizational structure increases the complexity as a result of frequently interaction between the different teams on-site, onshore and offshore. Moreover, tasks and related responsibilities of employees requires regular alignment between various on-site, onshore and offshore teams, which also increased the degree of asset specificity. The interviews with the vendor's respondent's show various examples in which asset specificity influence their organizational structure. The introduction, for instance, of IT infrastructure experts and IT architects expanded their functional organizational structure both on-site and offshore. This finding supports our second proposition.

5.3 Organizational Structure

Although the vendor is organized globally, the representatives experienced no obstruction with regard to the number of layers in hierarchy. This can be explained by the fact that the client-oriented team have the responsibility to act local. In each country where the global vendor is present an organization is built to support the client locally. In this way the vendor's organization can be considered as flat. Moreover, we found that the limited layers in hierarchy stimulate the process of decision-making in a positive way. Discussing the dimension of the level of horizontal integration, we found that the boundaries of the representatives' functions were clearly defined. After the adaptation to the client's business need, all vendor functions contain explicit single roles in order to create a maximum focus on the client organization. The technical functions, for instance, were also based on a single role. When additional functions are required in supporting the client, several employees will be involved, each with specific knowledge, skills and experience. In this case we found that the extent to which additional expertise was required by the client fits with the vendor's approach of lowering the level of horizontal integration. In particular, we found that the client-oriented team have a decision-making responsibility while they are able to communicate directly with their client's counterparts. The finding of the decision-making responsibility is contradictory to specific literature on services outsourcing which rely on a formal, top–down, systematic decision-making [40] [41]. More generic literature shows that organizations that operate with a high degree of environmental uncertainty may decentralize decision-making [42], rely less on formal rules and policies and flatten their hierarchies [28]. The locus of decision-making is perceived by the client-team representatives as twofold. The representatives have the opinion that they are authorized to make decisions that are directly related to their client. The interviewed participants involved in the client-oriented team argue that with respect to decision-making, their team operates almost independently of the global organization. On the one hand, they are able to focus completely on the client side, which is congruent with the vendor's strategy to create customer intimacy. On the other hand, the participants argue that this approach creates a difference between their team and the global delivery organization, which leads to tensions regularly.

'The importance of the organizational structure is significant. Just after the deal was signed, the transition period started. During that period, dimensions like decision-making and communication were not aligned properly with the client organization. When the formal delivery phase began, our organizational dimensions were rearranged which improved the performance towards our client'. (Source: a programme delivery manager).

5.4 Ex-post Transaction Costs

Interestingly, we found that all client episodes lead to an increase of the degree of asset specificity on the vendor side. The interviews with vendor representatives indicated that, as a result, the transaction costs expanded significantly. The explanation may be twofold. First, it can be assumed that vendor investments in specific assets increased the transaction costs significantly. For example, the introduction of the on-demand support service and expanding the number of employees in the client-oriented team, which are based on dedicated functions, required a higher degree of asset specificity. This finding is consistent with transaction cost reasoning. However, there may be another explanation for increased transaction costs. The vendor applied an extensive blended organizational form, deploying teams on-site, onshore and offshore. Hence, this organizational structure requires more resources and extends the mutual cooperation between the team members. Consequently, extending the organizational chain, which comprises centralized and decentralized client involvement up to the vendors geographically dispersed delivery units, will result in higher vendor coordination cost to fulfill the provisioning of IT services. This refers to the TCE logic of opportunity costs (transaction risk) that includes the costs of failures to align the transaction with changing circumstances [13]. The increase of opportunity costs, which can be expressed in terms of time, energy and money, arise from a larger part of management attention in managing the organizational chain, which became a recurring activity of the outsourcing arrangement. The vendor has to deal with this finding as neglecting the opportunity costs may lead to an unsatisfied client that might hazard a contract renewal. Interestingly, we found empirical evidence that the partial customization (idiosyncratic) of the organizational structure, which is fulfilled by the vendor's client-oriented team, influences the ex-post transaction costs. Preliminary to the partial customization all vendor delivery units were involved directly in the client arrangement while acting independently from each other. Additional alignment agreements on the vendor site were established to ensure the delivery of IT services. This mechanism lead to hidden costs that increased the overall transaction costs too.

The adjustment of vendor's organizational structure, however, indicated that the overall transaction costs decreased. This evidence underpins our finding that the vendor's functional organizational structure can be considered as a mediator in controlling the organizational chain and thus managing the ex-post transaction costs. Moreover, studying the financial business case, which was established at the start of the outsourcing arrangement, the interviews and document analyses revealed that only the production costs to produce the IT services were calculated. The episodes, however, show that the transaction costs increased substantially during the arrangement. We did not expect to find that the vendor neglected the calculation of coordination costs at all. It can be argued that the opportunistic behaviour of the vendor is the cause for neglecting the transaction costs. Offering standardized IT services, while ignoring the level of client customization (e.g. mixed or idiosyncratic), the transaction costs can be perceived as low. However, an important assumption of transaction cost reasoning is that environmental uncertainty and asset specificity will increase the transaction costs.

6 Conclusion

This paper has studied the influence of environmental uncertainty and asset specificity on organizational structure and the ex-post transaction cost. A longitudinal study was conducted to examine the effect of both determinants on a global vendor's organizational structure. As the vendor started their arrangement based on an 'one size fits all' approach, client specific circumstances were neglected. We did not expect to find a standard approach as our vendor under study has a long experience in the field of providing IT outsourcing services. Evidence was found that both environmental uncertainty and the degree of asset specificity influences the vendor's organizational structure. Findings show the effect of the vendor's potential opportunism that reflects to environmental uncertainty [13]. Since client circumstances changed over time, the degree of asset specificity increased, resulting in higher transaction costs. Consequently, the position of the vendor will be less attractive when compared to competitors or even to a client whose rationale was to outsource its IT-function in order to achieve cost reductions. It can be argued that our vendor under study has to find a balance between the extent of asset specificity and their market attractiveness. During the adaptability process the vendor invested in re-designing their organizational structure by establishing a more customized approach. As such, the vendor's functional organizational structure can be considered as a mediator in controlling the organizational chain and thus managing the ex-post transaction costs. It is important to note that our study is limited as we only studied the client case with a focus on the Netherlands. As a result, we have been able to discuss only a part of the global client case. A second limitation is the relatively small number of interviews. Nevertheless, the findings as described are promising. Yet, vendor executives need to deal with environmental uncertainty and asset specificity when developing a functional organizational structure to support their clients. To some extent, the vendor's organizational structure must manifest an idiosyncratic character to meet clients need. Consequently, vendor's need to take coordination costs into account when managing an outsourcing arrangement. Vendor executives and managers should need to reassess their organizational structure regularly to select the required governance mode. Specifically, vendors need to develop mechanisms to adverse the effect of potential opportunism. By using their functional organization vendors are able to manage the degree of ex-post transaction costs. Future research studies might examine how an increase of transaction costs influences the business case of vendors during the term of the arrangement. This provides insights of outsourcing arrangements form the perspectives of vendors are profitable over time.

References

1. IAOP, http://www.iaop.org/firmbuilder/articles/34/200/592/
2. Beulen, E., Ribbers, P., Roos, J.: Managing IT Outsourcing. Governance in Global Partnerships, 2nd edn. Routledge, London (2011)
3. Lacity, M.C., Khan, S., Yan, A., Willcocks, L.P.: A review of the IT outsourcing empirical literature and future research directions. J. of Inf. Tech. 25, 395–433 (2010)
4. Nahm, A.Y., Vonderembse, M.A., Koufteros, X.A.: The impact of organizational structure on time-based manufacturing and plant performance. J. of Oper. Mgt. 21, 281–306 (2003)
5. Dyer, J.: Effective inter-firm collaboration: how firms minimize transaction costs and maximize transaction value. Str. Mgt. J. 18, 535–556 (1997)
6. Lacity, M.C., Willcocks, L.P.: Interpreting Information Technology Sourcing Decisions from a Transaction Cost Perspective: Findings and Critique. Acc. Mgt. and Inf. Tech. 5(3), 203–244 (1995)
7. Watjatrakul, B.: Determinants of IS sourcing decisions: a comparative study of transaction cost theory versus the resource-based view. J. of Strat. Inf. Sys. 14(4), 389–415 (2005)
8. Aubert, B.A., Rivard, S., Patry, M.: A transaction cost model of IT outsourcing. Inf. and Mgt. 41, 921–932 (2004)
9. Barthélemy, J., Quelin, B.V.: Complexity of outsourcing contracts and ex post transaction costs: an empirical investigation. J. of Mgt. Stu 43, 1775–1797 (2006)
10. Williamson, O.E.: Markets and Hierarchies. Free Press, New York (1979)
11. Williamson, O.E.: Transaction cost economics: the governance of contract relations. J. of Law and Econ. 22, 233–261 (1979)
12. Lacity, M.C., Willcocks, L.P., Feeny, D.: IT sourcing: maximize flexibility and control. Harvard Business Review, 84–93 (May/June 1995)
13. Speklé, R.F.: Explaining management control structure variety: a transaction cost economics perspective. Acc. Org. and Soc. 26(4-5), 419–441 (2001)
14. Nicholson, B., Jones, J., Espenlaub, S.: Transaction costs and control of outsourced accounting: Case evidence from India. Mgt. Acc. Res. 17, 238–258 (2006)
15. John, G., Weitz, B.A.: Forward integration into distribution: an empirical test of transaction cost analysis. J. of Law.Eco. and Org. 4(2), 337–355 (1988)
16. Rindfleisch, A., Heide, J.B.: Transaction cost analysis: past, present, and future applications. J. of Mark. 61(4), 30–54 (1997)
17. Klein, B., Crawford, A., Alchian, A.: Vertical integration, appropriable rents, and the competitive contracting process. J. of Law and Eco. 21, 297–326 (1990)
18. Williamson, O.E.: The economics of organization: The transaction cost approach. Am. J. of Soc. 87(3), 548–577 (1981)
19. Dalton, D.R., Todor, W.D., Spendolini, M.J., Fielding, G.J., Porter, L.W.: Organizational structure and performance. Acad. of M. Rev. 5, 49–64 (1980)
20. Koufteros, X.A., Vonderembse, M.A.: The impact of organizational structure on the level of JIT attainment: towards theory development. Int. J. of Prod. 36, 2863–2878 (1998)

21. Daft, R.L.: Organization Theory and Design. West Publishing Company, MN (1995)
22. Bouwman, W.A.G.A., van den Hoof, B., van de Wijngaert, L., van Dijk, J.: Information and Communication Technology in Organizations. Sage Publications, Thousand Oaks (2006)
23. Carmeli, A., Tishler, A.: The relationships between intangible organizational elements and organizational performance. Str. Mgt. J. 25, 1257–1278 (2004)
24. Lawrence, P.R., Lorsch, J.W.: Organization and Environment, Homewood IL, Irwin (1967)
25. Zammuto, R.F., O'Conner, E.J.: Gaining advanced manufacturing technologies benefits: the roles of organizational design and culture. Acad. of Mgt. Rev. 17(4), 701–728 (1992)
26. Germain, R.: The role of context and structure in radical and incremental logistics innovation adoption. J. of Bus. Res. 35, 117–127 (1996)
27. Burns, T., Stalker, G.M.: The Management of Innovation. London, Tavistock (1961)
28. Walton, R.E.: From control to commitment: transforming work force management in the United States. In: Clark, K., Hayes, R., Lorenz, C. (eds.) The Uneasy Alliance: Managing the Productivity-Technology Dilemma. Harvard Business School Press, Boston (1985)
29. Doll, W.J., Vonderembse, M.A.: The evolution of manufacturing systems: towards the post-industrial enterprise. Omega 19, 401–411 (1991)
30. Davenport, T., Nohria, N.: Case management and the integration of labor. Slo. Mgt. Rev. 35(2), 11–23 (1994)
31. Paswan, A.K., Dant, R.P., Lumpkin, J.R.: An empirical investigation of the linkages among relationalism, environmental uncertainty, and bureaucratization. J. of Bus. Res. 43, 125–140 (1998)
32. Langfield-Smith, K., Smith, D.: Management control systems and trust in outsourcing relationships. Mgt. Acc. Res 14, 281–307 (2003)
33. Levina, N., Ross, J.: From the vendors perspective: exploring the value proposition in Information Technology Outsourcing. MIS Q. 27, 331–364 (2003)
34. Gonzalez, R., Gasco, J., Llopis, J.: IS outsourcing: a literature analysis. Inf. and Mgt. 43, 821–834 (2006)
35. Yin, R.K.: Case Study Research. Design and Methods. Sage Publications, Thousand Oaks (1994)
36. Orlikowski, W.J., Lacono, C.S.: Desperately seeking the 'IT' in IT research: a call to theorizing the IT artefact. Inf. Syst. Res. 12(2), 121–134 (2001)
37. Novak, J.D., Gowin, D.B.: Learning how to learn. In: Kotlarsky, J., Oshri, I., Fenema, P.C.V. (eds.) Knowledge Processes in Globally Distributed Contexts. Palgrave Macmillan, London (1984)
38. Lincoln, Y.S., Guba, E.G.: Naturalistic inquiry. Sage Publications, Beverly Hills (1985)
39. Weill, P., Ross, J.: IT Governance: How Top Performers Manage IT Decision Rights for Superior Results. Harvard Business School Press, Boston (2004)
40. Dibbern, J., Goles, T., Hirschheim, R., Jayatilaka, B.: Information systems outsourcing: a survey and analysis of the literature. DATA BASE for Adv. in Inf. Syst. 34(4), 6–102 (2004)
41. Cohen, L., Young, A.: Multisourcing Moving Beyond Outsourcing to Achieve Growth and Agility. Harvard Business School Press, Boston (2006)
42. Ruekert, R.W., Walker, O.C., Roering, K.J.: The organization of marketing activities: a contingency theory of structure and performance. J. of Mark. 49, 13–25 (1985)

Appendix A: Interview Questions

The following questions will be part of the in-depth interview sessions and will yield more profound information. First, some generic questions will be addressed. Secondly, specific questions that relate to the client case are discussed.

Generic Questions

Number	Question
1	Please do elaborate on the mission of the company that is strived for, strategic objectives (market leadership or cost leadership, differentiation strategy)
2	How important is providing outsourcing services for your company (focus and priority of the service within the organization)
3	Can you describe the characteristics of the market segment your client is involved in? (static or dynamic markets, simple or complex services required)

Specific Questions

Number	Question
4	How does your company deal with environmental uncertainty with regard to your client? How is this process established? Who is responsible within the organization to support this process? Who is discussing these developments with your client?
5	How did your company respond to these uncertainties over time?
6	Which bottlenecks can be addressed that restrain the organization for adapting to client developments? Who is responsible for removing the bottlenecks and on what level is this taking place?
7	How are the assets, as applied, influenced over time? How does your comapny deal with adapting these assets?
8	Please describe some events that affected the assets within your organization during the arragement?
9	To what extent is the functional organizational structure within your department influenced by environmental uncertainty?
10	To what extent is the functional organizational structure within your department influenced by the sourcing strategy of your client (e.g. sole sourcing, multi vendor sourcing)?
11	To what extent is the functional organizational structure within your department influenced by specific assets?
12	How are the organziational dimensions (number of layers in hierarchy , level of horizontal integration , locus of decision-making , level of communication) influenced by client uncertainties?

Appendix B: Excerpts of the Interviews

Document ID	Code	Question ID	Question	Vendor's response
			Construct organizational structure	
Global vendor	OS	OS01	To what extent is the functional organizational structure within your department influenced by environmental uncertainty?	Indeed, we notice the influence of environmental uncertainty on our organizational structure. The client strongly focuses on our capabilities when they have to decide to buy our application service offer. Our competition with provider Y is fierce as both parties are able to offer the same type of IT service. The capabilities applied are the differentator. The performance offered strongly relates to the ability and availability of our capabilities and how thaty are organized (technology, offshoring).
Global vendor	OS	OS02	To what extent is the functional organizational structure within your department influenced by environmental uncertainty?	The impact is high. Recent strategy decisions within our company will lead to more and fierce competition in the market. This requiers a strong focus at each level in our organzaition, which will have consequences for our capabilities and thus to our client.
Global vendor	OS	OS3	To what extent is the functional organizational structure within your department influenced by the sourcing strategy of your client (e.g. sole sourcing, multi vendor sourcing)?	Our organizational structure is more and more affected by our client strategy. By means of a recent change in our client strategy, from a fully centralized organziation towards a decentralized organzaition, each BU will have the right to develop their own sourcing strategy and accompanying policies. In practice, this means a change to a multivendor strategy. However, this will cost us business as we have a share-of-wallet of 65% related to the IT spend of our client. This new strategy definitly will have an impact on our capabilities and governance.
Global vendor	OS	OS04	To what extent is the functional organizational structure within your department influenced by the sourcing strategy of your client (e.g. sole sourcing, multi vendor sourcing)?	The sourcing strategy of our client will have a significant impact on our capabilities and assets. This relates to (1) number and type of capabilities (assets); (2) the size of the client within our firm(large/small); (3) relationship management (regional or central appraoch); (4) transition (more smaller transitions in stead of few large transitions).
Global vendor	OS	OS05	To what extent does specific assets and organizational structure affect each other?	We sure notice the relation between capabilities (assets) and organzaitional structure. Most importantly, we observe this relationship at our demanding client. The more demanding our client, the stronger the relationship between capabilies (assets) and organzaitional structure. For example, take the on-demand concept. Both the necessary capabilities and adaptation to the required organizational structure (communication, decision-making) lead to a more on-demand delivery model. High flexibility means that first we solve the problem and create a trouble ticket later. As a result, we changed our organizational design to the client environment (decision-making is low in our organzaition, direct communication).
Global vendor	OS	OS06	To what extent does specific assets and organizational structure affect each other?	There is a strong relationship which is influenced by the type of delivery that is applied. Our global proposition in combination with offshoring services influences our organzaition too. An other example is the fact that our client is quit demanding. Decision-making is low in our organization by means of the client-focus teams. Our blended organizational structure is based on a mix between on-site and local (domestic) support and global delviery teams. Despite the fact that many activities can be executed remotly, local presence is still important. On the other hand, our choice to implement a dedicated client-focus team contributes to establish the fit between capabilities and structure. The fit remains constant while client circumstances changes often.
Global vendor	OS	OS07	To what extent does specific assets and organizational structure affect each other?	Sure we notic the relation between both aspects. Our organizational design capability (clients WHAT question) decides our design and implementation of specific dimensions (decision-making, hierarchy). In particular, the client environment determines the organzaitional dimensions of our structure (HOW question). These dimensies can be seen as 'soft skills'. Remark: during the salesphase we discussed these governance aspects with the client (perception management). We noticed that this approach also requires to some extent the client appreciate this capabilities. Partially, it is about tacit knowledge, that is dependent on clients maturity. At the same time, developing our assets need to be a regular activity.

Cultural Emergence in Global IS/IT Outsourcing

Danai Tsotra*, Laurence Brooks, and Guy Fitzgerald

Department of Information Systems, Computing and Mathematics
Brunel University, Kingston Lane, Uxbridge UB8 3WE, UK
d.tsotra@gmail.com

Abstract. In the contemporary business environment, Global Outsourcing (GLOS) and global networks are used to achieve strategic and economic advantages, with customer-supplier relationships spanning across not only countries but also continents. In this global context, culture and culture-related issues are factors that affect GLOS relationships and collaboration. Building on areas of existing research, the paper examines literature on culture and IS/IT outsourcing, and focuses on the emergence of culture in a GLOS-specific context. GLOS culture is examined through a cultural systems perspective, which normative research shows to be able to effectively reflect issues of emergence, change, and dynamism. Using an interpretivist qualitative methodology and a thematic analysis of case studies of a customer-supplier automotive network across Europe and Asia, cultural emergence was found to be related to four categories of cultural attributes: ABC (attitudes, behaviors, and cognition), context, interactivity, and regulation. To address cultural emergence, the paper focuses on the analysis of specific mechanisms and processes that play a role towards the emergent GLOS culture. Understanding them through the dimensions of dynamism, scale, and motivation, the paper discusses their role in cultural emergence and discusses benefits for researchers and practitioners.

Keywords: Outsourcing, global outsourcing, culture, cultural systems, emergent culture.

1 Introduction

Outsourcing of Information Systems and Information Technology (IS/IT) describes the practice of transferring assets, leases, staff, and managerial responsibility for delivery of services from internal IS/IT functions to external third party providers [24, 27, 30]. Used both as a strategy and a business practice, it is defined through the difference in the location of the service recipient and the service supplier. With respect to variation in terms of geographical distance, the broad term of outsourcing has been divided into further categories, including onshore, nearshore, offshore, and farshore outsourcing [40,47], with the last three categories involving the relocation of business processes to places outside the client's national boundaries [20]. More specifically:

* Corresponding author.

J. Kotlarsky, L.P. Willcocks, and I. Oshri (Eds.): Global Sourcing 2011, LNBIP 91, pp. 99–114, 2011.

- Onshore outsourcing involves both the customer and the provider being located in the same country.
- Nearshore outsourcing involves outsourcing to countries close to the client company or to countries that are related by the same category of treaties or alliances.
- Offshore outsourcing involves outsourcing to countries or continents not necessarily connected by national boundaries or trade laws but characterized by compatibility in areas of culture, economic status, and capabilities.
- Farshore outsourcing involves countries separated by a distance larger than the distance encountered in cases of nearshore and offshore relationships.

For the purpose of the present research, the term Global Outsourcing (GLOS) is used. GLOS is defined as the relationship and the collaboration between two or more organizations, within the context of nearshore, offshore and farshore IS/IT outsourcing alliances, arrangements, or deals.

GLOS is an important aspect of the IS/IT business strategy [25] and has resulted in higher business expectations and new challenges for organizations while, from a managerial perspective, its management has become a "competency" that future managers "*must*" learn [14]. In terms of advantages and disadvantages of IS/IT GLOS, cost advantage can be achieved through access to large pools of IS/IT experts and low-salary workforce, while disadvantages usually exist as a result of increased coordination costs due to socioeconomical and geopolitical risks [7]. Compared to a traditional buyer-supplier outsourcing relationship (where both the customer and the provider are located in the same country), practical considerations in GLOS may include control and monitoring of the provider, constant communication, and rigorous definition of requirements [53]. Moreover, client organizations need to be aware of additional categories of costs, such as transaction costs, extra offshore costs, and hidden costs [13], before initiating a GLOS relationship and in order to better estimate in advance the overall impact of the potential outsourcing relationship [38]. Such costs and risks appear to also exist in traditional outsourcing, yet they pose a greater threat in cases of global outsourcing, due to the geographical distance factor [14, 52].

1.1 Research Background

Apart from the physical distance between suppliers and clients, GLOS collaborating organizations are also characterized by degrees of cultural compatibility and fit [50]. Researchers emphasize the importance of cultural distance, while cultural similarity is considered more important than the spatial affinity between organizations [21, 25]. Moreover, compatibility in culture is among the characteristics that play an important role in an outsourcing relationship, helping it move beyond a "narrow" geographical view that focuses only on financial benefits [57].

The importance of culture in IS/IT GLOS has been cited by many researchers who study outsourcing in the IS/IT field [25, 31, 34]. According to current research [1], success of global outsourcing projects often relies on achieving mutual cultural understanding, based on which the collaborating organizations can build trust and share knowledge. Moreover, in a list of the "top 12" offshoring issues, researchers consider the effects of cultural differences to be number two (after strategic organizational implication) in importance [32], while cultural compatibility is also addressed as a key issue when considering cultural issues in a GLOS project [50].

However, despite the importance assigned to culture, there are concerns regarding cultural issues in GLOS projects that are "not yet fully understood" [32], while the role of people and cultural change required to support strategic buyer-supplier relationships has been largely ignored [36, 43].

The present study examines cultural emergence in global IS/IT outsourcing and discusses *emergent GLOS culture*, as uniquely developed among the collaborating organizations of every GLOS relationship. The paper is organized as following: In the next section (section 2), it examines the topic of culture in IS/IT GLOS and applies a cultural systems perspective to the analysis of GLOS culture. Section 3 presents the methodology and section 4 shows the analysis of the data. Section 5 discusses the emergent GLOS culture as it evolves through the data analysis. Afterwards, in section 6, the paper analyzes cultural emergence, while the last section (section 7) presents the discussion and the conclusions of the study.

2 Culture in IS/IT GLOS

Culture and culture-related issues are frequently mentioned as factors that affect GLOS collaboration and relationships, being potential indicators of success or failure [6, 23, 33, 50, 51]. For example, in relation to IS/IT outsourcing, culture has been studied in success factors models [4, 23], effective sourcing partnerships [50], and potential risk [33, 51], while cultural characteristics have contributed to project failure through escalation of workforce and social risks [51], overlooking of personnel issues [5, 6], and ineffective relationships [45, 46, 54]. In addition, they are related to behavioral and trust issues [48], potentially resulting in inefficiency expressed in low productivity, poor commitment, ineffective communication, and lack of expertise and readiness.

In the field of cultural research, culture is a topic studied frequently in relation to various business/organizational issues and the importance of culture and cultural differences is evident in the increasing amount of research on the topic [42, 44]. However, at the same time, an increase can be observed in the number of studies that call for a change in the way culture is approached. Among the reasons for such a call for change is the belief that, in the contemporary modern environment, the traditionally used cultural concepts in anthropology and sociology are not capable to fully reveal aspects of the modern economy. This is mostly because of their focus on stability and their inefficiency in addressing organizational responses to globalization and modern competition [26, 42]. Therefore, in order to address this research issue, recent research has focused on discussing the need for new approaches to the study of culture, in order to address its nature as ongoing, contested, emergent, and influenced by the contemporary dynamic environment [60, 61]. Moreover, in terms of applying specific cultural perspectives to the field of IS/IT, the choice of between the use of either national or the organizational type of culture dominates the field [29], with Hofstede's taxonomy [28] being applied to more than 50% of the articles that examine culture at the national level [35]. However, Hofstede's theory has faced lots of criticism [26, 42], mostly in relation to the need for a paradigmatic shift in the way culture is studied (as discussed above), the stability of the theory regarding the existence of national characteristics within a specific nation/state, and the perceived inability of such characteristics to adjust and change.

Viewing the criticism of the currently most popular conceptualization of culture [28], along with the call for change in the way culture is approached and the need to address culture beyond static dimensions, leads to the rationale of the present paper, which is to develop a cultural perspective that reflects the emergent nature of culture in a global context. Consequently, in order to address the above-mentioned research issues, this paper examines the concept of emergence in GLOS, while building on two existing cultural types that recognize the concept of cultural emergence: The first is situating culture, which involves the way multiple cultural contexts interact in order to influence social behavior in the organizational environment [59, 61], and the second is negotiated culture, which emphasizes negotiations in terms of participation in new organizational settings, multicultural variability, and creation of a unique working culture within a specific organizational context [8, 9].

Expanding on the analysis of cultural emergence in a GLOS specific organizational context, organizational members of the collaborating organizations, after a period of interaction, tend to develop common sets of procedures and experiences that result in a context-specific and localized culture. Furthermore, the interaction between GLOS collaborating organizations reflects the expression and exchange of the organizations' unique sets of cultural characteristics and results in the development of a unique set that is *specific* to the GLOS context. Within this context, a new, distinctive, GLOS culture emerges, with the potential to dynamically change and adjust through interrelationships, interdependencies, and interactions of cultural characteristics of separate organizations within the GLOS deal.

IS/IT GLOS culture, in the present paper, is proposed to demonstrate the following characteristics:

- It is locally situated in the GLOS context of the relationship, the organization, or the broader business environment in which organizational members interact, expressing different cultural identities and affiliations.
- It is influenced by its stakeholders, both within and outside the organization and, by reacting to internal and external influences, the organization becomes dynamic, learning, and adaptable in terms of actual behavior.
- It is embedded in everyday, socially negotiated work practices, through which cultural change is behaviorally and dynamically expressed in the GLOS relationship.
- It emerges as a result of multicultural variability and interactivity and, by adapting to the social, organizational, and environmental influences, it becomes a unique emergent culture within the specific GLOS context.

2.1 GLOS Cultural Systems

In order to understand in depth the IS/IT GLOS cultural collaboration, the present paper adopts a cultural systems perspective. The reason is that, as an inherent characteristic, cultural systems express emergence, dynamism, interaction, and evolution, concepts also addressed within the field of culture and, more specifically , in relation to the need for culture to be perceived beyond static and stable concepts. Consequently, a GLOS relationship is viewed as a GLOS cultural system, which expresses its emergent GLOS culture as a result of the interaction between cultural characteristics associated with the collaborating organizations.

Cultural systems are defined as coherent sets of values, concepts, beliefs, rules, learned behaviors, expressed symbols, and ideals [49]. In addition, they distinguish a particular group from other groups by guiding and rationalizing its members' behavior through decision-making and accumulation of resources [19]. Components of a cultural system also include the various ways individuals organize their collective world experience, their scheme of cause-effect relationships, the hierarchy of their values, and the processes used to achieve desired features [16]. In terms of emergence, a cultural system develops and changes as a result of the inherent interaction and the contribution of its elements to the organizational context. Through interactions, interrelations, and interdependence, the cultural system has the ability to evolve and change. Thus, the emergent culture of a system, within a specific context (in the present study a GLOS cultural system within a GLOS-specific context) can be examined in terms of the ways that various components of the cultural system are interrelated [55], contradicting, complementing, or coexisting with each other, through methods of socialization, feedback, interaction, collaboration, and transmission [2].

Furthermore, a cultural system is characterized by a hierarchical context and multi-level layers of components existing within the system and also surrounding it [58]. According to the perspective of this paper, the larger environment to which the GLOS cultural system belongs is the external organizational or business environment, within which the GLOS context operates (further within which the GLOS cultural system expresses its emergent GLOS culture). Between these levels of hierarchy, communication and interaction can take place, resulting in a certain level (or lack) of information flow. The more information the GLOS cultural system acquires, the more freedom and flexibility it has in terms of availability of possible choices and potential for emergence and change [17]. Consequently, depending on its relation to the external environment, a system may be isolated from its environment and closed and, therefore, its final state will be determined by its initial conditions, manifested as cultural stability and lack of emergence. In contrast, an open system exchanges information with the environment, resulting in interaction and reorganization of the system's components, and subsequent emergence [39].

The present paper uses inherent characteristics of cultural systems. More specifically, systems are identified through the interactions and the interdependencies among their components, while the cultural system attempts to evolve, form a "whole" [58], and manifest its unique emergent culture according to the context in which it operates and the regulations it faces.

Theoretical aspects and characteristics of the systems literature that express the view of a GLOS relationship as a GLOS cultural system include the following:

- GLOS is part of a multilayered environment and functions as an open system that is subject to information exchange and flow.
- GLOS relationships include interactions and regulatory activities in order for the system to attain its goals.

- Eventually, a GLOS-specific culture emerges through regular interaction and interdependence of the integrated components of a GLOS cultural system.
- The business environment, the GLOS context, and various managerial, supervisory, and group activities provide regulation and feedback to a GLOS relationship.
- Management and supervision serve as control mechanisms to ensure the objectives of the GLOS cultural system are met.
- In order to survive or maintain equilibrium with respect to the environment and its goals, a GLOS cultural system 'moves' towards change, adaptation, and adjustment.

Overall, the cultural systems perspective seems appropriate for the study of IS/IT GLOS because, in order to describe the emergent GLOS culture, it uses inherent characteristics and concepts of cultural systems as addressed by systems researchers and examined in organizational studies [15, 37]]. GLOS, addressed through the unique and emergent nature of its culture, appears to exemplify by default such characteristics and concepts (i.e. emergence, change, dynamism), making, therefore, the cultural systems lens is a promising perspective in terms of its ability to address the emergent nature of the IS/IT GLOS culture. In addition, following the application of the cultural systems perspective, the concept of emergent GLOS culture can explain the GLOS relationship as a dynamic system of adaptation and evolution, containing elements that interact with one another and with(in) the environment. Moreover, the focus of the cultural systems perspective on emergence, interaction, and change is among the concepts *already* addressed by research and the systems theory, while GLOS, in relation to the unique and emergent nature of its culture, exemplifies such systems characteristics. Consequently, the cultural systems perspective is a promising perspective in terms of its ability to provide a theoretical background to the emergent nature of the GLOS culture.

3 Methodology

The paper, in order to analyze the emergent culture of a GLOS cultural system is using the philosophical perspective of interpretivism, which assumes that access to reality occurs through social constructions such as language, consciousness, and shared meanings [41]. In addition, it applies a qualitative methodology and a multiple case study approach.

The industrial setting of the case studies is the automotive industry, due to its increasing use of outsourcing to achieve tactical and strategic benefits, such as demand satisfaction, customization, Original Equipment Manufacturing (OEM) capabilities [11, 12]. Four companies were studied, all of them interrelated in a customer-supplier network involving the Electric System (ES) of buses and coaches. The network it involves the ES of a modern technologically-advanced type of coach that is composed of approximately 20 interconnected ECUs (Electronic Control Units) and a cable network, and is responsible for safety monitoring functions, (e.g. Antiblock Break System), security control (e.g. locking) ,comfort level of the passengers (e.g. heating, ventilation and air-conditioning), infotainment (information and entertainment), navigation (e.g. Global Positioning System), and electronic control of mechanical parts.

The complete production of the ES is performed in three phases, for each one of which the client (AC), located in a South European country, is using a different supplier (AS) in three different countries: a Northern European one (AS1) for design and development, a Central European supplier (AS2) for implementation and production, and an Asian supplier (AS3) for installation and industrialization. Apart from its focus on an industry (automotive) that is supportive of GLOS, the specific network was chosen because it offers the ability to 'follow' the ES throughout all the phases and related operations. In addition, it is based on countries with different economic and sociopolitical backgrounds. For example, the client company is based on a country where the specific industry sector is still developing, the country of AS1 is well known for its technical skills, AS2 is in the process of emerging economically within the EU, and AS3 has a particular interest in developing positive outsourcing relationships with EU-based countries because it aspires to enter EU.

Regarding the operations in the GLOS network, the specifications of the ES are first designed by a group of engineers in AC. Then, the design and the development, a process that lasts approximately 2 years, is outsourced to AS1, a company with advanced technological knowledge and capabilities. AS1 is responsible for creating the ES prototype (which includes writing the programming code and specifying hardware requirements) and carrying out the necessary tests to certify that the ES specifications meet regulatory standards in terms of safety, electromagnetic compatibility, and durability (a process known as homologation). After this phase is completed, the next phase involves the implementation and production of the system. In order to achieve this, AS1 sends to AS2 all the relevant "know-how" including drawings, software etc. Finally, the ES (consisting of all its specialized components, being 2 kilometers long, and weighting about one tonne) is sent to AS3, where the installation of the system and the industrialization take place before the bus is driven back to AC. Industrialization, in the specific engineering context, involves the phase when the production becomes a widespread and accelerated operation, with trustworthy productivity rates.

Semi-structured interviews took place in the interviewees' offices, through emails, or on the phone. Overall, 17 individuals from the client company were interviewed and 8, 7, and 9 in each supplier site, respectively. All interviews were conducted individually, tape-recorded, and transcribed. The interview agenda included five sections and focused on information regarding the interviewees, the company, general GLOS cultural issues, GLOS cultural emergence, and specific GLOS cultural issues.

4 Analysis

A thematic analysis was applied to the data [10, 22], involving the transformation of the qualitative data into insightful themes [10]. After the coding and the identification of the themes, a thematic network (figure 1) was developed in order to examine GLOS culture through grouping of the themes into three levels: global, basic, and organizing [3, 8].

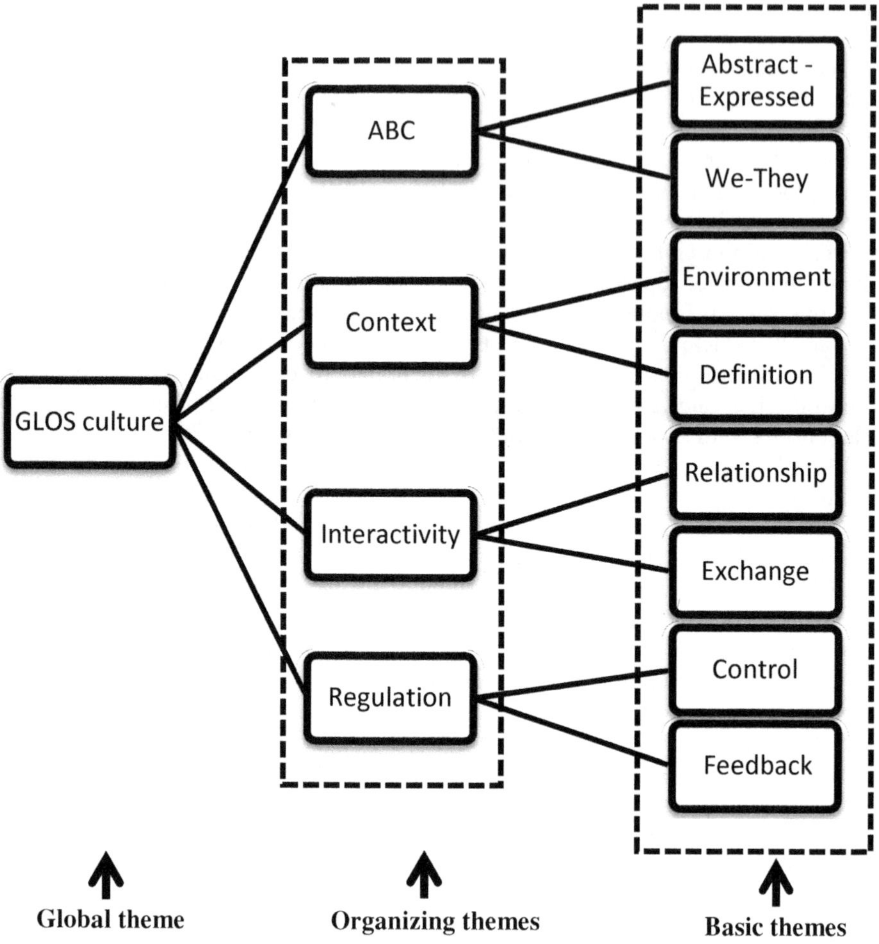

Fig. 1. Thematic network

The development of codes and themes started with a deductive approach. The codes emerged from the literature on culture and the initial themes emerged from the literature on cultural systems. Later, in the data analysis, an inductive approach allowed for the identification of additional codes and themes. The basic and the organizing themes related to GLOS culture (global theme) are further analyzed in figure 2, where the emergent GLOS culture in a GLOS cultural system is analyzed.

5 Emergent GLOS Culture

From the thematic analysis of the data, emergent GLOS culture is associated with four cultural attributes (organizing themes in the thematic network), each one characterized by further dimensions, as shown in the model in figure 2 and explained in the next sections.

According to the model, emergent GLOS culture 'emerges' from the GLOS cultural system, as it (the GLOS cultural system) results from the *combination* of cultural characteristics of separate organizations involved in the GLOS relationship. The cultural characteristics of separate organizations are depicted as cultural characteristics 1, 2, …, n, implying that the number of organizations that are part of the GLOS collaboration or the GLOS cultural system (as presented in the present model) is not restricted to two.

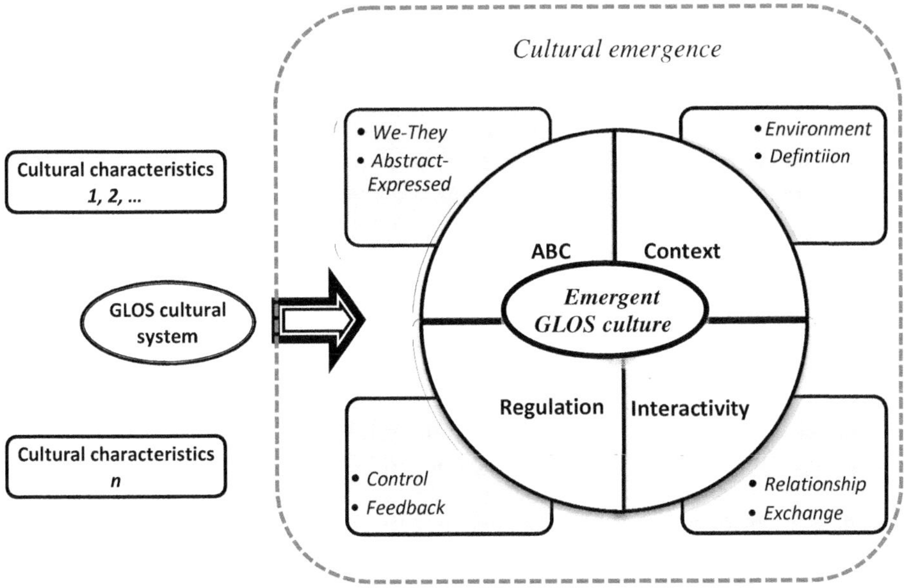

Fig. 2. Emergent GLOS culture in a GLOS cultural system

5.1 Attitude, Behaviors, Cognition

From the interviews, the organizing theme of Attitudes, Behaviors, and Cognition (ABC) is found to represent the following aspects of the GLOS culture.

- Attitudes (A) represent abstract, tacit, and internalized representations of the world, i.e. beliefs, concepts, ideals, values, norms, traditions, thinking.
- Behaviors (B) represent expressed, empirical, and externalized activities related to attitudes.
- Cognition (C) represents the cognitive processes related to both attitudinal and behavioral issues, and captures the process of change, which can be evident in terms of thinking (mental change) or doing (practical change).

From the interviews, two basic themes surfaced and were used as ABC-related dimensions, one involving a "we - they" link and one expressing "abstract – expressed" characteristics. The former (the "we - they" dimension) describes the way individuals and groups perceive and organize their world experience, become members of cultures and subcultures and, consequently, by acquiring roles within smaller or bigger social groups, adjust or differentiate their attitudes and behaviors from those of other groups. In the analysis, this dimension was reflected in statements that focused on comparing and contrasting between collaborating organizations. The latter (the "abstract – expressed" dimension) represents, on one side, tacit and intangible characteristics such as concepts, values, norms, beliefs and, on the other side, empirical behavioral expressions. In the data, this dimension was evident in statements regarding theoretical aspects of the employees' way of thinking, which can also be translated into related actions or workplace practices. For example, differentiating between seeing the wiring looms of the ES prototype on the table and actually fitting it to the coach.

5.2 Context

Context functions as an intermediary in the exchanges between the GLOS cultural system and the environment and it is also related to the system's definition.

Environment is perceived to represent the external business environment, as it exists beyond organizational boundaries, while it also operates at the cognitive level, affecting the individuals' thinking. Moreover, the external environment, apart from the economic and sociopolitical status, which tends to be stable unless major changes occur (e.g. wars, new laws, governmental changes), also includes stable concepts (e.g. objective expressions of time, holidays, schedules, language) for the understanding of which adjustments can be made, e.g. through appropriate standardization and documentation of agreed upon rules and procedures. In addition, apart from the existence of the external environment and the various interactions that operate within and around the GLOS system, another dimension that emerged was definition. The concept of definition is described as understanding and adjusting the system and its boundaries in relation to its goals and its needs. Goals and needs help define the GLOS relationship by being related to its initiation (i.e. signing of the specific outsourcing agreement), its everyday operations, and its broader functionality.

5.3 Interactivity

The organizing theme of interactivity is related to the dimensions of relationship and exchange.

More specifically, interactivity is associated with the coexistence of the cultural system's elements and it also refers to the exchanges that take place within or around the system, crossing different boundaries of the system's hierarchy. It should be noted that the existence of a relationship does not presuppose exchange, since elements of the cultural systems can work side-by-side (coexist) in a parallel way, without any need for further interaction or any pressure to change as a result of the relationship. This is the reason why relationship and exchange are treated as different basic themes (and consequently dimensions). Therefore, relationship refers to collaboration required by the formal aspects (e.g. the signing of the deal) of the arrangement and, depending on the relationship, exchange may take place or not.

5.4 Regulation

In the study, regulation implies the need for harmonization and relationship building, and is further characterized by dimensions of control and feedback.

In the analysis of the data, the concept of control was found to exist within the system as a prerequisite for organization and order, often expressed as responsibility and power within the system, caused by both internal and external factors. In addition, it also exists as a result of information exchange between the system and the external business environment and of the need to follow externally imposed demands and regulations. Moreover, feedback emerged as another dimension that describes regulatory functions and information exchange, found to exist both as an external and as an internal mechanism. External feedback, on one hand, is based on the interaction of the cultural system with the decision and policy makers at the executive level of the company or on externally imposed conditions, such as laws, policies, treaties, taxes, condition of the market. The internal feedback, on the other hand, would include observations, 360 degrees feedback, intergroup discussions, and meetings.

6 Cultural Emergence

From the analysis of the data, cultural emergence was related to mechanisms and processes by addressing the issue of "*how emergent culture emerges*". Relevant data, when analyzed in terms of dynamism (time), scale (expected size of the change), and motivation (reasoning and end result of the cultural emergence), seemed to fit into two categories:

- Mechanisms represent techniques of a short, maybe spontaneous nature, and refer to everyday work-related behaviors and resolutions of problems that may be solved through relatively small cognitive and behavioral adjustments.
- Processes emphasize techniques of a larger scale, with a long(er)-time perspective, organized and executed at the organizational level, possibly as part of the organization's strategy, and often including multiple phases.

For example, mechanisms such as updating of the software would normally take less than a day, while rewarding an employee with an extra paid day off on Christmas can be an impulsive act. In terms of examples of processes, seminars in language and terminology were expected to last 3 weeks in company AC and AS2, with optional registration to evening classes and additional seminars to refresh the employees' memory (especially on terminology) throughout the duration of the collaboration. Processes could also be of a strategic planning nature, for example manipulating motivation levels through changes in the compensation system (e.g. by changing the reward system from a basic salary to a bonus system) or demanding closer collaboration with the government and the Minister of Commerce to address the legal aspects involved in the case of AC contacting business with AS1, AS2, and AS3.

In other examples, emergence was related to the environment, especially to time, distance, and regulations. More specifically, time represents an objective understanding in terms of hours-minutes/day/year, distance represents physical distance in terms of measuring standards (e.g. kilometers, miles), and regulations (e.g. rules, taxes, treaties, laws) are related to explicit factors (e.g. the government, the HR employee book, the clauses and the conditions of the contract). Interestingly enough, these three characteristics of the environment, even though they are considered stable enough when examined objectively (e.g. the frequency of tax laws changes, the geographical distance between companies, export laws), the perception of them can change through awareness, standardization, and transparency.

From the analysis of the findings, examples related to cultural emergence that can be used as possible guidelines for applying specific mechanisms and processes to GLOS relationships include the following:

- The majority of M&Ps involve languages, education, and socialization either predefined by the company or according to individuals' comfort levels and their attitudes towards the opposite sex, age gap, social status.
- As a strategy for building core capabilities, mechanisms appear to be important for transference of critical skills, managerial systems, norms, and values.
- For critical concrete forms of skills (e.g. advanced programming skills), individuals tend to rely on formal educational channel, mentoring, and training, associating them with enhanced understanding and reduced misinterpretations.
- When dealing with practical issues, agreeing on common practices appears to solve everyday problems (e.g. for time/date problems using both the USA and European format).
- Standardization and documentation as business practices can increase the credibility of the company in the global market.

7 Discussion / Conclusions

The paper, using a thematic analysis of interview data collected in an industrial setting, discusses a model that addresses the emergent culture in IS/IT GLOS relationships.

From a theoretical perspective, the main contribution of the paper is the use of the cultural systems perspective in the area of outsourcing. Even though a systems perspective has been applied before to outsourcing research, the use of the *cultural* systems perspectives has not been applied to the sourcing field. In addition, the paper offers a model that demonstrates themes that can further analyze the emergent nature of culture, addressing issues of context-specificity, dynamism, and interactions.

For practitioners, the paper discusses a way of addressing questions on the role of culture in GLOS, by viewing culture as a byproduct of cultural characteristics of the collaborating organizations and by further breaking down the GLOS culture into specific cultural attributes. While it studies the emergent nature of culture, it discusses attributes that can be examined in a practical setting, beyond mere conceptual development. Consequently, the point of interest in a GLOS cultural study changes from the analysis of the general role of culture in the success/failure of GLOS projects to a question on the role of *specific* cultural attributes in the success/failure of intercultural projects.

In addition, the model of emergent GLOS Culture can be used to examine the transition period in GLOS relationships, from the existence of two separate systems into the emergence of a new GLOS cultural system. Through identification of specific cultural attributes, it can contribute towards relationship improvement and it can function as a tool for relationship governance. Furthermore, it offers a way to examine cultural competency in terms of its emergent nature, while different parties can examine their common understanding and definition of the cultural attributes that play a prominent role in the specific GLOS relationship. As a result, identification and definition of cultural attributes of a GLOS cultural relationship 'move' beyond mere translation of terms and subjective understanding by individual organizational members. This can contribute towards decrease of culture-related ambiguity and reduction of cultural resistance, since, on many occasions, cultural resistance occurs due to misunderstandings in the translation of tacit aspects of culture-specific concepts.

Furthermore, analyzing emergence in terms of mechanisms, processes, and the categories of dynamism, scale, and motivation (as discussed in the previous section), the following issues can be addressed:

- The dimension of dynamism can address time issues in terms of duration of a technique (either mechanism or process), duration of its impact, immediacy of impact, and potential to evolve, change, or be revoked.
- The dimension of scale can be extended to examine the impact change on various levels of the system, e.g. individual, group, departmental, organizational, and that of the external business environment.
- The dimension of motivation can explain reasons for adopting and promoting a mechanism or a process and its perceived/achieved end result.

Moreover, such aspects of the dimensions can be further examined in terms of their effect on specific cultural attributes, as the ones presented in the model of Emergent GLOS culture. This can lead to the development of guidelines (example of which were mentioned in the section on Cultural emergence), according to which certain types of mechanisms and processes (depending on their level of dynamism, scale, and motivation) can be more effective than others for the emergence of specific cultural attributes.

In terms of limitations, the present paper does not discuss concrete details regarding the data and their analysis, because of its focus, instead, on examining the emergence of GLOS culture. This is also the reason why no emphasis was given on how specific codes and themes were developed from raw data. Finally, it should be noted that the model of emergent culture does not claim that cultural norms change but, rather, that the expression of behaviors associated with them within a GLOS specific context can change as a result of the interaction of cultural characteristics of the collaborating organizations. In other words, the different aspects of the model can be manipulated through the use of appropriate Mechanisms & Processes and address the development and the emergent GLOS culture.

References

1. Abbott, P., Zheng, Y., Du, R., Willcocks, L.: From Boundary Spanning to Creolization: Cross-cultural Strategies from the Offshore Provider's Perspective. In: Proceedings of the Americas Conference on Information Systems, p. 274 (2010)
2. Archer, M.S.: Culture and Agency: The Place of Culture in Social Theory. Cambridge University Press, UK (1996)
3. Attride-Stirling, J.: Thematic Networks: An Analytic Tool for Qualitative Research. Qualitative Research 1(3), 385–405 (2001)

4. Aubert, B.A., Patry, M., Rivard, S.: A Framework for Information Technology Outsourcing Risk Management. Database for Advances in Information Systems 36(4), 9–28 (2005)
5. Barthelemy, J.: The Hidden Costs of IT Outsourcing. MIT Sloan Management Review 42(3), 60–69 (2001)
6. Barthelemy, J.: The Seven Deadly Sins of Outsourcing. The Academy of Management Executive 17(2), 87–98 (2003)
7. Beulen, E., Ribbers, P., Roos, J.: Managing IT Outsourcing: Governance in Gobal Partnerships. Routledge, Oxford (2006)
8. Brannen, M.Y.: Negotiated Culture in Binational Contexts: A Model of Culture Change Based on a Japanese/American Organizational Experience. Anthropology of Work Review 18(2-3), 6–17 (1998)
9. Brannen, M.Y., Salk, J.E.: Partnering Across Borders: Negotiating Organizational Culture in a German-Japanese Joint Venture. Human Relations 53(4), 451–487 (2000)
10. Braun, V., Clarke, V.: Using Thematic Analysis in Psychology. Qualitative Research in Psychology 3(2), 77–101 (2006)
11. Calabrese, G., Erbetta, F.: Outsourcing and Firm Performance: Evidence from Italian Automotive Suppliers. International Journal of Automotive Technology and Management 5(4), 461–479 (2005)
12. Capgemini: Application Outsourcing for Automotive OEMs: Realizing Cost Savings and Business Improvements Through a Structured Three-Phase Approach (2008), `http://www.capgemini.com/insights-and-resources/by-publication/application_outsourcing_for_automotive_oems` (retrieved October 10, 2010)
13. Carmel, E., Agarwal, R.: The Maturation of Offshore Sourcing of Information Technology. MIS Quarterly Executive 1(2), 65–77 (2002)
14. Carmel, E., Tjia, P.: Offshoring Information Technology: Sourcing and Outsourcing to a Global Workforce. Cambridge University Press, UK (2005)
15. Checkland, P.: Systems Theory and Management Thinking. American Behavioral Scientist 38(1), 75 (1994)
16. Chesebro, J.W., Bertelsen, D.A.: Analyzing Media: Communication Technologies as Symbolic and Cognitive Systems. Guilford Press, New York (1998)
17. Doktor, R., Lie, J., Poillon, C.: A Systems Theoretic Perspective Upon International Organizational Behavior: Some Preliminary Observations and Hypotheses. Management International Review 31, 125–133 (1991)
18. Elo, S., Kyngas, H.: The Qualitative Content Analysis Process. Journal of Advanced Nursing 62(1), 107–115 (2008)
19. Ember, C.R., Ember, M., Peregrine, P.N.: Anthropology. Prentice Hall, Upper Saddle River (2002)
20. Erber, G., Sayed-Ahmed, A.: Offshore Outsourcing: A Global Shift in the Present IT Industry. Intereconomics 40(2), 100–112 (2005)
21. Evans, J., Treadgold, A., Mavondo, F.T.: Psychic Distance and the Performance of International Retailers - A Suggested Theoretical Framework. International Marketing Review 17(4/5), 373–391 (2000)
22. Fereday, J., Muir-Cochrane, E.: Demonstrating Rigor Using Thematic Analysis: A Hybrid Approach of Inductive and Deductive Coding and Theme Development. International Journal of Qualitative Methods 5(1), 1–11 (2006)

23. Fjermestad, J., Saitta, J.A.: A Strategic Management Framework for IT Outsourcing: A Review of the Literature and the Development of a Success Factors Model. Journal of Information Technology Case and Application Research 7(3), 42–60 (2005)
24. Grover, V.: The Effect of Service Quality and Partnership on the Outsourcing of Information Systems Functions. Journal of Management Information Systems 12(4), 89–119 (1996)
25. Gurung, A., Prater, E.: A Research Framework for the Impact of Cultural Differences on IT Outsourcing. Journal of Global Information Technology Management 9(1), 24–43 (2006)
26. Hendry, J.: Cultural Theory and Contemporary Management Organization. Human Relations 52(5), 557–577 (1999)
27. Hirscheim, R., Lacity, M.: The Myths and Realities of Information Technology Outsourcing. Communications of the ACM 43(2), 99–107 (2000)
28. Hofstede, G.: Culture's Consequences: International Differences in Work-Related Values. Sage Publications, Beverly Hills (1980)
29. Karahanna, E., Evaristo, J., Srite, M.: Levels of Culture and Individual Behavior: An Integrative Perspective. Journal of Global Information Management 13(2), 1–20 (2005)
30. Kern, T., Willcocks, L.: Exploring Relationships in Information Technology Outsourcing: The Interaction Approach. European Journal of Information Systems 11(1), 3–19 (2002)
31. Khan, N., Fitzgerald, G.: Dimensions of Offshore Outsourcing Business Models. Journal of Information Technology Cases and Applications 6(3), 35–50 (2004)
32. King, W.R., Torkzadeh, G.: Information Systems Offshoring: Research Status and Issues. MIS Quarterly 32(2), 205–225 (2008)
33. Kliem, R.: Managing the Risks of Offshore IT Development Projects. Information Systems Management 21(3), 22–27 (2004)
34. Krishna, S., Sahay, S., Walsham, G.: Managing Cross-Cultural Issues in Global Software Outsourcing. Communications of the ACM 47(4), 62–66 (2004)
35. Leidner, D.E., Kayworth, T.: Review: A Review of Culture in Information Systems Research: Toward a Theory of Information Technology Culture Conflict. MIS Quarterly 30(2), 357–399 (2006)
36. McIvor, R., McHugh, M.: Collaborative Buyer Supplier Relations: Implications for Organization Change Management. Strategic Change 9(4), 221–236 (2000)
37. McLeod Jr., R.: Management Information Systems: A Study of Computer-Based Information Systems. Prentice-Hall, Inc., Upper Saddle River (1995)
38. Modarress, B., Ansari, A.: The Economic, Technological, and National Security Risks of Offshore Outsourcing. Journal of Global Business Issues 1(2), 165–175 (2007)
39. Mora, M., Gelman, O., Forgionne, G., Petkov, D., Cano, J.: Integrating the Fragmented Pieces of IS Research Paradigms and Frameworks: A Systems Approach. Information Resources Management Journal 20(2), 1–22 (2007)
40. Murthy, S.: The Impact of Global IT Outsourcing on IT Providers. Communications of the Association for Information Systems 14(6), 543–557 (2004)
41. Myers, M.D., Avison, D.E.: Qualitative Research in Information Systems. Sage Publications, London (2002)
42. Myers, M.D., Tan, F.B.: Beyond Models of National Culture in Information Systems Research. Journal of Global Information Management 10(1), 24–32 (2002)
43. Nicholson, B., Sahay, S.: The Political and Cultural Implications of the Globalization of Software Development: Case Experience from UK and India. Information and Organization 11(1), 25–43 (2001)

44. Nisbett, R.E., Peng, K., Choi, I., Norenzayan, A.: Culture and Systems of Thought: Holistic versus Analytic Cognition. Psychological Review 108(2), 291–310 (2001)
45. Oza, N.V., Hall, T.: Difficulties in Managing Offshore Software Outsourcing Relationships: An Empirical Analysis of 18 High Maturity Indian Software Companies. Journal of Information Technology Case and Application Research 7(3), 25–41 (2005)
46. Oza, N., Hall, T., Rainer, A., Grey, S.: Critical Factors in Software Outsourcing - A Pilot Study. In: Proceedings of the ACM Workshop on Interdisciplinary Software Engineering, Newport Beach (2004)
47. Palvia, S.C.J.: Global Outsourcing of IT and IT Enabled Services: A Framework for Choosing an (Outsourcee) Country. Journal of Information Technology Cases and Applications 6(3), 1–20 (2004)
48. Parker, D.W., Russell, K.A.: Outsourcing and Inter/Intra Supply Chain Dynamics: Strategic Management Issues. Journal of Supply Chain Management 40(4), 56–68 (2004)
49. Parsons, T., Shils, E., Smelser, N.: Toward a General Theory of Action: Theoretical Foundations for the Social Sciences. Transaction Publishers, Piscataway (2001)
50. Piachaud, B.: Outsourcing Technology. Research Technology Management 48(3), 40–46 (2005)
51. Rottman, J., Lacity, M.: Twenty Practices for Offshore Surcing. MIS Quarterly Executive 3(3), 117–130 (2004)
52. Rottman, J., Lacity, M.: Proven Practices for Effectively Offshoring IT Work. MIT Sloan Management Review 47(3), 56–63 (2006)
53. Rottman, J., Lacity, M.: A US Client's Learning from Outsourcing IT Work Offshore. Information Systems Frontiers 10(2), 259–275 (2008)
54. Stringfellow, A., Teagarden, M.B., Nie, W.: Invisible Costs in Offshoring Services Work. Journal of Operations Management 26(2), 164–179 (2008)
55. Vaccari, E., Delaney, E.: Cognitive Modeling in the Systems Theory Paradigm. Systems Research and Behavioral Science 16(3), 227–238 (1999)
56. Veiga, J., Lubatkin, M., Calori, R., Very, P.: Measuring Organizational Culture Clashes: A Two-Nation Post-Hoc Analysis of a Cultural Compatibility Index. Human Relations 53(4), 539–557 (2000)
57. Vestring, T., Rouse, T., Reinert, U.: Hedge Your Offshoring Bets. MIT Sloan Management Review 46(3), 27–29 (2005)
58. von Bertalanffy, L.: General System Theory: Foundations. George Braziller, New York (1968)
59. Weisinger, J.Y., Salipante, P.F.: Cultural Knowing as Practicing: Extending Our Conceptions of Culture. Journal of Management Inquiry 9(4), 376–390 (2000)
60. Weisinger, J.Y., Trauth, E.M.: Situating Culture in the Global Information Sector. Information Technology & People 15(4), 306–320 (2002)
61. Weisinger, J.Y., Trauth, E.: The Importance of Situating Culture in Cross-cultural IT Management. IEEE Transactions on Engineering Management 50(1), 26–30 (2003)

Should This Software Component Be Developed Inside or Outside Our Firm? - A Design Science Perspective on the Sourcing of Application Systems

Tommi Kramer, Armin Heinzl, and Kai Spohrer

University of Mannheim, 68131 Mannheim, Germany
{kramer,heinzl,spohrer}@uni-mannheim.de,
http://heinzl.bwl.uni-mannheim.de/

Abstract. From a national and global perspective, the sourcing of application systems has significantly matured and been widely adopted over the past years. However, little research has been conducted regarding the properties and contingencies of outsourced technological artifacts. In most scholarly published contributions, it is often difficult to find the IT artifact in the IS sourcing debate. Especially, it has not yet been explored on which rationales certain parts of an IS architecture are handed over to external vendors or kept in-house. In order to overcome this drawback, we focus in this paper on the outsourcing decision for components of IS architectures. This, in turn, directs the focus to the properties of software components and their surrounding contingency factors which may facilitate the decision to outsource a component or not. Thus, the unit of analysis will not be on an organizational or work group level, but rather on the level of a technological artifact itself: the software component which needs to be developed among others in order to achieve the desired system functionality. We are not aware of any research contributions in IS sourcing which have been conducted on a software component level so far. Thus, we aim to contribute towards an underexplored topic which is highly important since organizational decisions towards outsourcing are deeply rooted in the technical functionalities of the desired systems.

Keywords: outsourcing, decision making, software engineering, software development, design science, IT artifact.

1 Introduction

From a national and global perspective, the sourcing of application systems has significantly matured and been widely adopted over the past years. A vast variety of academic contributions has been offered up to now, largely focusing on the determinants, forms, transition modes, relationships and outcomes of such contracts [1,2,3]. However, little research has been conducted regarding the properties and contingencies of outsourced artifacts in particular. In most

J. Kotlarsky, L.P. Willcocks, and I. Oshri (Eds.): Global Sourcing 2011, LNBIP 91, pp. 115–132, 2011.

scholarly published contributions, it is hard to find the IT in the IS sourcing debate. Especially, it has not yet been explored on which rationales certain parts of an IS architecture are handed over to external vendors or kept in-house. If, for instance, the project manager of an IS application development project is seeking advice which modules or components should be developed within the firm and which parts of the architecture should be handed over to external vendors, the existing literature on IS sourcing will hardly be capable to assist him.

Consequently, our research focuses on the support of software companies which have to make the sourcing decision for distinct software components. In detail, we try to answer the following research question: *Which components of an IS architecture should be developed in-house and which can be outsourced to external vendors?*

This, in turn, directs the interest to the properties of a software component and its surrounding contingency factors which may heavily influence the decision to outsource this component or not. Thus, the unit of analysis will not be on an organizational or work group level, but rather on the level of a technological artifact itself: the software component which needs to be developed among others in order to achieve the required system functionality. We are not aware of any existing work in IS outsourcing research looking at software component level. Thereby, we aim to contribute to the body of knowledge about an underexplored topic which is highly important since the organizational decision to outsource is deeply rooted in the technical functionalities of the desired systems.

2 Methodology and Research Approach

In order to answer our research question, we intend to craft a novel method as well as a tool to support the make-or-buy-decision of software components. This paper focuses on the novel method only. Any research endeavor which intends to develop novel artifacts or instantiations of the respective artifacts demands a methodology which is not epistemological in nature but focuses on the design of the novel artifacts. Thus, a design science research approach is deemed to be appropriate in this case [4].

Conforming to this approach, we intend to inform our artifact design by suitable theories and concepts. On the one hand, systems theory and the concept of sub-systems design will be utilized in order to take various levels of interdependencies and the degree of component modularity into account [5,6,7]. Examples of such interdependencies are among others structural dependencies between different components as well as the structural dependencies between components and requirements. These dependencies will be referred to as structural characteristics of a component. On the other hand, we will draw on concepts rooted in transaction cost theory [8] to analyze properties within the single components. Such contextual characteristics are, for instance, the business process specificity, the technological specificity, and the functional specificity of the software components analyzed. They have repeatedly been found to be of significant influence in IS outsourcing [1,9,10].

Accordingly, we deduce a set of determinants from the existing literature base which are considered to be crucial for the component sourcing decision. The determinants are then combined and integrated with the help of a decision table as a simple but flexible heuristic. This heuristic for the software component insourcing versus outsourcing decision will then be applied in a case study. The intention of this case study is to evaluate the decision heuristic as well as to create an avenue for future development. The case study is conducted with a medium-sized enterprise software vendor to represent an adequate example for enterprises that intend to outsource. Finally, we outline the limitations of our novel approach, i.e. the component sourcing heuristic, and its instantiation, the respective component decision tool. In the remainder of this paper, we will refer to the component sourcing heuristic as our novel artifact and to implications for a component decision tool as this artifact's instantiation. Concluding, we elaborate on the implications of our research for theory and practice and provide an outlook for future research regarding this topic.

3 IS Software Engineering and Outsourcing

Since we explore technological dimensions of software development outsourcing in detail, we will offer a basic perspective on software engineering (SE) and IS outsourcing. In particular, we will focus on the rationales of these concepts as well as the challenges involved.

3.1 Software Engineering

Software engineering is often compared to engineering of buildings or mechanical as well as electrical systems. The term SE can be derived from other disciplines and may be defined as an engineering approach for software systems [11]. It comprises not only the production process which is composed by a set of development phases but also maintenance after the system's rollout [12]. In addition, a software creation process is characterized by a multi-stage and repetitive application lifecycle. Necessary stages of such a lifecycle primarily focus on the following activities [12]: Software specification is the activity in which the desired functions and limitations of the requested software product are defined. It is followed by the design and implementation phase during which the design and the creation of the actual software code take place based on the specification. Thereafter, executable programs are checked for the requested functionality and tested for errors in the scope of the software validation. In the final evolution phase, software is continuously adapted to changing customer requirements. Within this paper, the focus is set on the design phase. Designers and developers decide at this point about the type of implementation, the architecture used for coding the application, and the granularity of description. This phase is especially important for the conversion of the created specification to a specific system implementation on a particular platform.

The design phase of the development process is initiated by a decomposition of a complex system into several sub-systems and the creation of a framework to control each of them. Since this primarily describes the architecture of the whole system, it is called the architectural design. It is an important phase that links the requirements engineering with the software development as it defines the communication between all components of the system through the framework. An ingeniously developed architecture of the software serves as a profound fundament of discussion between a range of stakeholders at a single table [13,12]. Furthermore, in the design phase, stakeholders and designers decide about the granularity of the software's description (e.g. components or classes). On the basis of this decision, the software system is planned and designed. Thus, we consider the structural design of a software system as a decisive activity when it comes to the outsourcing question.

3.2 Outsourcing

This paper deals in particular with outsourcing decisions in the domain of application development and it seems necessary to clarify the meaning and type of outsourcing used in this research context as numerous sourcing options exist within the IS discipline.

We use the term outsourcing in a very particular way. In the IS discipline the term itself is widely adopted with a meaning that complete IS functions are shifted from internal provision to an external provider [1]. Numerous service providers that are specialized in specific IS functions have established and benefit from economies of scale. In this paper, we consider the fulfillment of development tasks for a software product by a third party as outsourcing, independent from its location. From the perspective of western countries, software development tasks have shifted to mostly Eastern European, Asian or South-American locations [14,15]. We do not differentiate between near-shoring and far-shoring, but we focus on outsourcing.

With regard to our sourcing decision approach, we provide a short overview of motivational factors for companies that intend to establish an outsourcing relationship. Even though there are numerous convincing factors for the sourcing of software components, several challenges are associated with external procurement of development services.

Rationale. The rationale of software development companies to outsource tasks of the development process to subcontractors is justified by several arguments in favor of outsourcing. Some examples of them are given in the remainder.

Cost savings play a significant role in application development outsourcing. Primarily, development tasks are outsourced to low-wage countries in order to have software developed cheaper. By signing a contract with an outsourcing partner, the software company outsources its risk and time constraints to the subcontractor as well. In case of failing (e.g. the software is not as requested or components are delivered late) the contracted company is held responsible, generally by charging penalty fees [16,17].

Globalization is a further motivating force to go into outsourcing, not only for large enterprises which have the financial power but also for smaller companies.

Internet and telecommunication devices enable them to get in contact with outsourcing partners and to exchange data easily. Thus, the development of foreign markets, the availability of cheaper work force, and the advantages of global partnerships attract firms likewise independent of their size [18].

The outsourcing relationship can aim at an increase of development speed, agility, and flexibility. Moreover, it also enables the exploitation of complementary human assets that are available in foreign locations. Especially, the utilization of new talents with specific abilities in certain technological domains plays an important role. In particular, software developing companies are reliant on creativity regarding the design of software within the development phase [19]. Finally, the lack of development resources onshore motivates companies to establish outsourcing partnerships with firms which can easily upscale development capacities offshore. Such outsourcing vendors are often located in countries with less regulated labor legislations and unions [19].

Challenges. As IS outsourcing often denotes a shift of software development tasks from onshore to offshore locations [20], established reasons for companies not going into outsourcing are language differences, the complexity of coordinating the outsourcing relationship, the complexity of control, as well as social and cultural issues [19,9,21]. While language barriers impede the exchange of essential project information between outsourcing partners, the complexity of coordination is a further challenge in outsourcing scenarios as well. Since software development consists of several complex and interdependent tasks until a software product can be released, developers must continuously exchange implicit knowledge, preferably while having a cup of coffee or tea [22]. In a distributed scenario, this type of communication is not feasible. A control breakdown is caused by giving away tasks into the field of responsibility of another company. Consequently, the liability and the execution of tasks are primarily controlled by the subcontractor and not by the outsourcer anymore. Finally, cultural differences can negatively affect outsourcing through misunderstandings, mistrust, or authoritative issues such as different reporting behavior of professionals to the management.

Whilst having the mentioned obstacles in mind, many companies are motivated to set up outsourcing partnerships or have already initiated outsourcing relations, which is also an observable trend in the software development domain [23]. Nevertheless, firms have difficulties in adopting outsourcing practices as their decision making process is not well defined. In the following section, we present existing approaches for the decision problem and elaborate how these approaches impact the development of our new artifact.

4 Existing Approaches to the Outsourcing of Software Development Tasks

Outsourcing of IS functions and thus of development tasks has been widely researched. Testing of software fragments, for example, has been one of the first tasks to be outsourced to external vendors. Over time the expertise of outsourcing vendors in foreign countries has increased. Thus, the outsourcing of development tasks is not only limited to testing any more, but also covers the whole set of development phases. This enables software companies also to outsource earlier phases than testing [24]. In this paper, we focus on the early phases, which are requirements engineering, design, and software development. The transition from the design to the development phase is particularly emphasized. Uncovering existing trends in software engineering that have an impact on our artifact and analyzing the state-of-the-art behavior in outsourcing decision making, we derive implications for our approach.

4.1 Software Engineering Trends

Within the SE domain, several major trends on how software is developed can be found. Mainly, current software development processes follow the principles of the Rational Unified Process (RUP) [25]. The RUP consists of phases consistent with the SE process described above, integrates elements from generic process models, iteration steps from models like the spiral model as well as UML diagrams that offer best support for analysis and design. Therefore, the RUP can be considered a hybrid process model combining static aspects (strongly defined core steps such as the development phases) with dynamic elements (stating the incremental character by phases such as inception, elaboration, construction, and transition) of software engineering [25,12]. Furthermore, the RUP shifts the single perspective mentality found in conventional models to a multi-perspective one [25]. Caused by this multi-perspective view, the application of the RUP requires the use of UML diagrams and models as well as component based development steps and, therefore, presumes the application of object-oriented programming languages. Even the automation of generating objects and classes directly from UML models is efficient to such an extent, that the use of object-oriented programming languages is recommendable and, therefore, already wide-spread [26]. As a consequence of object-orient programming, the required software product is structured in components, packages, and classes. This categorization has the impact that identified decision characteristics of software objects can be evaluated on the basis of either components or packages or classes. Furthermore, there is a trend in SE to follow the principles of agile software development [27,28]. In contrast to static software development process models, the agile approach is primarily described with *lightweight* methodologies and processes and has its roots in the definition of a completely different software development process, called *Extreme Programming* [27]. The lightweight approaches are primarily focused on the target of the project and a stakeholder-oriented solution. Thus, technical problems and social interactions hold the main focus of attention within agile approaches. Not the writing of exorbitant documentation and design models, but the concentration on stakeholders' requirements and on a deliverable solution is what supporters of agility mention. This is considered the main difference between agile methods and traditional process models. Typical implementations of agile development are *Extreme Programming* and *Scrum* [27]. One positive aspect of these agile approaches is the flexibility and ease of use, especially for smaller groups and projects. A key point of agile methods is that requirements are subject to prioritization [29]. The prioritization principle of requirements is currently recognized by popular requirements elicitation approaches [30,31,32]. The ranked list of requirements represents the functionality that has to be implemented first and which is of great importance for all stakeholders. Consequently, the priority of requirements has a decisive impact for the outsourcing decision and must be regarded in our new approach.

We also derive additional elements for our approach from Open Source Software Development. We have a particular focus on the modularity of such software systems and how these projects deal with modularity in the design and development phases. Within the Open Source Software Development, components and programs are created with voluntary contributions of individuals. The success stories of several Open Source projects (Linux, Apache, and FreeBSD) document the advantageous character of this approach [33]. This success is achieved by a large community of users whose task is to act as team members and co-developers and, hence, to correct software defects or to add new features to the software product. Collaboration of the community by following a peer review process is highly important for Open Source development and its success [33]. The crucial part of Open Source projects is their transition from an initial idea and formation phase to a continuously improving software project with numerous largely independent system components [33]. Thereby, small teams and individuals can maintain and develop code autonomously whilst being motivated to contribute. It becomes obvious that autonomy of system components plays a major role in such software projects [33]. Our newly developed approach, therefore, considers the coupling of and interdependencies between software objects when making the decision to outsource or not.

4.2 Decision Making in Outsourcing Scenarios

Besides current SE methods, the decision making process in the course of outsourcing plays also an important role in our approach. Outsourcing deals with the question of what to make and what to buy. Thus, 'making' denotes the internal development of software objects (representing all kinds of software artifacts, e.g. components, packages, etc.) and 'buying' represents the external procurement of these objects.

According to different literature analyses [1,2] the questions of the why, what, which, how, and the outcome of outsourcing has been researched. Several theories were reported to be applied for sourcing phenomena and the 'make-or-buy' question has been explored comprehensively from a broad perspective and by the use of many of these theories. However, when setting the research focus on the 'what' to be outsourced and how it can be identified, only a few theories are taken into account. Since this paper investigates the decision finding in a software engineering environment, transaction cost economics (TCE), as well as the resource-based theory serve as a basic framework for the 'make-or-buy' decision. Both theories suggest management to behave and decide at least to a certain degree rationally since the goal is making profit or gaining economic benefits. Furthermore, we apply the systems theory which considers the modularity of components [34,35,36]. Hence, this section demonstrates the theory-informed classification of important characteristics of a software object into different specificities and introduces existing research approaches.

Transaction Cost Economics. By adapting the TCE theory, we assume that human assets play a major role in outsourcing contexts. Since the competitive ability of software companies can primarily be based on the human capital of their employees, the company's intention to outsource specific components is always heavily related to considerations about respective transaction costs [1,37]. Components with complex production processes have significantly higher transaction costs than simple development tasks [9]. Consequently, the costs for managing the complexity of tasks and processes can overrun cost savings expected from outsourcing [9]. In our approach, we represent human asset specificity in form of three different specificities for software objects: business-related, functional, and technical. The business-related specificity denotes the required knowledge of a human regarding operational and management processes that are supported by the software product. Functional complexity aims at special knowledge that software companies need in order to translate specific types of business processes into a logical software design or that external developers need to understand the software code [10]. Technical specificity denotes all programming skills and techniques which are necessary to implement the desired software system.

Resource-based view. The resource-based view argues that the market is able to develop over time and to learn from the past. Thus, the market may provide independently created capabilities and routines based on available resources [35]. If an organization is not able to provide required resources for the creation of a product or service internally, the market resources can complement the firm's assets and may be useful for its strategy [38,39]. If there are no sufficient resources internally available, a company might be forced to outsource tasks, even strategic ones when offered by the market. However, resources with high strategic significance and highly heterogeneous distribution (in other words: high asset specificity) shall be kept in-house in order to protect own core competencies. This, of course, has an implication for the outsourcing decision.

Based on the TCE and the resource-based view of the firm, existing research work gives advice for handling outsourcing questions by suggesting to outsource non-core functions and to keep highly complex functions in-house. Therefore, Stratman [40] proposes to categorize well understood, standardized service processes, without strategic impact, as non-core and thus potentially suitable for outsourcing. In contrast to that, tasks that are complex, less defined, have no standardized procedure and, therefore, include profound and tacit knowledge, as well as complex decision finding, are considered core functions. Consequently, these tasks show more challenging and complex characteristics, which may endanger a project's success through additional transaction and production costs in case of outsourcing [9]. Consequently, TCE and the resource-based view provide rational to focus on the introduced types of specificities as a basis for the sourcing decision.

Closest to the software component development outsourcing is the research of Mirani [41] who states that small applications or components are more likely to be successfully delivered in an outsourcing relationship. The precondition for this success is a low complexity of the components and software fragments for which a specification is transmittable and whose development process is highly structured.

Systems Theory. The decision making analysis can be rounded up by an approach based on systems theory [7]. It makes use of the modularity of software elements which has been proven to be helpful for the development of complex systems such as software systems [36]. Since complex systems consist of a tremendous number of interdependent elements, the system developer's task is to guarantee the effective co-operation of all involved elements [7]. High interdependencies require specific organizational setups and experienced management in order to meet design and development decisions within this context. But instead of developing a solution with respect to direct influence on the interdependent elements through internal solutions exclusively, the division of labor and the specialization on knowledge-based processes lead increasingly to a distributed development of complex systems [42]. Several drivers, such as reduced communication and information costs or well-established standards, simplify the inter-organizational development of complex systems. But only by using modular product architectures, this operation method becomes efficient [43]. Modularity is reached decomposing a system into numerous subsystems or modules that have a minimal degree of interdependence and that only interact by defined interfaces [43]. The decomposition of a system paves the road to an independent development of each subsystem that can be executed by outsourcing partners or subcontractors. Finally, all subsystems can be integrated into a complete system. Hence, systems theory suggests that the separation of software modules alleviates the development of complex software systems. This leads to the implication that communication among software objects has to be reduced to a minimum, especially then, if the software objects are partially outsourced. Consequently, we include the interdependencies between software objects as well as the intensity of the required communication between stakeholders of the objects as further decision criteria for our new artifact.

Existing approaches for decison making. Furthermore, a few studies have already researched the *what* question from different perspectives. Carmel et al. [44] describe in their study a global triage process, an assessment methodology in which each system component or task is evaluated for its outsourcing fit. The final decision is represented analogously to a traffic light. While red indicates that a task is not appropriate for the outsourcing shift, green releases a task to the offshoring location. Various decision factors such as *client agreement*, *complete assessment cost estimate*, *interviews with application owners* and so forth illuminate the complexity of a sourcing decision, but do not specifically focus on characteristics of software components. Moreover, the outsourcing relationship of that study is a set of best-shore subsidiaries and not a third party vendor as our study focuses on as well. Another research study focuses on complex engineered systems and their global development [45]. While complexity is mainly defined by connections and interdependencies to other elements of the system, one of their findings reveals that core competences necessarily have to be kept in-house, even in captive offshoring scenarios. Unfortunately, a closer definition of *mission-critical* elements is not given in that study.

4.3 Implications

For the development of our approach, we have taken a position of two different perspectives: From the SE perspective we can derive that software companies mostly develop programs by the use of an object-oriented approach as well as by the adaption of agile process elements. Therefore, we presume that a priority order of requirements has to be established and can be used for the decision making process. The implementation itself is then described by the use of components, classes, packages, or other elements provided by the RUP. Finally, open source development is a demonstrative example for modularity in distributed systems development and we therefore deem the encapsulation of software objects highly relevant for our outsourcing approach. Well defined and mostly independent software elements play the key role in such scenarios.

From a 'make-or-buy' perspective, it can be stated that several theories and approaches indicate the challenges and issues that contribute to the success of outsourcing. As we have outlined above, we focus on business-related specificity, functional specificity, and technical specificity derived from TCE and the resource-based view. The systems theory approach additionally focuses on the granularity of and communication complexity between artifacts and developers which serves as a foundation for the following characteristics of software objects: Interdependencies between software objects and communication intensity among stakeholders of different software objects. Finally, we have classified the developed properties and contingency factors for software components as structural and contextual characteristics which are described in the following section.

5 Artifact Design: A Decision Support Approach

In this section, the development of an artifact as it is postulated by the design science research methodology is presented [4]. In detail, we provide the conceptualization of a decision support approach for outsourcing scenarios in software developing enterprises in the following.

In line with the conclusion of the previous section, the conceptual approach combines specific contextual and structural characteristics of a component for a largely objective decision making, based on numerous facts that can be derived from the project's knowledge base. Therefore, we start with essential requirements in this section in order to be able to create the proposed approach. Furthermore, we give a detailed description of the design of our technological artifact.

5.1 Requirements and Assumptions

We assume that the identified structural and contextual characteristics of a component are mainly related to common software development processes as introduced in the beginning of this paper. Furthermore we presume, as we can derive from software development statistics, that software is developed by using an object-oriented development process. Consequently, software design documents are either based on classes, packages, or components. Thus, structural models of software elements, behavioral information models about the interactions between these elements, as well as an architectural model are expected outcomes of the design phase (RUP). Furthermore, requirements have to be prioritized by the requirements management of the software project. Traceability information that shows the linkage of software artifacts to corresponding requirements is inevitable as well and assumes that software companies posses an established collaboration environment that provides the required traceability information for elements of the development process. Traceability information is meta-data about all kinds of objects, their relations among each other, as well as according attributes of their connections within a software development process. These data are mostly provided by collaborative software development platforms [46].

5.2 Process Description

Within this section, we propose our decision making approach based on existing literature and introduced theories coupled with previous assumptions. Reconsidering RUP and described software development models, software components seem to be adequate objects of analysis for achieving decision support in outsourcing scenarios. Looking back at the software process models, a component-based outsourcing analysis fits best between the design and development tasks of the planned software system. At this point, software objects have to be classified into different categories, which we define as structural and contextual characteristics of each software part. The classification and analysis result in a grading that exposes software components which are more appropriate for internal development and which are better suited for external procurement from a vendor.

In a first step of our approach, the input data for our sourcing decision has to be prepared in a way that a mapping from software objects to correspondent requirements or sets of them is possible and that a priority order of all requirements exists. This information should be provided by an underlying collaboration and traceability system which serves as a data base for objective information retrieval for software components. Furthermore, such a collaboration platform can provide information about communication paths of software objects either to other objects or to developers and further stakeholders. Thus, our derived set of structural characteristics, having its roots mainly in systems theory, can be used for the ranking evaluation of software components:

- Communication intensity between the component itself and stakeholders
- Priority and centrality of requirements for the component
- Interdependencies between a component and other components

These characteristics can be combined so they then represent the structural properties of a software component. In a second step, we then focus on contextual component properties with their roots in transaction costs economics and the knowledge based view of the firm:

- Technical specificity aligned to the underlying technology
- Business process specificity of the component
- Functional specificity of the component

Now, having the input factors declared, the decision making approach is prepared to start with the examination of all software components and result in an outsourcing potential classification according to Figure 1. By the use of simple heuristics, so called decision tables [47], each property of a component is classified in a largely rational and objective manner. For that, three different decision criteria (high/medium/low affection) can be applied. The aggregation of a component's decision tables results in the outsourcing potential of a specific component. Nevertheless, the knowledge of software experts, ideally design experts, is inevitable and influences the sourcing decision. The use of decision tables in a first step objectifies subjective ratings, while the final aggregation simplifies the complex problem of the decision finding. Both techniques are introduced in detail in the remainder.

Decision Tables. Decision tables are tabular means for describing decision processes [48]. Their formal character can be compared to a two-dimensional matrix with two different sections of rows. The rows denote the antecedences in the upper part and the consequences in the lower part of the matrix. The columns of a decision table contain all possible rules that emerge from the problem domain. The fields within the matrix describe, on the one hand, all possible combinations of the different conditions (as rules) in the upper part of the matrix and, on the other hand, the resulting consequences of each rule in the lower section (an example of such a matrix can be found in figure 2). In general, the combination of all conditions is executed with the *AND* operator [49]. After having introduced the general concept of decision tables, we now go more into detail of the decision making rules and process based on this technique. Derived from section 4.3 above, we differentiate between structural and contextual characteristics of software components. An objective evaluation of possible rules by the use of a decision table has to be ensured for each of them.

Beginning with the characteristics on the middle level of the aggregation model in Figure 1 (interdependencies between software objects and development resources, knowledge specificity), each of them is assigned to a different decision table with a specific set of values and conditions. This set is defined to contain the elements *HIGH*, *MEDIUM*, and *LOW*. Their use is more precisely defined in the following by prescriptive rules according to each condition. In order to offer a brief insight, we exemplarily present the set of conditions in the decision table for the characteristic of "*knowledge specificity*":

The condition part of *knowledge specificity* consists of: Functional specificity, business process specificity and technical specificity. An example condition for

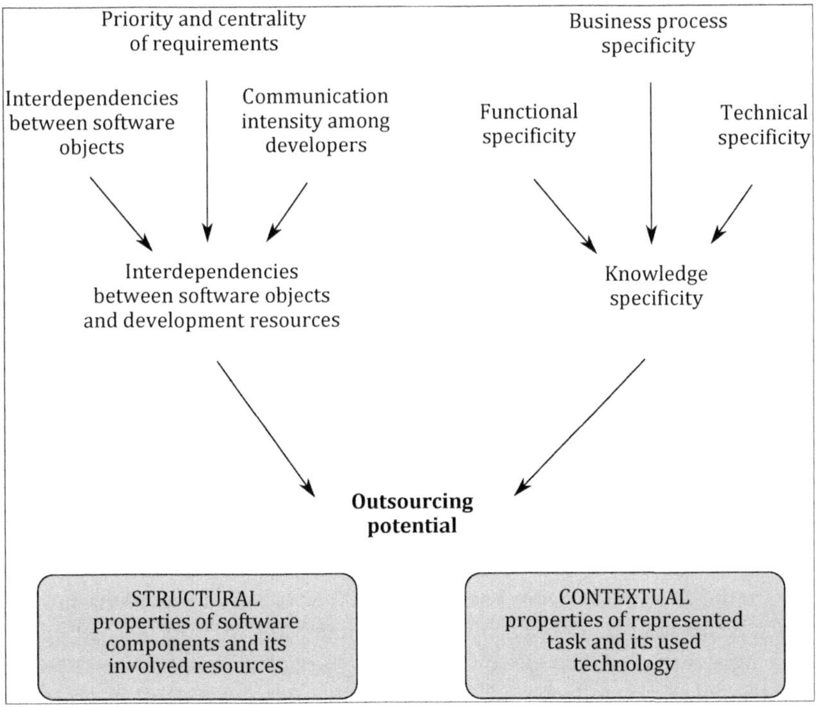

Fig. 1. Aggregation Model of contextual and structural characteristics of a software component

knowledge specificity is the following: "The more technical know-how is required for the implementation of a software object, the higher is the knowledge specificity of this object and vice versa." Similar rules are defined for functional and technical specificity, accordingly. Each row of the table then represents one possible rule which is active if all values of the conditions have been fulfilled indicated by this row. The resulting action is then indicated in the lower part of the matrix and defines the degree of the knowledge specificity. Only one rule can be active at a time. An example of a decision table for knowledge specificity can be found in Figure 2. Rule three (R3), for instance, is defined as follows: If business process specificity of a software component is 'high' and if its functional specificity is 'high' and if its technical specificity is 'low', then the knowledge specificity is classified as 'middle'. In our study, each decision table is weighted equally when it comes to the final determination of the outsourcing potential.

Outsourcing Potential. Another integral part of the decision process is the final result of the evaluation, the outsourcing potential analysis. It is derived from a business economics methodology which is based on the Pareto principle, called *ABC analysis* [50]. The purpose of this analysis is to finalize the decision making process with an ordered list of the analyzed software components. The resulting ranking of the software objects then represents a list of aggregated values

Knowledge specificity		R_1	R_2	R_3	R_4	R_5	R_6	R_7	R_8	R_9	R
B_1	Business process specificity	H	H	H	H	H	H	H	H	H	M
B_2	Functional specificity	H	H	H	M	M	M	L	L	L	H
B_3	Technical specificity	H	M	L	H	M	L	H	M	L	H
A_1	Knowledge specificity - High	X	X	-	X	-	-	-	-	-	X
A_2	Knowledge specificity - Middle	-	-	X	-	X	X	X	X	X	-
A_3	Knowledge specificity - Low	-	-	-	-	-	-	-	-	-	-

Fig. 2. Decision table for knowledge specificity

indicating the potential to outsource the respective object. Consequently, components with a high outsourcing potential are less crucial for the development of the analyzed software project.

The classification of the outsourcing potential in groups like *LOW*, *MEDIUM* and *HIGH* is also conducted by means of a decision table. A typical allocation of objects to the defined classes is derived from the Lorenz curve [51] and is, therefore, partitioned in the following way: LOW - 10% to 20% of the regarded objects contribute between 60% and 70% to the overall project success; MEDIUM - 30% to 40% contribute between 40% and 30% respectively; HIGH - 40% to 50% contribute from 5% to 10% respectively. The allocation of the percentages of the different classes may be defined by each company individually according to the outsourcing strategy and scope. Finally, the prescriptive rule for the outsourcing potential is defined as following: "The higher the outsourcing potential of a software component is, the better such a component is qualified for being developed by an external vendor and vice versa."

By classifying software objects according to the presented methodology, a set of components can be objectively identified that has the potential to be outsourced without having crucial consequences such as losing intellectual property, failing in mapping a business process into a software system, or having a tremendous communication overflow.

6 Considerations for Evaluation

The evaluation of the decision making approach, as introduced in this paper, has the purpose to prove its functionality and usability within its operational context. As we present research work in progress, we primarily focus on the evaluation of the conceptual approach of our developed technological artifact. Thus, we intend to measure the target achievement of our artifact by conducting a case study with several focused interviews of outsourcing experts [52].

The first step of the evaluation consists of an interview guideline with 28 questions about organizational data, personal experience, outsourcing expertise, and mainly about finding an outsourcing decision. Each question has been worded in a comprehensive way to give the respondents the possibility to fortify aspects of the outsourcing decision approach that we already think to be correct.

The first interview we have conducted so far shows that outsourcing is part of the overall company strategy and thus is an inevitable fact. The outsourcing country of our respondent is India and the team size is currently at a size of 10 software developers. The used software development process model is an agile approach with short iteration cycles, daily scrum meetings, weekly review meetings, and sprint review meetings for both teams, the German and Indian side together.

When it comes to the component outsourcing decision, the software company has defined competencies for the German and Indian development teams based on software systems responsibilities. In detail, the maintenance and extension of software systems that apply to the respective skills of the teams have been assigned accordingly. In case functional knowledge of experts or specific knowledge about the business process is essential for the development process of the software system, the project will be conducted and maintained in-house. In addition, if the communication intensity to stakeholders is very high, software systems are kept in-house as well. The interviewed software company makes its decisions on the basis of software systems that are widely independent and have only little or no connections to other systems.

Consequently, the result of the case study covers to a large extent the proposed characteristics of software components that have to be considered when companies decide on the outsourcing question. Thus, factors such as interdependencies between software objects and development resources as well as knowledge specificity and their respective sub-characteristics play a significant role in outsourcing decision making. In addition, the prescriptive rules of the sourcing recommendation have been affirmed by our interview partner. To sum it up, the case study in its premature state already inidcates the usability and functionality of the proposed outsourcing decision approach.

7 Conclusion and Outlook

By applying a design science approach for investigating outsourcing decisions in the context of software development enterprises, we developed a decision making heuristic for software components. Therefore, we identified properties and contingencies from well-accepted methods and existing theories in order to classify software objects with respect to their importance in outsourcing scenarios. As a result of this research work, the decision making approach, our new artifact, addresses relevant issues not only from a software engineering perspective but also from an outsourcing point of view. Both streams are integrated in an outsourcing approach which is designed for practical use in software development projects with outsourcing elements. The conceptualization of our artifact has been pre-evaluated in a case study. As our first interview indicates, primarily the opportunity of having the option to decide on rationalized basis which components are to be developed inside or outside the firm is of highest importance. Furthermore, our interview revealed that tool support for decision making would facilitate the work of software architects and project leads of software development companies to make more precise decisions of what to outsource and what to develop in-house.

Providing an outlook for further research, we will conduct further case studies with software enterprises that already have established outsourcing relationships. We intend to use these valuable sources of knowledge for further refining our decision heuristic. Once we have finalized the field work, we will develop a software tool that instantiates the proposed conceptual approach. The case studies to be undertaken might reveal additional criteria for the classification of the outsourcing suitability of software components which will be integrated into our approach.

References

1. Dibbern, J., Goles, T., Hirschheim, R., Jayatilaka, B.: Information systems outsourcing: A survey and analysis of the literature. Communications of the ACM 35(4), 6–102 (2004)
2. Lacity, M.C., Willcocks, L.P.: An empirical investigation of information technology sourcing practices: Lessons from experience. MIS Quarterly 22(3), 363–408 (1998)
3. Lacity, M.C., Khan, S.A., Yan, A., Willcocks, L.P.: A review of the it outsourcing empirical literature and future research directions. Journal of Information Technology 25, 395–433 (2010)
4. Hevner, A.R., March, S.T., Park, J., Sudha, R.: Design science in information systems research. Management Information Systems Quarterly 28, 75–105 (2004)
5. Baldwin, C.Y., Clark, K.B.: The architecture of participation: Does code architecture mitigate free riding in the open source development model? Management Science 52, 1116–1127 (2006)
6. Parnas, D.L.: On the criteria to be used in decomposing systems into modules. Communications of the ACM 15(12), 1053–1058 (1972)
7. Simon, H.A.: The architecture of complexity. In: Proceedings of the American Philosophical Society, vol. 106, pp. 467–482 (1962)
8. Williamson, O.E.: The economics of organization: The transaction cost approach. American Journal of Sociology 87(3), 548–577 (1981)
9. Dibbern, J., Winkler, J., Heinzl, A.: Explaining variations in client extra costs between software projects offshored to india. MIS Quarterly 32(2), 1–30 (2008)
10. Winkler, J., Dibbern, J., Heinzl, A.: The impact of software product and service characteristics on international distribution arrangements for software solutions. In: Proceedings of the 30th International Conference on Information Systems, Phoenix, Arizona (2009)
11. Shaw, M.: Prospects for an engineering discipline of software. IEEE Software 7, 15–24 (1990)
12. Sommerville, I.: Software Engineering, 8th edn. Addison-Wesley, Munich (2007)
13. Booch, G., Maksimchuk, R.A., Engel, M.W., Young, B.J., Conallen, J., Houston, K.A.: Object-Oriented Analysis and Design with Applications. Addison-Wesley, Upper Saddle River (2007)
14. Klimpke, L., Kramer, T., Betz, S., Nordheimer, K.: Globally distributed software development in small and medium-sized enterprises in Germany: Reasons, locations, and obstacles. In: Proceedings of the 19th European Conference on Information Systems (ECIS 2011), Helsinki, Finland (2011)
15. Olsson, H.H., Conchuir, E.O., Aegerfalk, P.J., Fitzgerald, B.: Two-stage offshoring: An investigation of the Irish bridge. MIS Quarterly 32(2), 257–279 (2008)

16. Apte, U.: Global outsourcing of information systems and processing services. The Information Society 7, 287–303 (1990)
17. Clermont, P.: Outsourcing without guilt. Computerworld 9, 67–68 (1991)
18. Herbsleb, J.D., Moitra, D.: Global software development. IEEE Software 18, 16–20 (2001)
19. Carmel, E., Tjia, P.: Offshoring Information Technology: Sourcing and Outsourcing to a Global Workforce. Cambridge Univ. Press, Cambridge (2006)
20. Krishna, S., Sahay, S., Walsham, G.: Managing cross-cultural issues in global software outsourcing. Communications of the ACM 47, 62–66 (2004)
21. Heeks, R., Krishna, S., Nicholson, B., Sahay, S.: Synching or sinking: Global software outsourcing relationships. IEEE Software 18(2), 56–60 (2001)
22. Kraut, R.E., Fish, R.S., Root, R.W., Chalfonte, B.L.: Informal communication in organizations: Form, function and technology. In: Oskamp, S., Spacapan, S. (eds.) Human Reactions to Technology: Claremont Symposium on Applied Social Psychology, pp. 145–199. Sage, Beverly Hills (1990)
23. Capgemini Consulting: Studie IT trends 2009. Capgemini, Study (2009)
24. Carmel, E., Agarwal, R.: The maturation of offshore sourcing of information technology work. MIS Quarterly Executive 1, 65–76 (2002)
25. Jacobson, I., Booch, G., Rumbaugh, J.: The Unified Software Development Process. Addison-Wesley, Boston (2003)
26. Tiobe Software, `http://www.tiobe.com/index.php/content/paperinfo/tpci/index.html` (retrieved 19/06/2011)
27. Beck, K.: Extreme Programming Explained: Embrace Change. Addison-Wesley, Reading (1999)
28. Agile Manifesto, `http://agilemanifesto.org/` (retrieved 19/06/2011)
29. Schwaber, K., Beedle, M.: Agile Software Development with Scrum. Prentice Hall, Upper Saddle River (2002)
30. Pan, G.S.C., Flynn, D.J.: Towards a stakeholder analysis of information systems development project abandonment. In: Proceedings of the 11th European Conference on Information Systems, ECIS 2003 (2003)
31. Rupp, C.: Requirements-Engineering und -Management, 4th edn. Carl Hanser Verlag, Munich (2009)
32. Sharp, H., Finkelstein, A., Galal, G.: Stakeholder identification in the requirements engineering process. In: Proceedings of the 10th International Workshop on Database and Expert Systems Applications (DEXA 1999), pp. 387 – 391 (1999)
33. Senyard, A., Michlmayr, M.: How to have a successful free software project. In: Proceedings of the 11th Asia-Pacific Software Engineering Conference, APSEC 2004 (2004)
34. Dibbern, J., Heinzl, A.: Outsourcing of information systems functions in small and medium sized enterprises: A test of a multi-theoretical model. WIRTSCHAFTSINFORMATIK 43, 339–350 (2001)
35. Langlois, R.N.: Capabilities and coherence in firms and markets. In: Montgomery, C.A. (ed.) Resource-Based and Evolutionary Theories of the Firm: Towards a Synthesis, Boston, USA, pp. 71–100 (1995)
36. Picot, A., Baumann, O.: Modularität in der verteilten Entwicklung komplexer Systeme: Chancen, Grenzen, Implikationen. Journal für Betriebswirtschaft 57(3-4), 221–246 (2007)
37. Williamson, O.E.: Transaction cost economics. In: Schmalensee, R., Willig, R.D. (eds.) Handbook of Industrial Organization, Amsterdam, Netherlands, pp. 135–182 (1990)

38. Grant, R.M.: The resource-based theory of competitive advantage: Implications for strategy formulation. California Management Review 33(3), 114–135 (1991)
39. Teng, J.T.C., Cheon, M.J., Grover, V.: Decisions to outsource information systems functions: Testing a strategy-theoretic discrepancy model. Decision Sciences 26(1), 75–103 (1995)
40. Stratman, J.K.: Facilitating offshoring with enterprise technologies: Reducing operational friction in the governance and production of services. Journal of Operations Management 26(2), 275–287 (2008)
41. Mirani, R.: Client-vendor relationships in offshore applications development: An evolutionary framework. Information Resources Management Journal 19(4), 72–86 (2006)
42. Thompson, J.D.: Organizations in Action. McGraw-Hill, New York (1967)
43. Baldwin, C.Y., Clark, K.B.: Design Rules: The Power of Modularity. MIT Press, Cambridge (2000)
44. Carmel, E., Dedrick, J., Kraemer, K.L.: Routinizing the offshore choice: applying diffusion of innovation to the case of eds. Strategic Outsourcing: An International Journal 2, 223–239 (2008)
45. Tripathy, A., Eppinger, S.D.: Organizing global product development for complex engineered systems. IEEE Transactions on Engineering Management, 1–20 (2011)
46. Hildenbrand, T.: Improving Traceability in Distributed Collaborative Software Development. Lang, Frankfurt (2008)
47. Pooch, U.W.: Translation of decision tables. ACM Computing Surveys 6, 125–151 (1974)
48. Heinrich, L.J., Roithmayr, F., Heinzl, A.: Wirtschaftsinformatik-Lexikon, 7th edn. Oldenbourg, Munich (2004)
49. Heinrich, L.J., Heinzl, A., Riedl, R.: Wirtschaftsinformatik - Einführung und Grundlegung, 4th edn. Oldenbourg, Berlin (2011)
50. Flores, B.E., Whybark, D.C.: Implementing multiple criteria abc analysis. Journal of Operations Management 7, 79–85 (1987)
51. Lorenz, M.O.: Methods for measuring the concentration of wealth. Publications of the American Statistical Association 9, 209–219 (1905)
52. Yin, R.K.: Case Study Research: Design and Methods. Sage, Beverly Hills (2006)

Getting Agile Methods to Work for Cordys Global Software Product Development

Jos van Hillegersberg[1], Gerwin Ligtenberg[2], and Mehmet N. Aydin[3]

[1] University of Twente
School of Management and Governance
P.O. Box 217, 7500 AE Enschede, The Netherlands
j.vanhillegersberg@utwente.nl
[2] Cordys Research & Development, The Netherlands
gligtenberg@cordys.com
[3] Department of Information Technologies,
Işık University, Turkey
mnaydin@isikun.edu.tr

Abstract. Getting agile methods to work in global software development is a potentially rewarding but challenging task. Agile methods are relatively young and still maturing. The application to globally distributed projects is in its early stages. Various guidelines on how to apply and sometimes adapt agile methods have been proposed. However, systematic literature reviews reveal that detailed evaluative studies are scarce and limited to small and medium sized projects. This study presents a framework that integrates best practices of adapting and applying agile methods reported in the literature. The framework is applied to analyze the experiences of global software product development company Cordys in a seven year longitudinal case study. Both the framework and the experiences of Cordys documented in this paper will be of value to other larger projects that aim to be successful in applying agile in globally distributed projects.

Keywords: Global Software Development, Agile Methods, XP, Scrum, Global Teams, Offshoring, Globally Distributed Software Engineering.

1 Introduction

1.1 The Rise of Agile Methods for Systems Development

Agile methods for software development were introduced around the beginning of the new century. The increasing business need for fast creation of internet and mobile applications was a key driver for the introduction of these light weight and nimble development processes. Traditional waterfall based methods had often resulted in large, bureaucratic and slow development processes. In many dramatic cases, sizeable project teams had burned significant amounts of money merely creating documents and reports rather than working software. In the rare event that working software was produced, the customer and end user had often been forgotten in the process, resulting in products that did not meet requirements and expectations. Already in the late 1980s and 1990s, innovations in systems development methods focused on more dynamic,

J. Kotlarsky, L.P. Willcocks, and I. Oshri (Eds.): Global Sourcing 2011, LNBIP 91, pp. 133–152, 2011.

adaptive and user centric ways of working. The Agilemanifesto.org, published in 2001, contains twelve principles that synthesize the ideas underlying agile methods. These include welcoming changing requirements, close collaboration of business people and developers, self-organizing teams, a focus on delivering working software and face-to-face conversation as the preferred way to transfer knowledge.

Abrahamsson et al. [2], in their review of agile methods, characterize these as incremental, cooperative, straightforward, and adaptive: "Incremental refers to small software releases, with rapid development cycles. Cooperative refers to a close customer and developer interaction. Straightforward implies that the method itself is easy to learn and to modify and that it is sufficiently documented. Finally, adaptive refers to the ability to make and react to last moment changes". Well known examples of agile methods include Scrum development Process [22],[23]. Extreme Programming (XP) [4] and Feature-Driven Development (FDD) [18]. Scrum and XP are among the most well known agile methods. They are often seen as complementary as XP provides specific engineering techniques and Scrum essentially works as a wrapper for such techniques [8],[10]. While agile methods have increased in popularity, they do not yet provide integral support for systems development. Different agile methods cover different phases of the software development life-cycle. Moreover, Project management support by agile methods is limited and limited emphasis is put on how to operate and tailor agile methods to specific organizations and situations [2],[3].

1.2 Agile Methods in Globally Distributed Development

Whether agile methods and distributed development can be combined to harvest the benefits of both is a subject of much debate. It has been widely recognized that geographical distance and the time zone and cultural differences associated with global distribution have caused problems for globally distributed software teams in achieving successful collaboration (e.g. see [15]). Agile methods use short iterations, frequent builds, and continuous integration that all require very frequent communication, coordination and trust. A theoretical analysis by Turk et al. [25] predicts that several agile process principles, such as self-evaluation, frequent customer and team face-to-face meetings, short time intervals between releases, focus on code rather than documentation and team spirit seem to be impractical in a global setting. The temporal, geographical and socio-cultural distance in distributed development makes the application of agile methods a complex task [16]. Paasivaara and Lassenius [16] summarize the key questions as:

> *In the global software development literature, communication is often seen as the most challenging problem of distribution whereas the agile methods basically rely on communication, preferably face-to-face communication, instead of documentation. The application of agile principles to global software development poses several questions regarding communication: How could daily communication be arranged effectively? What kind of communication practices and media are suitable for supporting different agile practices? How could informal communication, that is important to agile methods, be encouraged? How could the risk for misunderstandings, e.g. regarding requirements, be minimized? How could trust be built and retained between teams to ensure open communication?*

Based on a systematic literature review, Hossain et al. [11] conclude there is no clear description or understanding of how the use of agile practices can reduce global software development (GSD) risks and improve project communication, coordination or collaboration processes. They further state that "current research provides limited evidence of the effective use of agile practices in minimizing risks of global software development processes". Holmström [10] states that "the more common view is that agile methods are not applicable for GSD". Some authors report risks and limitations when using agile methods in a globally distributed setting. Sarker and Sarker [21], based on a case study of developing agility in a distributed IS development setting, find that many of the guidelines or prescriptions for agile methods could not be used effectively (and sustained) in distributed teams. The authors suggest that "agile methods need suitable adaptation for effective adoption/use in a distributed ISD setting". Sakthivel [20] puts forward that agile methods are only suitable for small scale offshore development projects. "Due to their high task dependencies and required face-to-face interaction with users during their iterative analysis, design, and trial stages, they are not suitable for mid- and large-size offshore projects". Hossain et al. [11] concludes based on a recent systematic literature review that: "we do not know the risks of using Scrum in a GSD project with a large number of project personnel, or an increased number of distributed sites". Moreover, the risks when using Scrum in GSD may vary according to project contextual factors.

Ramesh et al. [19] state that combining agile and distributed development introduces five challenges. First, agile development relies more on informal interactions than explicit documentation which poses a real challenge in achieving the communication formality that may be needed to assure effective communication between sites. Second, how can fixing quality requirements to guide the remote team be balanced with the agile principle of ongoing customer developer discussions. Third, what would be the appropriate balance between the formal process-oriented control typically used in distributed development and the more people oriented informal agile practices? Fourth, what is the appropriate level of formality in developing contractual agreements in agile development? Fifth, how can team cohesion be improved given the constraints of a distributed environment? Holmström [10] concludes that what is needed is an increased understanding of the characteristics of agile methods and how these can be applied to reduce the negative influence of distance in GSD.

The experiences of using specific agile methods reported on in the literature are scarce and mixed [26]. For example, based on a case study of a development team located in Sydney and Malaysia, Hossain et al. [12] find that daily Stand-up meetings, with the aid of various communication tools, help to build mutual understanding among distributed project stakeholders. Sprint review meetings increased project visibility and transparency and "Test Driven Development (TDD)" helped to maintain a shared standard development view. Based on case studies of global projects at HP and Intel, Holmström et al. [10] conclude that agile practices are valuable in reducing some of the challenges of globally distributed development. In particular, XP and Scrum practices were found useful for improving communication, coordination, and control within GSD teams. However, Sarker and Sarker [21] find that daily Scrum meetings are difficult to hold or organize in distributed settings where stakeholders are (often) located in different time zones. Their case analysis further reveals that the use of Scrum sprints (i.e., achieving short deadlines), and the maintenance of daily burn-down charts and stringent monitoring rules can become difficult in a distributed setting, because of a variety of unanticipated complexities associated with local cultures, infrastructures of varying quality, and temporal differences. Sarkar and Sarkar [21] find that the use of agile methods in some cases led to: "dysfunctional stress and work-life balance challenges, with negative impact on morale and productivity".

Paasivaara et al. [17] note that while there is increasing interest in applying agile methods to global projects, there are only a few reported experiences on industrial projects and even fewer case studies. This is confirmed by a recent systematic literature review by Jalali and Wohlin [13] of peer reviewed conference papers or journal articles published between 1999 and 2009. Most of the 77 papers identified have appeared recently and a majority of the current literature is in the form of experience reports, in which practitioners have reported their own experiences on a particular issue and the method used to mitigate it. The majority of them have not documented the characteristics of their empirical study and the context under which the project was running. Only three out of the 77 papers were jointly written by academics and practitioners. Jalali and Wohlin note that although experience reports are useful, more evaluation and validation research is needed to establish foundations for a more mature area. Moreover, they find that existing literature mainly consists of reports on small to medium sized projects.

It is the objective of this study to address the open questions in how to apply agile methods in a globally distributed software development project. As the above discussion reveals, more evaluative studies are needed, especially to learn how agile methods and practices should be implemented successfully in a global project. Current literature is usually lacks longitudinal research. As we have studied the continuous adaptation of agile methods in the global project at Cordys over a longer time period, we can better document lessons learned compared to a single snap-shot case study. Moreover, we focus on a large project where most reported experiences so far were limited to small and medium sized projects..

1.3 Research Method

As many open questions exist in applying agile methods to large globally distributed software development projects, this study adopts a longitudinal case study research approach. Theory building is in its early stages and the evolution of agile methods and the lack of knowledge on how to adopt them in GSD do make a qualitative case study a suitable choice [7].

As we learned that Cordys was among the first companies that adopted agile methods in a large global development project in 2004, we contacted them for conducting a case study research. Cordys showed interest in sharing their experiences in their journey and in collaborating with researchers in sharing knowledge. From the early steps at Cordys with implementing agile methods more than six years ago till today we have been exchanging experiences and ideas. We have conducted interviews with Cordys management and developers in 2005, 2008, 2009 and 2011 to assess the status and adaptations to the agile processes. In the interview we had in November 2005 at Cordys with Hans de Visser, VP services and Steven ten Napel, VP operations, the initial experiences with agile methods were discussed, including the reasons to adopt agile methods and the implementation strategy. In 2008, a workshop was held at the Cordys headquarters with several developers and project managers to share the experiences and future plans. Annual presentations were given by Gerwin Ligtenberg, program manager at Cordys, to us to discuss the ways the methods were tailored and supported with tools to fit the global setting. In 2011 an additional interview was held with Gerwin Ligtenberg in which he reflected on the key steps taken and changes made to the teams, organization, methods and tools. By serving as a second author of this paper, he also directly contributes to documenting the lessons learned at Cordys.

In order to organize the rich data we collected over the years, a comprehensive framework was needed. Especially over the last few years more studies had become available that provide various ways to analyze the use of agile methods in GSD. However, a comprehensive framework is still lacking. Therefore, we constructed such a framework based on a recent overview of the literature. The framework consists of reported issues that can arise in using agile methods in a global setting and practices that have been used to mitigate these. In the next section we present this framework. Next, we use this framework to analyze the Cordys case study. We report how Cordys, based on their experience, adapted practices, teams, organization processes or tool support to make agile methods work. We contrast this to the strategies listed in the framework. Finally, we summarize key findings and discuss potential further extensions to agile methods for use in GSD.

2 Challenges and Best Practices

2.1 Challenges in Global Agile Development

Hansen and Baggesen [9] describe experiences of using Scrum in a distributed setting between Denmark and Bangladesh. To implement Scrum effectively, it was first introduced to the local teams and later, after experiences was gained, implemented in the global teams. Onsite training sessions in Scrum were held by the CTO. Very experienced senior developers and consultants were moved into global Product Owner roles to establish a more structured flow of tasks and collaboration. "Proxy product owners" were introduced as anchor points for each offshore team. To increase understanding of the product requirements and context with the offshore teams, several domain knowledge sessions in Bangladesh were held. As trust between teams became a problem, onshore and offshore teams were merged into a single team with a single backlog of work. Sprints within sprints were introduced to break down user stories into smaller ones. Daily Scrum meetings and global code reviews created trust. The physical task board was quickly converted into a web-based virtual task board. Efficiency and relationships were further improved by introduction of automated testing and code reviews. Code built in Denmark was inspected by a team mate in Bangladesh and vice versa. To bridge cultural barriers, and build social relationships, people were moved around between both locations.

Ramesh et al [19] based on three company case studies of multiple mid size distributed projects elicit successful practices to slightly adjust and customize agile practices to make them work in a global setting. We summarize their findings here. Rather than starting with informal agile processes from the start, devote the first two or three iterations of a project to finalize critical requirements and develop a high-level architecture. Instead of relying exclusively on informal means for project tracking and monitoring utilizing a product/process repository better supports knowledge sharing. Build well understood functionality first to create an atmosphere in which both the developers and the client representatives were acclimatized to the processes, tools, and

Table 1. Challenges and Reported Practices of Global Agile Development

Challenge	***Practices***
Synchronous communication	S1. Synchronize work hours [19],[11]
	S2. Make meetings short and effective by posting three daily Scrum questions or develop backlog (feature list) before attending the distributed meetings [11]
	S3. Constant communication [19]
	S4. A scrum team allows additional distributed meetings along with Scrum master meeting attended by technical lead or design architect of each local Scrum team [11]
	S5. Distributed daily Scrum meetings are cut down to twice-a-week meetings [11]
	S6. XP pair programming can help to increase time overlap and reduce temporal distance [10]
	S7. Reduce the dependency between sites. Each role in a team at one site has a counterpart on the other site [16].
Collaboration and coordination Difficulties, lack of trust	C1. Informal communication through formal channels [19]
	C2. Frequent visits by distributed partners. Visits should be long enough to allow for informal chat and building social ties [19],[11],[16]
	C3. Build cohesive team culture [19]
	C4. Focus on well understood requirements rather than critical new functionality [19]
	C5. Document requirements at different levels of formality [19]
	C6. Maintaining valuable documentation [19]
	C7. Scrum simple planning can help increase "teamness" and reduce geographical distance [10]
	C8. XP pair programming and Scrum pre-game phase can help increase mutual understanding and collaboration within and between teams and reduce sociocultural distance [10]
	C9. Scrum team gathers and performs few initial sprints at one site before distributed development starts [11]
	C10. Scrum team are gathered quarterly or annually for few days [11]
	C11. Mandatory demo presentation during retrospective sessions to reduce offshore silence [11]
	C12. Scrum teams may move from a collocated project to a distributed project gradually through several stages (i.e., evaluation, inception, transition and steady state) [11]
	C13. A business/software analyst interfaces with the customer on the other site. The proxy customer can make decisions on behalf of the real customer [16]

Table 1. (*continued*)

Communication Bandwidth	B1.	Use "multiple communication modes" to ensure that a Scrum team with distributed project stakeholders is supported with various options of communication tools (phone, web camera, teleconference, video conference, web conference, net meeting, email, shared mailing list, Instant Message (IM), Short Message Service (SMS), and Internet Relay chat) [11],[16]
Large Team	L1.	Autonomous sub teams are allocated work based on features, functions and so on that ensure each sub team is allocated independent architectural subsystems with well defined interfaces project teams are geographically [11],[16]
	L2.	Autonomous Scrum teams are formed locally and each site conducts their own scrum. A Scrum of Scrums is attended by a key touch point member for each team to ensure inter-team communication. Independent architectural subsystems with well defined interfaces are allocated to each team to reduce inter site communication [11]
	L3.	Offshore teams can be geographically isolated and are not cross-functional and may not use Scrum processes [11]
	L4.	A Centrally located management team" in which management persons of each Scrum team are located in a central site [11]
Office Space	O1.	Each Scrum team is allocated to a single room so that they can communicate with each other [11]
	O2.	Each site has a separate meeting room with all necessary network connectivity and tools while attending a distributed meeting [11]
Evolving Quality requirements	Q1.	Trust but verify [19]
	Q2.	Distributed Quality Assurance [19]
	Q3.	Supplement informal communication with documentation [19]
Transformation Change and Learning	T1.	Scrum first introduced to the local teams and later, after experiences was gained, implemented in the global teams [9]
	T2.	Rotating gurus provide initial training and mentoring to the other site [16]
	T3.	Conduct "initial Scrum training," "technical Scrum" to clarify new technology issues, reinforce the value of Scrum and improve team collaboration while using Scrum practices [11]

the application. Instead of short time boxing typical in agile methods, allow for a flexible short-cycle approach in which two to three development cycles are used. Synchronize work hours instead of trying to establish 24x7 schemes. Facilitate informal communication through formal channels to prevent miscommunications. More than custom in co-located agile projects, coordination roles of project managers/leads are important. Constant (meaning almost 24h) communication using mail and videoconferencing is required. Trust is even more important in the absence of formal control. Frequents visits of senior management, customers and product managers to developing sites or the reverse are needed to build trust. Agile working in a distributed fashion requires a cohesive team culture. Trust needs to be supplemented with on-site verification. Quality assurance and supplementing informal communication with formal documents can assure this.

Hossain et al. [11] conducted a systematic literature review to identify challenges of using the prime agile management method Scrum in global software development. They initially identified 366 published papers which they reduced to 20 primary papers. Based on the frequency that a challenge is reported in the literature, they identify and rank seven challenges. In Table 1 we combined the challenges of the studies discussed above and listed practices reported on these papers. Tool support for agile distributed development is a complicated topic that has recently received more attention. Therefore we dedicate a separate section to this topic.

2.2 Tools for Globally Distributed Teams

Globally distributed teams that use agile methods need a variety of tool support. Dullemond et al. [6] discuss the advantages and challenges of the combination of agile software development and GSE with a focus on how these be supported with technological aids. They present five types of technology requirements for tools used in global projects. Abbattista et al. [1] provide an overview of various current and emerging tools for supporting global teams. In Table 2, we integrated both studies to provide an integrated overview of technology requirements and available tool support.

Table 2. Requirements for technology support and sample tools

Requirements [6]	*Description*	*Examples of tools [1]*
Facilitates direct contact between colleagues	F1. Technological support which facilitates direct communication between two or more actors.	Email is the most-widely used and successful collaborative application email can support conversations, but also operate as a task/contact manager. Recently, chat and IM have been spreading more and more in the workplace because, unlike email, they are 'socially translucent', providing a lightweight means to ascertain availability of remote team members and contact them in a timely manner. When rich communication is required audio and video conference may be applied Collaborative development environments (CDE). A CDE provides a project workspace with a standardized toolset to be used by the global software team. Earliest CDE were developed within open source software (OSS) projects because OSS projects, from the beginning, have been composed of dispersed individuals (e.g. SourceForge). Some CDE also include facilities for transparency and continuous integration and build.

Table 2. (*continued*)

Facilitates knowledge sharing among colleagues	F2. Technological support which facilitates the sharing of *technical* project knowledge.	Knowledge center. This function is mostly document-driven and web-enabled, and allows team members to share explicit knowledge across a work unit. A knowledge center includes technical references, standards, frequently asked questions (FAQs) and best practices. Some CDE's include wiki's and blogs to facilitate the creation of a project memory. Researchers have also experimented with social tagging of source code in a collaborative environment
Facilitates transparency of the project status	F3. Technological support which facilitates the sharing of *organizational* project knowledge.	Software Configuration management (SCM). A software configuration management tool includes the ability to manage change in a controlled manner, by checking components in and out of a repository, and the evolution of software products, by storing multiple versions of components, and producing specified versions on command. (example: SVN)
Facilitates quality assurance	F4. Technological support which facilitates quality assurance functions to monitor and guarantee the quality of the product.	Bug and issue tracking. This function is centered on a database, accessible by all team members through a web-based interface. Other than an identifier and a description, a recorded bug includes information about who found it, the steps to reproduce it, who has been assigned on it, which releases the bug exists in and it has been fixed in.
Facilitates continuous integration and frequent builds	F5. Technological support which eases the process of continuously integrating the system as well as producing builds frequently.	Build and release management. It allows projects to create and schedule, typically through a web interface, workflows that execute build scripts, compile binaries, invoke test frameworks, deploy to production systems, and send email notifications to developers. are essential tools to perform continuous integration, an agile development practice that allows developers to integrate daily, thus reducing integration problems

3 Cordys Case Study

The benefits of agile processes to enable a lean and flexible development process sound appealing, especially to a software product company that has to deliver competitive products in a rapidly changing market. Cordys is such a company. Founded in 2001, Cordys initiated a venture to develop from the ground up a Business Collaboration Platform, based on the principles of a Service Oriented Architecture covering an

Enterprise Service Bus (ESB), Business Process Management (BPM) and an Integrated Services Environment [5]. The product would allow existing IT assets to be exposed, embedded, deployed and managed from a business-driven, process perspective. Now, after ten years and thousands of man-years of development, the company's recent release is viewed by analists as a significant player in the BPM market [24].

Cordys employs 560 people globally. Roughly 320 are based in India, 110 in the Netherlands, 50 in Germany, 20 in UK, 30 in China, and 30 in the Americas [24]. Cordys has deployed a globally distributed product development process from the start in 2001. From 2001-2005 Cordys focused entirely on new product development financed by venture capital. Over the last five years, gradually more customers were attracted and implementation partners were added to the Cordys ecosystem. Customers include KPN, the World Bank, AXA financial services and Equens. Partners of Cordys include Accenture, Infosys, Cap Gemini and Atos Origin [24].

In search of a development process that would support its highly innovative environment and would focus on delivering high quality software code in short delivery cycles Cordys started to explore agile methods in 2004. Cordys has been a very early adopter of an agile development process in a globally distributed setting. Over the past seven years they have learned and adapted their agile process and diverged from the known agile practices that were typically designed for a co-located project team. In the following sections we use the challenges and practices reported in the literature (Table 1 and Table 2) to analyze the seven years of experience of using agile methods in globally distributed product development at Cordys.

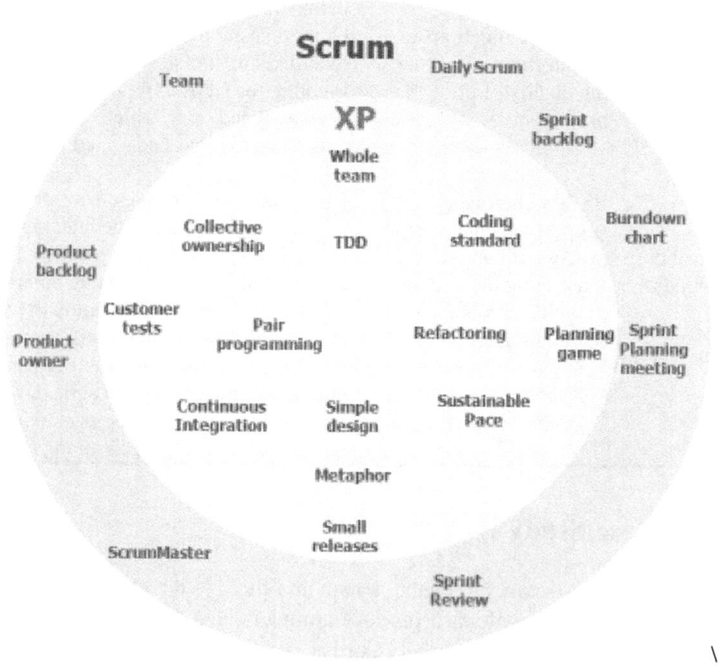

Fig. 1. Combining Scrum and XP: (Source: [14])

3.1 Synchronous Communication

Starting in 2004, Cordys globally implemented Scrum combined with the agile practices of eXtreme Programming (XP) [4]. Cordys quickly rolled out Scrum to its entire development team that at that time had approximately 40 developers in Putten, the Netherlands and 230 in Hyderabad, India. As is demonstrated in Figure 1, Scrum and XP provide complementary agile practices. Where Scrum offers typically a framework for planning and coordinating work, XP provide collaborative practices for design and development work.

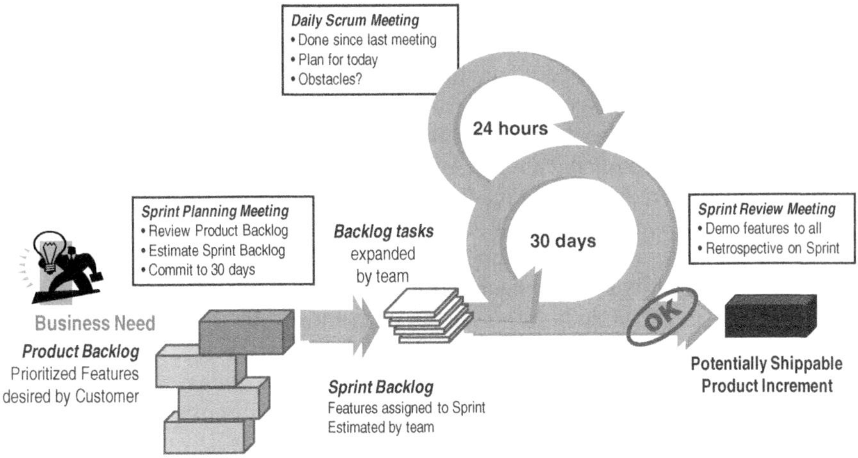

Fig. 2. Scrum process (Source: Cordys)

Cordys adopted a mostly standard Scrum cycle (see Figure 2) that includes agile practices such as daily team meetings and a central product backlog that guides activities. Work towards a new set of functionality is organized in fixed length "Sprints". A sprint starts with planning and ends with a review. A sprint planning meeting is a time-boxed meeting dedicated to developing a detailed plan for a sprint. Project stakeholders attend sprint review meetings to review the state of the business, the market and technology. A daily Scrum meeting is a short daily meeting (usually up to 15 minutes long) in which each team member is expected to address three questions: what did I do yesterday, what will I do today and what impediments are in my way? Three artefacts, namely: product backlogs, sprint backlogs and burn-down charts are produced. Backlogs consist of customer requirements while daily burn down charts show what cumulative work remains. Cordys set the meeting frequency to quarterly business plan reviews and initially 6 week sprints. Later this was reduced to 4 weekly and eventually 2-weekly sprints to get requirements implemented faster and increase productivity. According to the program manager one can not immediately start with short sprints from day one. “You need to build up experience with the process to be able to come up with working demo’s in a short timeframe”. Cordys teams consist of 6-10 persons with various roles like Software Engineers, Product Engineers, Architect(s) and a Program Manager. Management is mainly concerned with identifying deficiencies or impediments in the development process and practices. Essential to Scrum is that it is goal-driven and gives a high level of personal responsibility and empowerment to developers. For example, developers get the freedom to choose specific software development techniques, methods, and practices.

Synchronizing work hours (S1, **Error! Reference source not found.**) was feasible as Putten and Hyderbad have only a 4½ hour time difference allowing for sufficient overlap to organize joint meetings during regular work hours. XP user stories play a central role in Sprint meetings. A joint repository with user stories helps to create a joint view on the project and its backlog (S2). In an interview in 2008, the program manager noted: "It is important to get the user story ready in time before the sprint starts, as it is delineates the requirements to execute in the sprint and plan the steps appropriately".

Cordys minimizes required communication by empowering local teams. The team structure and work distribution closely resembles the product architecture. Scrum meetings are mostly held locally on site. However, scrum of scrum meetings still require distributed communications. Also, dependencies between modules do exist. Dependencies that require attention are identified in a sprint meeting and are usually logged in the bug tracker and followed up by frequent email and chat communication between engineers, architects, team leads and release management (similar to S3). When issues gradually escalate conference calls or a video conferencing is organized to resolve the issue. In addition to standard scrum meetings, all new requirements, their user stories and their impact on the component architecture are discussed between architects and team leads in a video conference (similar to S4). Dependencies between requirements and architectural components are discussed in a global sprint meeting. In these meetings work is assigned to teams and to upcoming or future sprints.

3.2 Collaboration and Coordination Difficulties, Lack of Trust

While teams have a certain level of autonomy, the product backlog is centrally monitored (C1). An example of a product backlog chart is shown in Figure 3. Cordys supports the agile principle that Face-to-Face interaction is the most productive method of communicating with customers and among developers. In our interview in 2005 Mr. ten Napel said:"we do believe this is true. We have never attempted to run Scrum meetings using collaborative tools such as videoconferencing. The Scrum master needs to read and even smell emotions of his team members". Fortunately, Cordys' component-oriented architecture enables Cordys to apply Scrum. Ownership of a specific component if is fully given to a single co-located team. The teams pick up tasks from the centrally administrated back-log list that concern their component. As a result, virtually all scrum meetings are co-located. When team members of the remote site do need to be present, they organize a video conference or travel to the site (C2).

As Cordys develops a generic product without a direct customer, the agile principle of direct interaction with the customer is impossible to implement. User requirements are set through bundling and generalizing request from current customers and predicting the needs of new markets. De Visser: "it is essential to have somebody to play the customer role in scrum team meetings. We usually involve somebody from product marketing to play this role." (similar to C13). Later (from 2008) this role was taken by Product Management. A close collaboration between Product Management and Marketing exists.

Although agile methods direct that developing extensive (relatively complete) and consistent documentation and software models is counter-productive, Cordys does recognize a need for documentation. Ten Napel:"documenting is still important but should not be done only because the method prescribes it. Only if the team sees clear added value to develop diagrams and models, these should be created. We do provide various templates to facilitate this". In addition, Cordys created a configuration management and process support platform using the Cordys product itself. The process can thus be described as a mix of central coordination and local freedom (C5, C6). In an interview in 2008 the program manager stressed: "The requirements need to be articulated till the level that developers can understand them and be sufficiently precise to be a start of the extreme programming process" (C5).

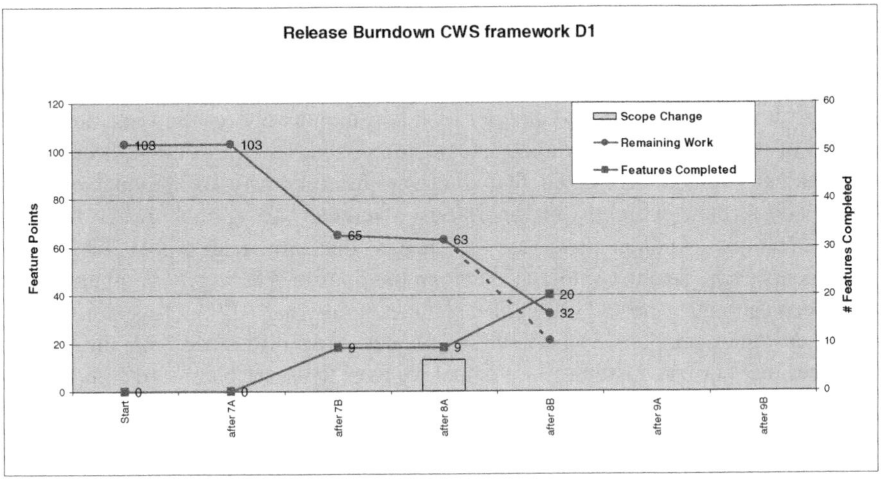

Fig. 3. Example of Cordys' burndown chart (Source: Cordys)

3.3 Communication Bandwidth

Cordys did adopt the practice of "multiple communication modes" to ensure that a Scrum team with distributed project stakeholders is supported with various options of communication tools (phone, web camera, teleconference, video conference, web conference, net meeting, email, shared mailing list, Instant Messages and Internet Chat). The program manager (2011 interview) explains that engineers use chat daily. Complex issues get a functional and business owner and regular video conferences are organized with the teams involved. All designs are maintained on a wiki. As the teams collaborated for multiple years most developers know each other and are flexible in picking the proper communication tools (B1). To discuss dependencies between teams a Scrum of Scrums meeting was held usually using a telco. “In this evaluation meeting of the last sprint it is important to have rich communication”, the program manager stressed (2011 interview).

3.4 Large Teams

The program manager recalls (2011 interview) that when Scrum and XP were introduced, all the handbooks talked about teams of typically 8, 10 or 12 people. “We had more than a hundred developers, how should we implement agile practices? No guidelines existed for this project scale. So we started to standardize on documenting component interfaces (API’s) as small descriptions that could be demoed. We left the process to arrive in time at such demos to the teams” (this is in line with L1). “One of the most important lessons we learned is that sound component architecture of the product is key and teams need to work dedicated to components in order to make distributed agile work”. “Components that grew too complex were split as team size needed to stay in the range of 8 to 12 people to remain effective”. Over time the Cordys product was spilt into more components: from four large components initially, to more than ninety components today. This process was not easy. An initial attempt to split the product in multiple components failed and the teams had to move back to the original structure. A second attempt took two months but resulted in a successful split up of the product in more independent components. It was a tough decision but management eventually realized that this was the only way the product could be developed further without an enormous overhead in global team to team communications. Today, there are 15 teams that are responsible for several components each. Teams communicate along the lines of API to API communication. They keep each other posted of planned changes in internal API’s. “It is almost like a vendor-customer relationship between teams. The only difference with the external interfaces that our end customers use is that we have to assure backward compatibility for those. Within the product that is not needed”. Components that get more radically new interfaces will continue to offer the deprecated API for some weeks till the consuming teams have migrated to the new component interface.

Offshore teams are allowed freedom as to how they exactly implement scrum meetings and processes (L2, L3). Cordys has learned that enforcing a precise process is not the right way towards effective collaboration. Cordys does not co-locate management in a single site (no L4).

To keep the component architecture simple business requirements are translated to user stories that should map to a small set or preferably a single component.

3.5 Office Space

Project teams share a work room (Figure 4). Separate video conferencing facilities are used for the sprint review meeting. “Only a real collaborative whiteboard remains on our wish list to support joint design and planning meetings. The technology is maturing now” (O1, O2).

Fig. 4. Project room during an architecture meeting (Source: Cordys)

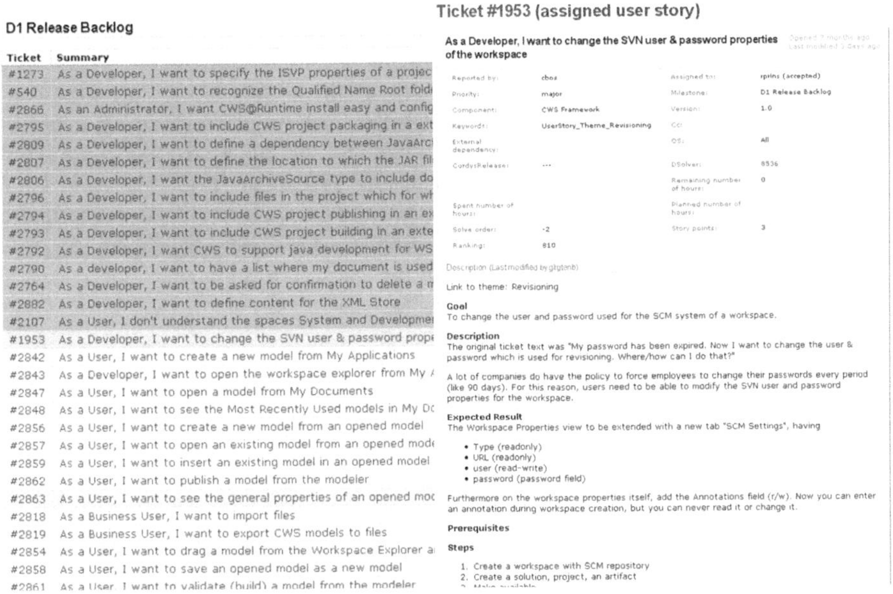

Fig. 5. Example of Cordys user story overview and a user story (Source: Cordys)

3.6 Evolving Quality Requirements

The setting of a product company ensures that trust can be built up over many years of development. Some developers have worked together for decades (also in the former Baan Company). Initial ideas to establish process standards within teams were quickly abandoned. The program manager (2011 interview) recalls why this was not a feasible route: "each time it was different in terms of style and way of working.

Teams work on different parts of the product that consists of different technologies. Each team had their own problems and issues". Management introduced a methodology of empowerment and focused on the quality of the business plan the team produced and the team quality improvement over time". No between teams comparisons were made on quality or productivity.

3.7 Transformation Change and Learning

Cordys experimented in a single team first with the agile approach. In November 2005, Hans de Visser, VP services and Steven ten Napel, VP operations look back on how Scrum and XP were introduced: "Teams are able to and willing to evaluate themselves. When Scrum was introduced in Cordys in 2004, this was not yet common practice". The company was in the process of moving up the CMM ladder. Most developers and architects had a history of working in Baan (the former company of Cordys Founder Jan Baan) that had also heavily invested in achieving high CMM levels through establishing standard methods and processes, measuring quality and predicting progress. De Visser: "adopting Scrum was a shift in mindset. Although we did not throw everything we set the quality focus overboard, the focus changed to innovation and communication...Currently, we manage by setting priorities in the product backlog, the teams themselves decide how many features they will implement in the next Sprint and how". Scrum, became firmly embedded across the organization. Mr. Ten Napel summarizes key steps in achieving this: "You should unconditionally believe in the process. Although it is tempting, never implement an agile process informally. For example, Sprint timelines should really be fixed; Scrum teams should not become too large, etc. Do not start with an insignificant pilot but immediately apply the process in a critical project (not fully in line with C4). Also, we had an enthusiastic Scrum champion; we trained Scrum masters, and established a program office that has supported the full transition. Scrum training was organized in

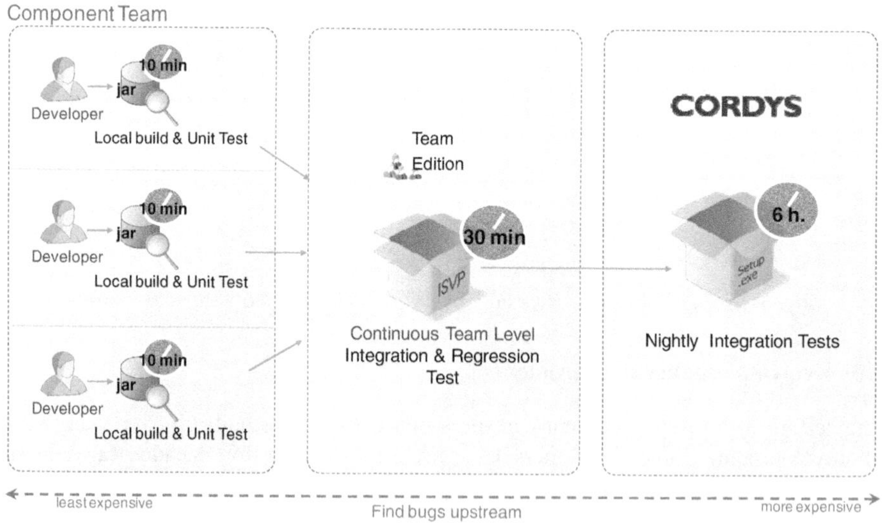

Fig. 6. Continuous local builds and team level integration and testing (Source: Cordys)

Hyderabad and Putten for architects and team leads. Last but certainly not least, from the start Jan Baan, then our CEO, viewed the Scrum process to fit our core goal of being innovative" (T3). In 2011, the Program manager looks back with confidence that initially starting with Scrum in one local team was a good decision (T1). "Still initially, many team managers thought this was yet another management fad that would pass by, they did talk about Sprints and Scrums but hadn't actually changed much in their processes. It took time to get accustomed to the new way of working".

Active Builds > Regression Test Results > **Test Report Summary**
Server: **srv-ind-vbeb** (Windows 2003/IIS/MSSQL/OLEDB)
Build: **std1 #234**

Component	TestCase Count						Success %	
Name	Total	Executed	Timeouts	Failures	Errors	Success	Executed	Total
Installer	7	7	0	0	0	7	100.00	100.00
Binary Parser	23	23	0	0	0	23	100.00	100.00
Scheduler	228	228	0	0	0	228	100.00	100.00
XDS	260	260	0	0	0	260	100.00	100.00
CCF	378	347	0	0	0	347	100.00	91.80
Data Mapper	283	248	0	0	0	248	100.00	87.63
ESB	1012	851	0	1	0	850	99.88	83.99
XML	1673	1279	0	1	0	1278	99.92	76.39
Coboc	212	141	0	0	0	141	100.00	66.51
Notification	229	154	0	14	0	140	90.91	61.14
WS-AppServer	343	204	0	4	8	192	94.12	55.98
Rule Engine	163	92	0	0	1	91	98.91	55.83
DBConnectors	5772	2671	0	0	4	2667	99.85	46.21
TestFramework	72	7	0	0	0	7	100.00	9.72
BPM Runtime	277	0	0	0	0	0	N/A	0.00
BPM Modeling	226	0	0	0	0	0	N/A	0.00
XForms	172	0	0	0	0	0	N/A	0.00
State Machine	5	0	0	0	0	0	N/A	0.00
SecurityServices	24	0	0	0	0	0	N/A	0.00
Classic Studio	0	0	0	0	0	0	N/A	N/A
SSO	0	0	0	0	0	0	N/A	N/A
CWS	0	0	0	0	0	0	N/A	N/A
Undefined	0	0	0	0	0	0	N/A	N/A
ALL	**11391**	**6512**	**0**	**20**	**13**	**6479**	**99.49**	**56.88**

Fig. 7. Report of automated regression tests (Source: Cordys)

3.8 Tools for Global Software Teams

Over the years Cordys invested much in tools to support the agile way of working. Initially very limited and simple tools were used but as the product increased in size various tools were introduced. In order to gain more productivity, each step, feature or functionality is tested. The program manager (2011 interview) notes that "in order to make the approach work we established a central code repository. We found that each team needed to have a code branch that they could individually test and in addition we needed to make sure that every one or two weeks a commit was made to our configuration management tool SVN so that integration tests could be run (F3, F5 in Table 2). We further established continuous integration tests for team branches and the entire product. It took us half a year to make sure that new code could be added to the trunk (the main body of development, originating from the start of the project until the present) and from this automatically several builds could be generated and tested (Figure 6)(F4). Each team has to comply to the rules so that when they add to the trunk the build is not allowed to break and install and the functionality should pass the tests. "The only way to get to shorter sprints is to have automated testing". Bugzilla was used to report bugs and assign them to teams (F4). A single installation allowed management to keep an overview of bug statuses. The Auto Pilot tool is used to create daily builds, to execute all the static and dynamic tests automatically, to monitor the build quality, and to compare the quality with previous builds. The project manager also knows the test coverage; in which line that developer or programmer found difficulty and how much time they tested it. When evaluating the tools used by Cordys against those we listed in Table 2, than we can conclude that most categories have been implemented. Only a true collaborative development environment is not yet in place (CDE). This can be explained as teams work on various components using different technologies and a fully integrated CDE would be of limited added value.

4 Conclusion and Discussion

Getting agile methods to work in global software development is a potentially rewarding but challenging task. Agile methods are relatively young and still maturing. The application to globally distributed projects is in its infancy. The debate whether agile methods are suitable for such projects is ongoing. The literature provides mixed results and recommendations as to how and under what conditions agile methods can bring added value. Various guidelines on how to apply and sometimes adapt agile methods have been proposed. However, systematic literature reviews reveal that detailed evaluative studies are scarce and limited to small and medium sized projects. This study contributes to both theory and practice. The theoretical contribution includes a framework that integrates best practices of adapting and applying agile methods to GSD reported in the literature. It integrates various experience reports and systematic reviews on practices and tools. The framework is applied to analyze the experiences of Cordys in a longitudinal case study. To our knowledge, no other studies exist on large projects using longitudinal data. The experiences from Cordys documented in this paper will be of value to other larger projects that aim to be successful in applying agile in GSD.

Several key lessons have been learned at Cordys in seven years of applying agile methods in a global setting. Introducing agile is hard in a big bang fashion. A gradual approach though firmly supported by management works better. It is essential not to try to standardize the details of agile methods across global teams. Agile is all about trust, empowerment and some freedom should be allowed to local teams to tailor their process and documentation style. A mix of central coordination and local freedom and empowerment works best. Although the deadline of a sprint should be firm, one should not be too dogmatic about the length of sprints. It takes time to move to short sprints especially as many teams are jointly working on a complex product. Co-located scrum meetings are far more effective than distributed scrums. Teams should ideally share an office space. To achieve as much local scrums as possible, the product architecture should be component based and local teams should remain small and work only on a limited set of components. Communication between teams should follow the lines of the product architecture. Multiple communication modes should be adopted by the project and distributed scrum meetings absolutely require high quality tool support. The role of tools is vital in constructing a complex product globally. Getting configuration management, bug reporting, automatic integration and testing in place is critical to success. It is a significant investment but worth every effort in the longer run. Cordys did not find all Scrum/XP practices equally useful. Collective code ownership could cause confusion and mixed responsibilities and was not adopted. Pair programming was found too expensive and inefficient and is not practiced at Cordys.

We can conclude that the framework compiled in this study (Table 1, Table 2) is effective for analyzing the use of agile methods in large global software development projects. The findings from the Cordys case reveal that the practices included in the framework are sometimes directly applied, adopted over time, adapted to the context or not applied at all. Remarkably, some of the practices were not found effective at Cordys and alternative practices were invented. To understand how agile practices should be introduced and adapted to fit the project context and stage of maturity we plan to study more global projects that are in the process of adopting, tuning and adapting agile methods. We also aim to continue to follow the further experiences and adaptations of agile methods at Cordys.

References

1. Abbattista, F., Calefato, F., Gendarmi, D., Lanubile, F.: Incorporating social software into distributed agile development environments. In: 1st International Workshop on Automated Engineering of Autonomous and Runtime Evolving Systems, and ASE 2008 the 23rd IEEE/ACM Int. Conf. Automated Software Engineering, pp. 46–51 (2008)
2. Abrahamsson, P., Warstab, J., Siponenb, M.T., Ronkainena, J.: New Directions on Agile Methods: A Comparative Analysis. In: Proceedings of the 25th ÍEEE International Conference on Software Engineering (2003)
3. Aydin, M.N., Harmsen, F., Slooten van, K., Stegwee, R.: On the Adaptation of An Agile Information Systems Development Method. Journal of Database Management, Special issue on Agile Analysis, Design, and Implementation 16(4) (November-December 2005)
4. Beck, K.: Embracing Change With Extreme Programming. IEEE Computer 32, 70–77 (1999)
5. Cordys Website, `http://www.cordys.com/`
6. Dullemond, K., Van Gameren, B., Van Solingen, R.: How technological support can enable advantages of agile software development in a GSE setting. In: Proceedings 4th IEEE International Conference on Global Software Engineering, ICGSE, pp. 143–152 (2009)
7. Eisenhardt, K.M.: Building theories from case study research. The Academy of Management review 14, 532–550 (1989)
8. Fitzgerald, B., Hartnett, G., Conboy, K.: Customising agile methods to software practices at intel shannon. European Journal of Information Systems 15(2), 200–213 (2006)
9. Hansen, M.T., Baggesen, H.: From CMMI and isolation to scrum, agile, lean and collaboration. In: Proceedings of the Agile Conference, AGILE, pp. 283–288 (2009)
10. Holmström, H., Fitzgerald, B., Ågerfalk, P.J., Conchúir, E.Ó.: Agile practices reduce distance in gloral software development. Information Systems Management 23(3), 7–18 (2006)
11. Hossain, E., Ali Babar, M., Paik, H.: Using scrum in global software development: A systematic literature review. In: Proceedings - 4th IEEE International Conference on Global Software Engineering, ICGSE, pp. 175–184 (2009)

12. Hossain, E., Babar, M.A., Paik, H., Verner, J.: Risk identification and mitigation processes for using scrum in global software development. In: Proceedings - Asia-Pacific Software Engineering Conference, APSEC, pp. 457–464 (2009)
13. Jalali, S., Wohlin, C.: Agile practices in global software engineering - A systematic map. In: Proceedings - 5th International Conference on Global Software Engineering, ICGSE, pp. 45–54 (2010)
14. Kniberg, H.: Blog on Combining Scrum and XP, `http://blog.crisp.se/henrikkniberg/2007/10/13/1192249140000.html`
15. Kotlarsky, J., Oshri, I., Van Hillegersberg, J., Kumar, K.: Globally distributed component-based software development: An exploratory study of knowledge management and work division. Journal of Information Technology 22(2), 161–173 (2007)
16. Paasivaara, M., Lassenius, C.: Could global software development benefit from agile methods? In: Proceedings - IEEE International Conference on Global Software Engineering, ICGSE 2006, pp. 109–113 (2006)
17. Paasivaara, M., Durasiewicz, S., Lassenius, C.: Using scrum in distributed agile development: A multiple case study. In: Proceedings - 2009 4th IEEE International Conference on Global Software Engineering, ICGSE, pp. 195–204 (2009)
18. Palmer, S.R., Felsing, J.M.: A Practical Guide to Feature-Driven Development. Prentice-Hall, Englewood Cliffs (2002)
19. Ramesh, B., et al.: Can distributed software development be agile? Comm.of the ACM 49(10), 41–46 (2006)
20. Sakthivel, S.: Managing risk in offshore systems development. Communications of the ACM 50(4), 69–75 (2007)
21. Sarker, S., Sarker, S.: Exploring agility in distributed information systems development teams: An interpretive study in an offshoring context. Information Systems Research 20(3), 440–461 (2009)
22. Schwaber, K.: Scrum Development Process. presented at OOPSLA 1995 Workshop on Business Object Design and Implementation (1995)
23. Schwaber, K., Beedle, M.: Agile Software Development With Scrum. Prentice-Hall, Englewood Cliffs (2001)
24. Thompson, M.: Technology audit Business Operations Platform 4, Cordys, Butler Group (June 2009)
25. Turk, D., France, R., Rumpe, B.: Assumptions Under lying Agile Software Development Processes. Journal of Database Management (JDM) 16(4) (October-December 2005)
26. Woodward, E., Surdek, S., Ganis, M.: A Practical Guide to Distributed Scrum, Deployment and Advanced Configuration. IBM Press (2010)

Global Software Development Coordination Strategies - A Vendor Perspective

Sadhana Deshpande, Sarah Beecham, and Ita Richardson

Lero- Irish Software Engineering Research Centre,
University of Limerick, Ireland
{Sadhana.Deshpande,Sarah.Beecham,Ita.Richardson}@ul.ie

Abstract. Global software development (GSD) is often impeded by global distance which may be geographical, cultural, temporal or linguistic. This results in the requirement for specific strategies to coordinate a range of activities between client and vendor teams in the GSD environment which are different from a collocated setting. GSD literature recommends many coordination strategies, but tends to take the client viewpoint. However, these should also be viewed from the vendor perspective. This paper addresses this gap by presenting coordination strategies which we identified from GSD literature and an empirical research study which we carried out with vendor companies in India. Comparing these coordination strategies with relevant strategies in the human resource management section of the PMBOK® Guide, we have defined a set of strategies which can be used by GSD Project Managers when coordinating a project.

Keywords: Global Software Development (GSD), Coordination, Project Management, Human Resource Management, Client, Vendor.

1 Introduction

Over the last two decades software development has become increasingly geographically distributed across the globe [1]. Various business motives such as local skills shortage, cost saving, mergers and acquisition, gaining competitive advantage in existing markets and entry into new markets drive organisations towards distributed or global software development (GSD) [2]. Given the highly competitive environment in which companies operate, the client who is outsourcing and the vendor who is receiving this work have to equip themselves to operate successfully across geographical, national and international boundaries. However, GSD is often impeded by global distance that can be categorised as interior and exterior distance [3]. Exterior distance is caused by geographical, cultural, linguistic and temporal differences [3][4]. Whereas, interior distance is formed by organisational, technological and knowledge differences that may exist at various organisations [5]. Organisational distance occurs when structures and business processes of collaborating organizations are different [5]. Differences in their methods of work, management of human resources, knowledge and software development process may

J. Kotlarsky, L.P. Willcocks, and I. Oshri (Eds.): Global Sourcing 2011, LNBIP 91, pp. 153–174, 2011.

also exist [6]. Where a software application is being developed, there may be inadequate domain knowledge. This triggers knowledge distance and knowledge gaps within organisations [5]. Using disparate technology across development sites causes difficulty in developing and maintaining the software which in turn creates technological distance [5]. All these distances make GSD and the management of GSD projects exceptionally complex and difficult.

One result of having these distances in GSD is that they draw out communication, coordination, culture and control issues [7]. When team members are collocated these issues tend to get resolved quickly and informally. However, in the GSD environment, these issues can spiral out of control as it can be difficult to know the right person to contact for resolving such issues. The empirical literature on GSD gives evidence as to how various tactics are applied to alleviate communication, cultural, coordination and control issues created by global distance. While each of these is of interest to GSD researchers, the research presented here particularly focuses on coordination. A fundamental problem of GSD is that many of the mechanisms that function to coordinate the work in a co-located setting are absent or disrupted in a distributed project [8].

With globalisation, problems related to the coordination of distributed software projects, teams and team members are regularly investigated. From the available literature on GSD, it is evident that several effective strategies are implemented and followed to overcome the coordination issues within those companies engaged in GSD projects. Some strategies followed are original and innovative but are not prevalent, their occurrences in practice are random and vary according to the circumstances as and when they are essential. Therefore in this ongoing research study we aim to bring together effective coordination strategies that are followed to manage the GSD projects.

A systematic literature review (SLR) [9] completed by the authors has been presented in a previous paper [10]. In that paper, we investigated coordination strategies followed by GSD client and vendor companies. We observed that only 14% of studies on coordination strategies have been carried out from the vendor view point. The objective of the research presented in this paper is to develop a *GSD Coordination Model* that will facilitate vendor companies to overcome various coordination issues while operating in the GSD environment. To do this, we use the Project Management Body of Knowledge, the PMBOK® Guide (2008) [11].

This chapter is structured as follows; Section 2 presents the background of coordination in GSD and Section 3 gives an overview of the PMBOK® Guide. Section 4 describes the Research Methods we used to answer our research question and explains the rationale for using the PMBOK® Guide to underpin our study. Section 5 compares coordination strategies used by practitioners and presented in the GSD literature with the PMBOK® Guide. We discuss our research findings in Section 6, and present our conclusion in Section 7.

2 Background: Coordination in GSD

Coordination between software development teams is one of the very difficult aspects of software engineering [12]. Furthermore, the effectiveness of various coordination mechanisms differs in collocated, distributed and time-separated context [13]. The need for coordination is less when activities are carried out independently but, when there is a substantial dependency among various activities, there is huge need for coordination [13]. In the case of GSD projects, coordination needs are high because various activities are distributed and dependent on many other ongoing activities, therefore introducing substantial dependency. If proper analysis with a fine-grained level of detail about the dependencies of each task and activities is done and well understood, it becomes easy to identify different coordination mechanisms to manage these dependencies [13].

Coordination per se is an interdisciplinary subject. Regular studies are carried out in various disciplines such as management, computer science, organization theory, operations research, economics, linguistics and psychology as they are important for understanding the cooperative work environment. In computer science, coordination study is essential because it involves both humans and machines. Malone & Crowston [14] have studied coordination for computer science and define coordination as 'the act of working together harmoniously and managing interdependencies between activities to achieve goal in which several actors are involved and multiple activities are performed' [15]. They state that coordination has four main components - goals, activities, actors and interdependencies. Thus, identifying goals, mapping goals to activities, assigning activities to actors and managing resources and interdependencies are the processes which should be included in coordination. To firmly hold on to the project goals and policies, effective control over groups, tools and standards are essential in GSD [3].

Offshoring is an arrangement when a company operates from a new location which is outside the home country [16], while in outsourcing a vendor company from a different country performs the tasks and processes to provide services to the client company [17]. Outsourcing and offshoring tasks have become the norm in software development [18]. Problems relating to the coordination of distributed software projects should be analysed and formalised. The GSD literature has revealed several effective coordination strategies that are implemented and followed within companies that manage the GSD projects. These strategies facilitate software companies in dealing with various coordination issues related to teams and team structuring [19], inter and intra team coordination [12], task allocation [20], bridging [21], cultural differences [22] communication and many more. In GSD, when teams and team members from various geographical locations work together to achieve project success through software development, they need high level of coordination [13]. Geographically distributed teams can take any size but, having the right balance between the team size at every geographical location is very important in GSD for effective coordination and communication [23]. For example, team size can affect the choice of technology to support GSD projects [23]. Uneven team size on both the client and vendor side can obstruct coordination process therefore it is necessary to understand the effects of team size on distributed development as they are still largely unknown [23]. The assessment between having small team size and large team size can help to uncover the issues that impede coordination in the GSD projects [23].

Team knowledge or team awareness is the detailed information of each teams work domain and team members expertise. In GSD, maintaining such information facilitates project managers and team members to contact exact person from other team hierarchy for effective coordination and communication [24]. With the emergence of advanced technologies team members can share team knowledge effectively [25] and this team knowledge helps to find expertise within the teams setup for the project, which will help to foresee task issues accurately and coordinate more efficiently [24]. Collective knowledge of team members and their tasks can counterbalance communication deficiencies and help team members to coordinate more effectively even if the intensity of their communication is reduced by geographic distance [24]. Apart from team size and team knowledge, it is also essential to have a proper understanding of intra and inter team coordination in GSD [12]. Complex tasks in large scale software development projects have many high interdependencies, and effectively coordinating these dependencies is critical to project success particularly when team members are in multiple geographic locations [24]. Team members follow different methods for intra and inter team coordination since the dependencies differs in both types of teams [12]. When the dependency is inter team, members prefer paying a personal visit to the other members' workplace to unblock the dependency.

In relation to this, onsite visits [26] is one of the major strategies suggested in the GSD literature. These are visits made by members of client sites to the vendor sites or by members of the vendor sites to the client. Scheduling onsite visits to the location of the other teams serves to resolve issues and misunderstandings [27] that may have happened prior to meeting each other and thus establish relationships amongst members of teams from different geographic locations [28]. Onsite visits should be planned meticulously by taking into consideration various aspects of the GSD projects. The visiting team members are termed as ambassadors [29], onsite coordinator [26], cross-site delegates [28][27], liaisons and gatekeepers [30][31]. They travel among sites for improving cross-team communication and the primary role of these visiting members is to coordinate activities between distributed teams [29]. They help to manage the dependencies that facilitate coordination in the GSD projects [32]. Moreover they promote to build relationships amongst various teams, provide a mechanism to create trust and transfer knowledge, communicate lessons learned and set future direction for the project [29]. On return to their original teams, these delegates become 'point people' for cross-site coordination in establishing communication across sites [28]. The onsite coordinator's relationship, knowledge of personalities and culture acts as a short-cut between the teams allowing for complex and subtle communication to flow in both directions [29].

Bridging is another significant approach suggested in the GSD literature that helps to overcome coordination issues by linking together or 'bridging' teams from various sites. Holmstrom, et al. [33] and Milewski et al. [21] have studied bridge type arrangements and found that bridges can facilitate in the successful coordination of the GSD projects [21]. In GSD projects, specific sites receive work from the primary client and outsource work further to other sites (vendors) and experience of being both customer and vendor in two-stage outsourcing relationships [33]. Being a bridge site allows such teams to understand and potentially help when dealing with relations of both client and vendor sites. Bridging helps in successful knowledge management and coordination of GSD projects [34]. While examining bridges and the bridging tactics, Holmstrom, et al. [33] and Milewski et al. [21] suggest the consideration of various attributes that are involved in building bridges and that bridges must be established when there is a high need for real-time interaction and when there is interdependency between each site's goal and objectives.

In addition to the strategies discussed above which specifically focus on GSD, there are other strategies which can be used, coming from the more general software development literature. Various standards and multitude of software process capability maturity models [35] have been developed in last two decades that are best applicable to the software industry. These standard documents and capability maturity models have helped put together vast bodies of knowledge about good software practices into a form that is easy to work with [35]. Therefore it becomes essential to identify precise standard documents and capability maturity models that are relevant to the GSD area in order to compare the identified strategies.

We have confirmed that while there are strategies available for project management in software engineering (SE), there is no particular focus on GSD. Although they do not specifically focus on GSD, vendor companies use standards such as the Capability Maturity Model Integrated (CMMI), ISO9000 and the Project Management Body of Knowledge (PMBOK® Guide, 2008). While the role of the research we present in this chapter is to benefit the GSD community for continued and effective management of projects, we believe that it is also important to use proven project management that relate specifically to coordination strategies.

To support our findings within the empirical research it was essential to identify a specific software process and standard which could be used as a basis for the provision of a strategy for overcoming GSD coordination issues and challenges encountered by vendor. Therefore, we held a focus group with five expert practitioners who have knowledge about software project management standards. Facilitated by one of the authors, the experts discussed guidelines for coordination strategies that were found to work in practice. While we recognize that software engineering models have some cognizance of coordination included, following this focus group's advice and taking into account the literature and existing practice, we have chosen the PMBOK® Guide as the basis for the GSD coordination model that we are developing. On the basis of this, this chapter focuses on the following research question:

Can the PMBOK® Guide help to address coordination issues and challenges in GSD projects from the vendor perspective?

3 Project Management Body of Knowledge

The Project Management Body of Knowledge, the PMBOK® Guide (2008), is a recognised standard for project management. It describes the established norms, methods, processes, and practices for a range of industries including the software industry and defines project management and related concepts. 'Good practices' in the PMBOK® Guide are generally recognised and applicable to projects and there is consensus about their value and usefulness [11, pg 4]. It is identified that the application of the PMBOK® Guide's skills, tools and techniques can enhance the chances of success over a wide range of projects. However, the knowledge described cannot always be applied uniformly to all projects and it is up to the project management team to determine what is appropriate for any given project [11, pg 4].

We carried out an in-depth review of the PMBOK® Guide, 2008 to understand its overall composition. There are three main sections – *The Project Management Framework; The Standard for Project Management of a Project* and *The Project Management Knowledge Areas.* Each section includes chapters that cover various topics. Section I which is *The Project Management Framework section* consists of the Introduction and Project Life Cycle and Organisation chapters. Section II, *The Standard for Project Management of a Project,* covers a chapter on Project Management Processes for a Project. Section III, *The Project Management Knowledge Areas,* includes chapters on the topics Project Integration Management, Project Scope Management, Project Time Management, Project Cost Management, Project Quality Management, Project Human Resource Management, Project Communications Management, Project Risk Management and Project Procurement Management. While we are interested in each of these topics, our objective was to know which good practices could be useful for coordination. By comparing the PMBOK® Guide and the coordination strategies used in GSD we identified specific chapters which would be useful for this purpose.

We established that the Project Human Resource Management chapter includes 'the processes that organise, manage and lead the project teams' and the project team is comprised of the team members who are assigned specific roles and responsibilities for successfully accomplishing the project [11]. From the GSD perspective, this chapter is important because the process described here includes the plans, tools and techniques that are useful in the management of the human resource required for the project – and this is where many of the issues and challenges arise in GSD. Therefore, in this book chapter we explicitly focus on *Project Human Resource Management* to answer our defined research question.

4 Research Methods

To answer our research question, and following our literature review, we needed to understand what coordination issues and challenges exist in GSD practice. We were then interested in how existing vendor companies deal with these issues and challenges. We could then compare our output with the PMBOK® Guide.

4.1 Data Collection

Initially, we followed Strauss and Corbin's grounded theory approach [36] using an exploratory multiple-case sampling method following an inductive grounded theory approach. This qualitative approach allowed our findings to emerge directly from the data. In the past, we have seen that this has been a successful approach when used in similar studies [37] [38].

Sampling involves decisions not only about which people to observe or interview, but also about settings, events and social processes [39]. Usually, qualitative research needs to be carried out on small samples, as the samples tend to be purposive, rather than random [40] [41]. For this research work, we studied small but focused samples within five multinational companies and one national company based in India as listed in Table 1.

Our population of interest was those people who are involved in management and decision-making for the teams – mainly Project Managers and senior staff. To contact these people, we approached three software companies in India where we had personal contacts. With the help of these contacts, we created a cluster of samples to perform the research. Therefore, the cases chosen for this research work are, to some extent, opportunistic [40]. We interviewed 15 individuals in different roles ranging from Junior Project Manager to Vice President (Software Projects) within these companies. A point to be noted is that the Junior Project Managers and Team Leads whom we interviewed performed a dual role of Software Engineers for the GSD projects. For confidentiality reasons we use pseudonyms for the participating companies.

Table 1. Summary of Organisations Researched

Name	Total Employees	Persons Involved: Online interview, Questionnaire, Face-to-face interview
Top-Info Technologies Ltd.	100,000	2 Senior Project Managers 1 Junior Project Managers
Dream Moon Software	110,000	Vice President Assistant Vice President 2 Senior Project Managers 1 Team Lead
Mega Technology Software	70,000	Chief Consultant 1 Senior Project Manager 1 Team Lead
Cyber Epoch India Ltd	12,000	Junior Project Manager
FJ Software	160,000	1 Senior Project Manager 1 Team Lead
Vision India Software	25-50	Senior Project Manager

Our approach included the compilation of questionnaires and interview questions based on the literature review and research question. These gave interviewees a chance to articulate their experiences and views on various issues which exist while managing outsourced GSD projects.

In the first instance, we used online questionnaires for data collection. This allowed us to gather initial information such as demographic details and to complete the groundwork for the research. The questionnaire was distributed amongst all the participants mentioned in Table 1 and was completed and returned by each one, achieving a response rate of 100%. Among others, we asked questions to establish how teams are setup to work on the GSD projects. For example, we questioned about

- What are the key elements that are required for a successful Indian based team?
- What are the most important factors you look for when selecting your team members?
- What are the key activities that need to be undertaken when establishing a cohesive Indian based team? (E.g. Training)

After receiving the completed questionnaires, we conducted the second phase of the research, within a period of next 15 days. Adopting a semi-structured approach, we carried out telephonic interviews with each of the same 15 participants. Each interview lasted more than 90 minutes and was recorded with the interviewee's permission. We probed deeper into the responses from the questionnaires. For example, team building exercises were stated as an activity to set up cohesive teams. In order to understand more about team building we enquired further about:

- How often are the team building activities carried out for the members working on the GSD projects?
- What positive strengths are built on? What negative issues have to be addressed?
- What are the different training programs conducted for the GSD team members?

The response for the telephonic interviews was very enriching. Following analysis of the data from the two initial data collection phases, one of the authors conducted on-site face-to-face interviews in India. During the visits in the software companies, the researcher had an opportunity to spend around 5-7 hours in each organisation observing and interviewing the participants in their software company. These face-to-face interviews were conducted again with the same participants who had answered the questionnaire and were interviewed online. Based on answers received during these research phases, a set of specific questions had been developed for the face-to-face interviews. Following from the previous example, it was important for us to identify how exactly the team building exercises and training programs help GSD teams. We also wanted to know more about the team meeting process. Therefore to understand more about all these activities we asked following questions –

- What advantage do you gain by conducting the training programs? Are the team members always willing to take these training? Can you give more detail on the setup of your training university/department?
- How is the brain storming session (as part of the team building exercise) helpful for the team members working on the GSD projects?
- Explain more about the proceedings/activities that happen in the weekly meeting?

These queries allowed a more in-depth exploration of the challenges, issues and solutions which had been identified. For example, one of the senior project managers explained details about team building exercise and other activities that are carried out to help reduce the attrition levels. The interview allowed for other aspects related to this to be made known. It would have been difficult to gain this understanding without this face-to-face interview. In addition to the one-on-one interview with each participant during her visit, she also took the opportunity to observe them while they performed their task working on the GSD projects. This allowed the researcher to observe at first-hand in the manner the tasks are executed by each member when working on the GSD projects and also to understand how various issues are resolved that crop up while coordinating work with the distributed team members.

All interviews were semi-structured. Therefore, while the interviews remained focused, the respondents were not constrained in their responses or the topics they raised and the researcher had the opportunity to probe further into various issues. Questions based on the observation were also asked to the participants. The participants freely expressed and shared their experiences while also presenting new ideas and suggestions. The discussion with the participants was recorded whenever possible and notes were written up.

4.2 Data Analysis

Following our data collection, the data from the questionnaire, telephonic interviews and face-to-face interviews was transcribed. We performed content analysis [39] on the transcribed data. The text was first divided into manageable categories to generate a set of codes (start list) [39]. The start list for this research work included codes such as TEAMS, COMMUNICATION, CULTURE, TEMPORAL DIFFERENCES, CUSTOMER and VENDOR. These codes were further broken down into sub-codes. For example, the TEAMS code included sub-codes as TEAM SELECTION, TEAM STRUCTURE, TEAM BUILDING, TEAM ISSUES AND TEAM MANAGEMENT. The transcribed text was examined using this list of codes and sub-codes. These codes and sub-codes have allowed us to abstract the data into more meaningful and prudent groupings which has given a deeper insight into a variety of topics under study.

4.3 Gap Analysis

The recognised 'good practices' mentioned in the PMBOK® Guide is a set of knowledge and practices applicable to various projects and are contributed by the project management practitioners. The scope of the PMBOK® Guide extends over a wide range of topics relating to project management therefore it was necessary to understand its relevance to our research study. The research discussed in the current chapter focuses on the Project Human Resource Management chapter of the PMBOK® Guide (2008). We conducted a comparative analysis of coordination processes from this chapter and the data obtained from our literature and primary study. The analysis focused on three distinct comparisons which:

- i Identified PMBOK® Guide processes that are also performed by GSD teams;
- ii Identified PMBOK® Guide processes not performed by GSD teams;
- iii Identified processes carried out in GSD situations which are not PMBOK® Guide processes.

While our focus was on the Project Human Resource Management chapter, for (iii) above, we also examined the full guide to ensure that these processes did not exist in any of the other PMBOK® Guide chapters.

5 Mapping GSD and PMBOK® Guide

As stated in the previous section, we carried out a mapping between our GSD research and the PMBOK® Guide. From the PMBOK® Guide perspective, this mapping focused particularly on the Project Human Resource Management chapter, but for (5.3) below, we established that the GSD process we identify did not exist at any point in the guide.

5.1 Processes in the PMBOK® Guide Performed by GSD Teams

We established that six processes are common to both GSD and the PMBOK® Guide.

Networking - Networking between the team members is essential to manage and coordinate project activities and has an influence on the effectiveness of projects [11, pg222]. Networking process mentioned includes proactive correspondence, luncheon meetings, formal and informal conversations during meetings and events. Networking is also important in GSD projects. One of the project managers we interviewed stated that:

> *"Networking helps to build on effective communication, create good team dynamics and bring team members out of their boundaries to integrate them professionally and socially with other teams and team members".*[1]

Along with the cases we studied, GSD literature has revealed various networking process which have been implemented for distributed teams and team members involved in GSD projects. Techniques we have noted in our research include easily coordinated activities such as giving team members an opportunity to spend time together socially so that they can discuss their project as well as matters relating to the project. Different social activities are organised for the team members that includes hosting team lunches and dinners and celebrating team members' religious festivals. These all help to develop interpersonal relations and exchange ideas for collocated team members which ultimately improve team performance.

Team Building - In the PMBOK® Guide, team building processes are emphasised. They are necessary to improve interpersonal relationships within the teams as they help build trust and establish good working relationships. As a consequence, this supports team members in working together efficiently [11, pg232]. The guide also states that 'team building strategies are particularly valuable when team members operate from remote locations without the benefit of face to face contact' [11, pg232]. This results in easier handling of project team problems, effective team discussion and resolution of issues which may arise. Our research demonstrates that GSD vendors utilise similar strategies. When analysing the cases we studied, we observed that the software project managers conduct regular team meetings to develop team dynamics. Additionally project issues are discussed. In some cases, where the problem has been resolved before the team meeting, its resolution is discussed. If it has not been resolved, members discuss its potential resolution, thus harnessing prior knowledge. We have also seen that regular team meetings, interactive sessions, brainstorming sessions, induction programs are also carried out as part of the team building exercise. One of the interviewees has stated that -

---

[1] Quotes that are drawn directly from our primary study are given in italics.

"Establishing a cohesive team at the outsourcing destination is important for the global software development...team building exercise brings stability within the team and largely helps in successful completion of the project. It helps to build united and integrated software development teams".

Training – Training, also mentioned specifically in the PMBOK® guide, is important to improve team performance and consequently to achieve project success. Training can be formal or informal as it is essential to develop team competencies. Before training is implemented, it is important that project managers formulate a proper plan for scheduling training programs for the team members.

In the GSD situation, training is an important activity for all of the software companies we studied. Our analysis revealed that regular training activities are carried out for the team members working on GSD projects and most of the companies maintain training calendars. One of the project managers we interviewed explained that -

"When senior team members are due for promotions...they encourage their subordinates to take-up such trainings...so that the subordinate can be chosen to take up higher position".

We noted that project managers include relief from duties by team members in their project plans so that they can undertake the training programs. Training sessions are conducted at various stages within the project. This includes training of new team members, with sessions specifically conducted to brief them about project details and the roles and responsibilities. Other training programs include enhancement of technical and communication skills of the team members and specific technology training. It is normally expected that each team member undertakes specific hours of training every year which helps them to work successfully on the projects. Training can also be used as a solution to filling skills gaps [11, pg232] and can be helpful to overcome attrition that hugely affects GSD projects.

Cultural Differences - The PMBOK® Guide acknowledges that project managers operating in global environments have to manage cultural differences [11, pg230]. GSD team members come from various cultural backgrounds, speak multiple languages and possess different industry experience. They operate in the 'team language' (often English), which is different from their native language [11, pg230]. The PMBOK® Guide very specifically emphasises that project managers should 'capitalise on cultural differences' [11, pg230]. It is expected that project managers should be able to encourage working together interdependently in a climate of mutual trust to help develop team spirit in a culturally diverse environment [11, pg230]. This is important for improving individual and team productivity while working on projects in global environment.

The cases we studied were all based in India, the most culturally diverse nation [42]. Despite this, we have observed project managers there managing diverse cultural and religious backgrounds [22]. To do this successfully, project managers should have comprehensive knowledge of the prevailing cultural diversity, and be able to take advantage of it to effectively accomplish their GSD goals.

"We have never felt that cultural background of any team member is an issue for team management…in fact we have certain advantages with the team members religious background…..as they work on each other's festive holidays…the strength is that team members work is an multicultural environment….they learn lots of various aspects of different religions and culture".

Interviewees from the Indian software companies discussed how they set up backup teams to leverage this cultural diversity. They can be used, for example, to overcome the potential loss of support and communication during festive and religious holidays, providing support 365 days per year, thus transforming cultural differences into strengths.

Team performance assessments - Team performance assessments are necessary to increase the probability of achieving project objectives in the desired timeframe [11, pg237]. Conducting an evaluation of the team's overall performance helps to gauge the existing competency within the team. It becomes particularly significant when teams and team members are distributed as in the case of GSD projects and it is essential that individual team performance is evaluated. This allows the project manager to take necessary steps to improve team performance, in turn helping to avoid consequences that may affect the overall project.

Our research demonstrated that Indian vendor software companies conduct such performance assessments on a regular basis.

"The project manager or team leads prepare the performance card to identify the positive or negative elements of each team and team member's performance. Based on the weakness appropriate steps are taken to enhance the skills".

In the PMBOK® Guide this activity is mentioned for collocated team members but the empirical data reveals that the GSD vendor software companies perform this assessment on two levels – for the entire GSD team and for the team members within site teams. This allows detailed analysis of team performance and gives the project manager the opportunity to take necessary steps to overcome any issue that can affect the project outcome.

Recognition and Rewards - The PMBOK® Guide includes recognition and rewards for team members, stating that plans relating to team member reward schemes should be part of the human resource management process [11, pg234]. It also allows for the consideration of 'cultural differences' when determining these. Teams and team members of GSD projects in the case study companies are motivated through the use of appropriate recognition and rewards. In team motivational schemes, the whole team is rewarded which help to create rapport within teams. Individual team members within the teams can also be rewarded:

"To motivate our teams and team members we have reward-based system…we give rewards to an outstanding team and also excellent team performer…who has done something special beyond his or her responsibility…that is related to project…we also have spot awards…which is a surprise to the team members….and is given at that individuals desk….so such small rewards do help us in motivating our team members".

Monetary rewards may also be given to the teams and team members for their special achievements. We studied one case where team members were given special remuneration for working in various time zones. However, it is important that the project manager, while rewarding teams and individuals, maintains the cohesiveness of the GSD team.

5.2 Processes in the PMBOK® Guide Not Performed by GSD Teams

While there are project human resource management process in the PMBOK® Guide performed within GSD teams, there are some process in the guide for which we have no evidence of use in the GSD environment. These four processes are discussed in this section.

Organisational charts: Within the PMBOK® Guide organisational charts have been presented as a tool to document team members' roles and responsibilities. They can also be used to explain the position of various teams and team members within the GSD project. Such project charts should include a graphic display of project team members and their reporting relationships. These charts can either be formal or informal, highly detailed or broadly framed based on the project needs [11, pg223]. Mostly such charts can be made for individual teams within the project. There have been calls by GSD researchers to define such roles and responsibilities when setting up GSD teams [43] and in the cases we studied; we observed that the exercise of creating project charts is very rarely carried out in GSD projects. In GSD, creating such project charts can help project managers to track the activities of GSD teams and team members. These charts would also support the creation of an appropriate project communication plan and the tracking of individual project team members. They can help to keep a repository of available skills and competencies throughout the project duration which can be utilized effectively within the project. Using such charts would also help project managers to plan in advance for the acquisition of required skill sets and the relocation of team members within the distributed project sites.

Staff acquisition and management plan: The PMBOK® Guide affirms that human resource plan must describe the requirements of human resource for the project. The plan should detail:

- How and when the human resource requirements for the project will be met
- The number of team members expected to work full-time on the project.

From a GSD perspective these guidelines support the requirement to have a clear plan of team members in both collocated and geographically distributed teams. This in turn can help to control cost of the project to some extent as the project managers will know in advance the required human resource for the project. The project managers can also plan and schedule in advance for the training programs and other activities required for building teams for the project.

Resource Calendar - In relation to staff acquisition and management, the PMBOK® Guide states that a resource calendar must be maintained to estimate the level of expertise available for the project. The calendar must have description of all the team members involved in the project and can help to [11 pg231]:

- Document the duration that each team member needs to work on the project
- Identify proper times when team members can participate in team development activities
- Track each activity of the team members and the progress of the project
- Understand each team members schedule, availability including personal holidays and necessity on other projects.

It should also be updated regularly during the project life cycle to guide the acquisition, release and development actions of team member.

While it is prominent within the PMBOK® Guide, maintaining the resource calendar is not an activity documented in the GSD literature review nor have we noted it during our empirical research. However, the introduction of a resource calendar could help to manage the available resources in GSD and overcome the issue of attrition. The project managers could use it to track available resources within the project and build up in-house resources amongst the existing team members. This would allow them to immediately take over new responsibilities from the team members who leave the project. A resource calendar would also assist mobility of team members between various locations as per the project needs, providing updated information on the available resources and helping to plan in advance for acquisition and release of team members. It would be useful when –

> *"We have to make sure that sufficient team members are available to work in shifts as per the client time zones and on holidays to provide 24/7 support. Not all team members are eager to work in shifts…or they cannot work all the time from evening 10pm to morning8am….its practically not possible….so we have to find team members who can replace and give this support…to work as per clients time zone".*

In such situations maintaining a resource calendar can be very useful for project managers. It could also be the basis for training, team building process.

Roles & Responsibilities: The human resource plan mentioned in the PMBOK® Guide provides guidance on how project human resources should be staffed, managed and controlled. This plan in turn helps to precisely define roles and responsibilities for every team member involved in the project and achieve project success. A role is the "label describing the portion of a project for which a person is accountable" [11, pg222] and each role must have clarity pertaining to "authority, responsibilities and boundaries" of each team member [11, pg222]. The guide also states that team members must be made aware of their right to apply project resources and make decisions about the methods for completing a task and that they should be well informed about acceptable quality standards and what responses they should make to project variances [11, pg223]. Responsibilities would mention the work that a team member is "expected to perform in order to complete the project activities" [11, pg223]. For project managers to ensure that project activities are completed effectively, they must be aware of the competencies of each responsible team member. If team members do not possess required competencies, proper action needs to be taken – otherwise the performance of the project can be affected. When incompetence is identified, positive approaches such as training, hiring new people, changes in scope and schedule must be brought about. There have been calls by researchers to precisely define and include roles and responsibilities to explain the position of teams and team members in the GSD projects [43]. Clear definition of roles and responsibilities can help planning and tracking of distributed project and team activities in GSD. It can also assist project managers to assign appropriate tasks to team members as per their interest and skill sets as it is important for GSD project managers to -

> *"look for the skill set of the resource that can match the project requirement in order to assign them specific tasks".*

Hence exactly defining roles and responsibilities can assist project managers in selecting team members who can be assigned tasks in the GSD projects. Clarity in roles and responsibilities is essential to coordinate distributed activities and to bring homogeneity within teams and team members across various sites of GSD. Hence it becomes vital that roles and responsibilities are defined clearly in GSD.

Effective usage of the PMBOK® Guide would solve this issue. Definition of roles and responsibilities must include position, skills and competencies that are essential for the project.

5.3 Processes Not in the PMBOK® Guide Performed by GSD Teams

When completing our primary research and literature review we identified four GSD coordination process that should be considered by GSD project managers although they are not included in the PMBOK® Guide. The GSD literature provides evidence of successful coordination strategies which have been supported by our empirical research conducted within software companies based in India.

Onsite Coordinators: A solution to GSD coordination problems, as noted in the literature, can be met by the 'onsite coordinator' [44 Carmel, 2006]. We have also noted the existence of this position in our empirical research, where a project manager explained:

> *"We have onsite coordinators stationed at the client site....so that they can manage the work load whenever required.....the advantage of having onsite coordinators is that we mostly do not have communication issue....they take care of clients and other issue if any".*

The role of the onsite coordinator is to plan, coordinate and manage the work between different geographically located teams and team members. Therefore they need an understanding of the software development project and are mostly senior team members who are positioned at the client site to act as a liaison across team for the development project. They can also help to manage cultural diversity [44] through bridging the cultural and linguistic differences between teams and facilitating organizational flow of communication [3], improving cross-team communication [29] and sometimes becoming the main communication channel for the non-collocated teams [27]. Their role may also include the arbitration of team conflicts and resolution of miscommunications that happens between team members. They try to build relationships amongst various teams and provide a mechanism to create trust and transfer knowledge. They also communicate lessons learned and set future direction for the project [29].

The onsite coordinator usually visits the client locations where they carry out onsite work. Apart from having an understanding of the software development project, they need to have sufficient global knowledge and a willingness to travel between locations. They may also go to other distributed sites for specific time periods and can be regularly rotated between various geographical locations to create homogeneity between sites. Natives of a particular country who previously emigrated can serve as the cultural liaison with an offshore site [3]. On return to their original teams, these delegates become 'Point People' for cross-site collaboration in establishing communication across sites [28] and their knowledge of personalities and culture can act as a communication short-cut between the teams, thus allowing for relevant communication to flow in both directions [29]. Onsite coordinators have also been labeled as cross-site delegates [28], panel points [27] or ambassadors [29].

Bridging: Bridges for GSD teams are normally groups of heterogeneous workforce available within a reasonably short geographical and temporal distance and become nodes to manage two or more separated work sites that exist on either side of their location. They receive work from one site and outsource work further to other sites. Therefore they have the experience of both outsourcing and insourcing in a two-stage outsourcing relationship [33]. Being a bridge site allows teams to understand and potentially help when dealing with projects between sites, increasing knowledge management and coordination [34]. Our empirical research has identified companies that have established bridges. Their GSD projects include the provision of support 365 days per year and bridge locations have been setup to monitor the flow of work from one location to another within time zones. Where software companies have development sites throughout the globe, the bridge sites take care of activities within their vicinity by managing daily overlapping working hours. During these overlapping hours, team members from two sites hand on tasks to the next site during "*hand-on and shake off*" sessions.

> *"There are always overlapping hour between two team sites to cover 'hand-on and shake-off' sessions. This process is followed between other team's sites throughout the day. During these overlapping hours members from departing team communicate about the work they have carried out and what needs to be done further".*

The interdependencies such as each site's goal and objectives that are dependent on the other sites have to be taken into consideration while building bridges [33]. The bridge teams should match the bridging function and team members must be compatible with the cultures they are interacting [21]. A particular location has to be selected based primarily on the existing or real availability of the experienced staff that can support the staffing requirements [26]. Physical closeness such as distance and time zone between sites is also important – thus allowing overlap in working hours.

Management of Attrition: Attrition is intrinsic to any business or industry and is an issue within the Indian software industry because the industry is young, thriving and growing. Managing attrition levels is important within the companies we researched. Appropriate steps include the understanding of triggers, and subsequently the management of this attrition.

In our empirical research we found that team members aspire to progress in their career through extending their skills and work experience. Team members may have different priorities in their life as they look for useful and exciting work in the initial stage of their career. Satisfying, supportive and varied work opportunities are shown to be important to the practitioner and may be more of a hook than competitive salary packages.

In some cases team members prefer to be close to their home town. Therefore they look for suitable opportunities. In other cases, team members look for new and more challenging jobs which will increase their knowledge -

> *"We have understood the main reason for attrition…..it is because people want to explore new opportunities that are available in the industry and they also look for new and more challenging jobs to work on at the initial stage of their career."*

As there are various opportunities available in the software industry internationally, Indian software professionals are often mobile, especially when they are young and have less family responsibilities. We have also observed that entry level professionals or fresher's change their jobs quite often as they get better benefits within each change. However, it is expected that once the software industry matures, the level of attrition will gradually fall.

There are various measures taken to overcome attrition levels in Indian software companies. Project managers must ensure task allocation is based on interest, work satisfaction and skills development. Team members are often allowed work hours to suit their particular circumstance. Job rotation can be introduced so that team members can continually develop their competencies. Additionally, project managers should try to develop multiple skill sets within their teams with the intention that team members can be replaced on any task.

Task Allocation: Appropriate task allocation is important while coordinating various tasks in software development projects. Allocation of task to the resources in the distributed teams is important to harness the potential of the 24-hour software development model and minimize the completion time of a GSD project [20]. The objective of task allocation must be to assign tasks to the available resources so as to complete the project in shortest duration. Task allocation can be a moderating variable to improve coordination between teams in GSD projects [45].During our empirical research we found that, in order to coordinate between tasks, they are often broken down and subdivided before they are assigned. The project managers take into consideration the strengths and interests of the team members while allocating tasks to them. Technical and domain knowledge, work experience and personal interest, skills sets and capabilities of the team members is considered. Project managers judge task allocation as important so that the team members can enjoy their part of work within the project.

Various other strategies are followed when allocating tasks. Job rotation is the main strategy practiced by project managers. This helps them to enhance various skill sets, allocate resources efficiently, and plan towards training, skills development and future resource allocation. As mentioned under attrition above, this will also contribute towards the reduction of staff turnover. A flexible yet strategic approach to task allocation is clearly shown in this quote from one of the project managers we interviewed -

> *"If a team member is not very keen on coding part of the project and is more interested in communicating with the clients or customers...then we allocate him the communicator's role within the project.... Thus understanding their working interest and behavior helps us analyse and make such decisions".*

The consequence of this is that project managers must be able to understand and analyse available skill sets, interests of the project team members and project requirements when allocating tasks.

Appropriate task allocation helps to coordinate activities more efficiently within the project. It also helps to build cohesive teams within the project and overcome conflicts and other issues that can arise in the project.

6 Discussion

The study carried out has allowed us to identify what happens in GSD practice in vendor sites. This is a viewpoint which has not often been presented in GSD literature. It has been important to carry out this research, as we have identified a number of strategies which have not been publicized in literature. For instance, the team selection process has identified approaches taken while selecting team members to work on the GSD project. Similarly, the team building process has helped us, as researchers, to understand what steps vendors take to build cohesive teams to work on the GSD projects. The empirical study has also allowed us to throw light on various strategies revealed within the literature and also to understand the issues that impede GSD, particularly from the vendor perspective. The study has presented how the vendor companies manage temporal differences by scheduling *hand-on and shake-off* sessions given the client's time zone. One of the substantial finding of this empirical research study is that of managing cultural diversity that exists within the GSD projects by setting up *backup* teams. India is a large and diverse nation with many religious and culturally diverse groups. This study has revealed how the project managers cope with the demands of cultural differences imposed by a geographically distributed environment [22]. These backup teams' help to coordinate various tasks and overcome the potential loss of support and communication during festive and religious holidays, providing support 365 days per year, thus transforming cultural differences into strengths.

So, what answer can we give to our research question: *Can the PMBOK® Guide help to address coordination issues and challenges in GSD projects from the vendor perspective?*

In the first instance, there are some sections in PMBOK® Guide which can indeed help to address GSD coordination issues and challenges, and we have presented evidence to show that these can and do work in practice. Secondly, there are PMBOK® Guide sections which have not been presented previously in GSD literature and we have not observed them in practice. We propose that these can be useful to the GSD vendor community. Thirdly, this research has shown that the PMBOK® Guide is not complete for GSD. This is not a surprising result, as the PMBOK® Guide was not developed for GSD. So, yes, the PMBOK® Guide helps to address coordination issues and challenges in GSD projects from the vendor perspective, but, currently, this is not sufficient as there are strategies, not in the guide, which are needed.

The process mentioned in the human resource management section and performed in practice by GSD teams assist us to emphasise their importance to manage and coordinate software development teams in GSD environment. The team building activity is necessary to improve interpersonal relationships within the teams and help team members' work together and establish good working relationships across geographical boundaries. The emphasis given by the PMBOK® Guide on taking advantage of cultural differences supports our assertion of transforming cultural differences into strengths [22]. Team performance assessments help to gauge the existing competency within the team. These processes are crucial and have an influence on the effectiveness of GSD project success.

We have also documented particular processes mentioned in the human resource management section of the PMBOK® Guide but not used in the GSD environment. In answer to our research question we found that the Guide does indeed help us to address coordination techniques in GSD projects by highlighting some new areas to consider. These processes can help to improve coordination in GSD projects. An organisational chart is one of the essential processes that must be followed in GSD projects. Organisational charts can explain the position of various teams and team members and display their reporting relationships. They can also help to precisely define and include roles and responsibilities and the position of teams and team members within the GSD project. Also, a resource calendar can be maintained to estimate the level of expertise available for the project.

The coordination practices such as onsite coordinators, bridging the sites, managing attrition and task allocation are not mentioned in the human resource management section of the PMBOK® Guide. Onsite coordinators help to manage cultural diversity by bridging the sites through cultural and linguistic differences between teams and facilitating organizational flow of communication.

Understanding the triggers that cause attrition can help both client and vendor companies to take necessary steps to overcome it. In task allocation it is essential to consider the strengths and interests of the team members. This helps in motivation and team members can enjoy their part of the work within the project. These practices are well established and followed by vendor companies and are endorsed by the client companies in GSD. Therefore these practices need to be acknowledged and included as part of regular practice to ensure the success of the GSD project.

7 Conclusion

While the PMBOK® Guide is the standard document for project management process, the results of our comparative analysis focusing on coordination strategies indicates that its scope is limited when applied to GSD projects, as it does not take all the challenges and issues of GSD into account. Therefore, this research has identified the need for a structured set of standards which focus specifically on coordination in

Global Software Development. It has proved useful to identify processess that will support coordination between geographically distributed software development sites, and following from this research, we are developing a GSD coordination model which uses the PMBOK® Guide as a basis. This will support project managers in overcoming GSD coordination challenges and issues, and, given the origin of the research within industrial practice, this should be a useful model with GSD vendor sites.

References

1. Sengupta, B., Chandra, S., Sinha, V.: A research agenda for distributed software development. In: Proceedings of the 28th International Conference on Software Engineering (ICSE 2006), Shanghai, China, May 20-28, pp. 731–740 (2006)
2. Herbsleb, J.D., Moitra, D.: Global Software Development. IEEE Software 18(2), 16–20 (2001)
3. Carmel, E., Agarwal, R.: Tactical Approaches for Alleviating Distance in Global Software Development. IEEE Software 18(2), 22–29.26 (2001)
4. Casey, V., Richardson. I.: Uncovering the Reality within Virtual Software Teams. In: International Conference on Global Software Engineering, ICGSE 2006 (2006)
5. Ralyte, J., Lamielle, X., Arni-Bloch, N., Leonard, M.: A framework for supporting management in distributed information systems development. In: Proceedings of Second International Conference on Research Challenges in Information Science, RCIS, June 3-6, pp. 381–392 (2008)
6. Bass, M., Paulish, D.: Global Software Development Process Research at Siemens. In: The 3rd Int. Workshop on Global Software Development (co-located with ICSE 2004), `http://www.icse-conferences.org/2004/` (2004)
7. Deshpande, S., Richardson, I.: Management at the Outsourcing Destination –Global Software Development in India. In: International Conference on Global Software Engineering (ICGSE 2009), pp. 217–225. IEEE, Limerick (2009)
8. Herbsleb, J.D.: Global Software Engineering: The Future of Socio-technical Coordination. In: Future of Software Engineering (FOSE 2007). IEEE, Minneapolis (2007)
9. Kitchenham, B.: Procedures for Performing Systematic Reviews, Keele University and National ICT Australia Ltd., Technical Report Keele University Technical Report TR/SE-0401 and NICTA Technical Report 0400011T.1 (June 2004)
10. Deshpande, S., Beecham, S., Richardson, I.: A Literature Review of Coordination Strategies in Global Software Development, LERO, The Irish Software Engineering Research Centre, Technical Report 2010-07 (January 2011)
11. PMBOK® Guide. 4th edn., Project Management Institute, New Town Square, Pennsylvania (2008) ISBN-10: 1933890517 & ISBN-13: 978-1933890517
12. Begel, A., Nagappan, N., Poile, C., Layman, L.: Coordination in large-scale software teams. In: Proceedings of 2009 ICSE Workshop on Cooperative and Human Aspects on Software Engineering (CHASE), pp. 1–7. IEEE Computer Society, Washington, DC (2009)
13. Espinosa, J.A., Carmel, E.: The Effect of Time Separation on Coordination Costs in Global Software Teams: A Dyad Model. In: Proceedings of the 37th Annual Hawaii International Conference on System Sciences (Hicss 2004) - Track 1, January 5-8, vol. 1. IEEE Computer Society, Washington, DC (2004)
14. Malone, T.W., Crowston, K.: What is coordination theory and how can it help design cooperative work systems? In: Proceedings of the Conference on Computer-Supported Cooperative Work CSCW 1990. ACM Press, Los Angeles (1990); reprinted in Marca, D.,

Bock, G. (eds.): Groupware: Software for Computer-Supported Cooperative Work. IEEE Computer Society Press, Los Alamitos (1992); also reprinted in Baecker, R.M. (ed.): Readings in Groupware and Computer Supported Cooperative Work. Morgan Kaufmann Publishers, San Mateo (1993)

15. Malone, T.W., Crowston, K.: The interdisciplinary study of coordination. ACM Computing Surveys 26(1), 87–119 (1994)
16. Carmel, E., Tija, P.: Offshoring Information Technology: Sourcing and Outsourcing to a Global Workforce. Cambridge University Press, Cambridge (2005)
17. Goles, T., Wynne, W.C.: Information systems outsourcing relationship factors: detailed conceptualization and initial evidence. SIGMIS Database 36(4), 47–67 (2005)
18. Herbsleb, J.D., Mockus, A., Finholt, T.A., Grinter, R.E.: An empirical study of global software development: Distance and speed. In: Proceedings of International Conference on Software Engineering (ICSE 2001), Toronto, Canada, May 15-18, pp. 81–90 (2001)
19. Narayanan, S., Mazumder, S., Raju, R.: Success of Offshore Relationships: Engineering team structures. In: Proceedings of the IEEE International Conference on Global Software Engineering, ICGSE, October 16 - 19, pp. 73–82. IEEE Computer Society, Washington, DC (2006)
20. Jalote, P., Jain, G.: Assigning Tasks in a 24-Hour Software Development Model. In: Proceedings of the 11th Asia-Pacific Software Engineering Conference, APSEC, November 30 - December 3, pp. 309–315. IEEE Computer Society, Washington, DC (2004)
21. Milewski, A.E., Tremaine, M., Egan, R., Zhang, S., Kobler, F., O'Sullivan, P.: Guidelines for Effective Bridging in Global Software Engineering. In: International Conference on Global Software Engineering (ICGSE 2008), Bangalore, India, pp. 23–32 (2008)
22. Deshpande, S., Richardson, I., Casey, V., Beecham, S.: Culture in Global Software development - a Weakness or Strength? In: IEEE International Conferences on Global Software Engineering (ICGSE 2010), Princeton, USA, August 23-26 (2010)
23. Bradner, E., Mark, G., Hertel, T.D.: Team size and technology fit: Participation, awareness, and rapport in distributed teams. IEEE Transactions on Professional Communication 48(1), 68–77 (2005)
24. Espinosa, J.A., Slaughter, S.A., Herbsleb, J.D., Kraut, R.E.: Coordination Mechanisms in Globally Distributed Software Development. In: First International Conference on Management of Globally Distributed Work, Bangalore, India (2005)
25. Keith, M., Demirkan, H., Goul, M.: Understanding Coordination in IT Project-Based Environments: An Examination of Team Cognition and Virtual Team Efficacy. In: 42nd Hawaii International Conference on System Sciences, HICSS, pp. 1–8 (2009)
26. Battin, R.D., Crocker, R., Kreidler, J., Subramanian, K.: Leveraging Resources in Global Software Development. IEEE Software 18(2), 70–77 (2001)
27. Begel, A., Nagappan, N.: Global Software Development: Who Does It? In: International Conference on Global Software Engineering (ICGSE 2008), Bangalore, India, August 17-20, pp. 195–199 (2008)
28. Bass, M., Herbsleb, J.D., Lescher, C.: Collaboration in Global Software Projects at Siemens: An Experience Report. In: Proceedings of the International Conference on Global Software Engineering ICGSE 2007, August 27-30, pp. 33–39. IEEE Computer Society, Washington, DC (2007)
29. Hogan, B.: Lessons Learned from an eXtremely Distributed Project. In: Proceedings of the Conference on AGILE 2006, July 23-28, pp. 321–326. IEEE Computer Society, Washington, DC (2006)

30. Pichler, H.: Be successful, take a hostage or "outsourcing the outsourcing Manager". In: Proceedings of the international Conference on Global Software Engineering, ICGSE, pp. 156–161. IEEE Computer Society, Washington, DC (2007)
31. Cataldo, M., Herbsleb, J.D.: Communication patterns in geographically distributed software development and engineers' contributions to the development effort. In: Proceedings of the 2008 International Workshop on Cooperative and Human Aspects of Software Engineering, CHASE 2008, Leipzig, Germany, May 13, pp. 25–28. ACM, New York (2008)
32. Sangwan, R., Bass, M., Mullick, N., Paulish, D.J., Kazmeier, J.: Global Software Development Handbook. Auerbach Publishers (2006)
33. Holmström Olsson, H., Ó Conchúir, E., Ågerfalk, P., Fitzgerald, B.: Two-Stage Offshoring: An Investigation of the Irish Bridge. MIS Quarterly 32(2), 1–23 (2008)
34. Boden, A., Avram, G.: Bridging knowledge distribution - The role of knowledge brokers in distributed software development teams. In: Proceedings of the 2009 ICSE Workshop on Cooperative and Human Aspects on Software Engineering (CHASE), May 17, pp. 8–11. IEEE Computer Society, Washington, DC (2009)
35. von Wangenheim, C.G., Hauck, J.C.R., Zoucas, A., Salviano, C.F., McCaffery, F., Shull, F.: Creating Software Process Capability/Maturity Models. IEEE Software 27(4), 92–94 (2010)
36. Strauss, A., Corbin, J.: Basics of Qualitative Research: Techniques and Procedures for Developing Grounded Theory. Sage Publications, Thousand Oaks (1990)
37. Casey, V.: Leveraging or Exploiting Cultural Difference? In: The 4th IEEE International Conference on Global Software Engineering (ICGSE). IEEE, Limerick (2009)
38. Ojha, N.V., Halla, T., Austen, R., Greyb, S.: Trust in software outsourcing relationships: An empirical investigation of Indian software companies. Information and Software Technology 48, 345–354 (2006)
39. Miles, M.B., Huberman, A.M.: Qualitative Data Analysis: An expanded sourcebook, 2nd edn. Sage, London (1994)
40. Kuzel, A.J.: Sampling in qualitative inquiry. In: Crabtree, B.F., Miller, W.L. (eds.) Doing Qualitative Research. Research Methods for Primary Care Series, vol. 3, pp. 31–44. Sage, Newbury Park (1992)
41. Morse, J.: Qualitative nursing research: A contemporary dialogue. Sage, Newbury Park (1989)
42. Library of Congress. Federal Research Division – Country Profile: India (December 2004), `http://lcweb2.loc.gov/frd/cs/profiles/India.pdf` (retrieved August 11, 2009)
43. Richardson, I., Ó HAodha, M., Casey, V.: Software Testing and Global Industry: Future Paradigms. Cambridge Scholars Publishing, Cambridge (2008) ISBN: 97801-4438-0109-6
44. Carmel, E.: Building your Information Systems from the Other Side of the World: How Infosys manages time differences. Management Information Systems Quarterly -MIS Quarterly Executive 5(1) (2006)
45. Amrit, C.: Coordination in software development: the problem of task allocation. SIGSOFT Softw. Eng. Notes 30(4), 1–7 (2005)

Shared Services Centres: A Case Study on a Dispersed Services Oriented Organization

Irman Nazri Nasir[1], Pamela Abbott[2], and Guy Fitzgerald[2]

[1] No. 8, Jalan Baru 15, Taman Bukit Kajang Baru, 43000, Kajang, Selangor, Malaysia
irmannazri@yahoo.co.uk

[2] Department of Information Systems and Computing, Brunel University, Kingston Lane, UB8 3PH, United Kingdom
{pamela.abbott,guy.fitzgerald}@brunel.ac.uk

Abstract. The provision of shared IT services is a process-focused intra-organisational arrangement that serves clients within the larger parent organization, achieving economies of scale through the creation of specialized knowledge centres. Although there is considerable research on shared services with regard to its conceptual underpinnings, implementation strategies and rationales, research is limited on the actual operation and challenges of the model. Given the importance of a services mindset to modern economies, an in-depth investigation of an IT services organisation is timely and will provide useful insights. This paper reports on a particular instance of a shared services centre using the concept of "service competency" developed in the paper. The paper also draws out the commonalities and differences between the provision of shared services and common outsourcing models. The findings demonstrate the complexities of attempting to provide a service orientation where organisational and operational issues obstruct and conflict with these efforts.

Keywords: Shared services, outsourcing, Malaysia, service competency, service quality, value creation.

1 Introduction

The provision of shared services is an organizational arrangement that seeks to consolidate and streamline commonly used internal business functions and to provide them from central points within an organization [7], [55]. The motivation for a shared services approach stems from the strategic move towards an organisational focus on "core competencies" and rationalisation of resources [1], [7], [20]. Indeed, some of the rationale relates back to the centralisation vs. decentralised organisational structure debates of the 1960s and '70s, as shared services are essentially centralised units delivering services to decentralised units. Child suggested that the risks of greater decentralisation would be compensated for by the formulation of procedures, rules and standards by senior management [13]. Donaldson et al. described this as a "compensatory relationship between greater delegation of decision making and

J. Kotlarsky, L.P. Willcocks, and I. Oshri (Eds.): Global Sourcing 2011, LNBIP 91, pp. 175–200, 2011.

greater structuring through bureaucratic controls" [17]. There was empirical support for this from various studies, albeit in the context of manufacturing organisations. Shared services are concentrated within one or more business units of an organization where the particular specialty resides. The idea is to create services based on process-oriented approaches to organising which may use IT platforms as a means of implementation. Shared services are expected to achieve economies of scale through the creation of these separate specialized entities providing services to internal clients [7], [29].

Shared services can be as seen both an alternative to outsourcing as well as an interim step towards full outsourcing of services [1], [63]. Where the governance arrangements allow for the shared service provider to be a sub-unit or fully owned subsidiary of the host organisation, the arrangement is seen to be similar to insourcing [1], [32]. In this case, there are two configurations: the shared services centre, (one business unit that only offers services to other units which are all receivers of those services) and the shared services network (several business units that offer and/or receive services from/to other business units [6]. The shared service provider can also be a 3rd party-owned business unit, in which case it can be referred to by the more generic term, shared services organisation [1].

Shared services configurations tend to focus on public administration, human resources services, IT services and support, back-office processes, customer services and call centres [20], [24], [38], [59], [68]. Regardless of the governance structures, issues found pertinent in the outsourcing literature to sourcing arrangements also pertain to shared services, e.g. production versus transaction costs, politics and power in client/provider relationships and strategic considerations [31]. Where the shared services units are geographically dispersed, issues related to distance, cultural barriers and client relationships are likely to be just as relevant and challenging as they are in the outsourcing literature. In-depth case studies related to the functioning of shared services centres, however, are sparse. This paper intends to fill that gap by reporting on a particular instance of shared services centre in Malaysia. In this context the paper addresses the issues of shared services and positions them in relation to the literature and the domain of outsourcing, with which they are often compared. In particular, the paper addresses the service concept in shared services relating to competencies and suggests that there is a neglected competence category that is identified as "service competency".

SSC emphasizes standardisation, best practices and specialized knowledge to achieve customer benefits, however, the success or failure of an SSC as a service organisation relies largely on employees' capabilities in delivering quality and reliable services. This capacity in turn, is related to the contractual conditions and governance mechanisms in place between the client and supplier units [24]. To investigate these issues further, this paper will explore (1) the notion of SSCs as a form of services organization, and (2) the relationship between models of sourcing (outsourcing, insourcing) that exist in the literature and the shared service model. With regard to (1) the paper will introduce the concept of "service competency" and illustrate through the case study how this concept may work in practice. In relation to (2) the paper will draw out the commonalities and differences between the provision of shared services and common outsourcing models of governance and compare how the case study organization accommodated these models of governance. The guiding research questions are therefore: (1) in shared services arrangements what structures and capabilities/competencies are in place to provide customer benefit and (2) how do these relate to the more familiar outsourcing models?

The paper is organised in the following way. The literature review investigates three aspects of shared services: capabilities and competencies necessary for interfacing with customers effectively; how service-related competencies fit within this background; and comparisons of outsourcing and shared services models. The methodology section presents the context and the case study organisation along with the method used in the research. The results section outlines the findings of the case while the discussion and conclusion sections discuss the implications of the findings and their relevance to practice.

2 Literature Review

The emergence of "services" as a cornerstone of contemporary economic activity in advanced economies has recently received much scrutiny and attention in a variety of literature across multiple disciplines e.g. marketing, economics, information systems [4], [11], [12], [25]. Information and Communication Technologies (ICTs) are also seen to be pivotal to the growth and sustainability of a services-based economy [3]. The processes of globalisation, another recent phenomenon, are thought to be propelled by the ubiquity and extent of ICT proliferation and to play a part in the growth of the services industry mainly through the internationalisation of the labour market [11], [66]. Organisations that adopt a service-oriented view seek to benefit from their core competencies and specialist knowledge, market to clients who could benefit from these competencies, collaborate with customers, and rely on financial returns as a key indicator of customer satisfaction [66]. But in order for client and vendor in a services-based exchange to realise value there must be an understanding between them as to what constitutes value and how the capability of the vendor can meet the client's needs [12], [25], [66]. Value is the benefit a client perceives from the interaction with the service provider and value creation is a collaborative process between the service organisation and the client [25], [67]. Therefore, the value proposition of the service organisation is itself open to negotiation and essentially serves to provide a match between specialised knowledge (from the service provider) and negotiated expectations (from the client's side). This is achieved through the development of capabilities and competencies on the part of the service provider.

2.1 Competencies and Capabilities in IS Service Provision

The most common functions provided by SSCs are IT services and support, back-office processes, customer service and call centres, and human resource activities [20], [38], [59]. The need to develop and support e-government and procurement facilities has also encouraged the public sector to apply this service delivery model [28], [30], [44]. This paper looks specifically at SSCs that specialise in consolidated IT-enabled back-office services. As such, these SSCs core competencies lie in acquiring the knowledge and skills required to enable smooth operation of the IT-enabled functions and their distribution in a seamless manner throughout a dispersed organisation. This may be likened to providing an intra- or inter-organizational IS function. Hence, in order to investigate competencies and capabilities likely to be associated with these types of shared service centres, a discussion of the capabilities and competencies related to the IS function would be useful and relevant. Below are organisational perspectives on IT/IS competencies taken both from the internal IS function and the external third-party service provider viewpoints.

The development of capabilities and competencies intra-organizationally within the IS function has been a long standing topic in the IS literature related to strategy and competitiveness [8], [47]. The literature has focused on establishing descriptions of IT competence/capability at the individual and organizational levels [5], [53], [54]. A number of these sources take a resource-based perspective emphasizing the development of particular IT competencies and capabilities. Ross et al., for example, relate a strong IT capability to the development of IT assets (human resources, technology infrastructure and the relationship between the IS function and the business side) [49]. Feeny and Willcocks develop a framework of nine IS capabilities that organizations need to embrace when attempting to exploit IT for strategic benefit. These nine areas are grouped into three broad categories: Business and IT vision, Design of IT Architecture and Delivery of IS Services [19]. Bharadwaj reviewed IT-related resources of the firm and concluded that IT capability lies in a firm's IT infrastructure, its human skills and its ability to use IT for intangible benefits, such as improved customer service [8]. Peppard and Ward claim that the development of IT capability is contingent on the acquisition of appropriate resources and the development of competencies. Their competency framework covers six macro areas: formulating strategy, defining the IS contribution, defining the IT capability, exploiting IS, delivering solutions and managing the supply chain for IS capacity [47].

There is also a stream of IS literature that engages with capabilities and competencies from the inter-organizational standpoint of IT/IS service providers and IS outsourcing vendors and their relationships with their clients [58]. It can be argued that since shared services centres have elements in common with outsourcing and insourcing models, these competencies and capabilities are also relevant for discussion. From the outsourcing literature, Goles identifies technological and relationship management capabilities as key to customer satisfaction with vendor performance [21]. Levina and Ross posit that complementarities between the vendor's and client's core competencies helps to promote a value proposition that is favourable to the client [40]. From a Business Process Outsourcing (BPO) perspective, where the prime consideration is the delivery of IT-enabled business services, Feeny et al. identify twelve specific supplier capabilities considered critical in order for an outsourcing vendor to supply contracted services [18]. The twelve capabilities are organised into three competency categories: delivery (the ability to match the customer's service expectations); relationship (the ability to match client's needs over time) and; transformation (the ability to work with the client to achieve improvements to business processes and performance). Five competencies have also been identified in another study [9], namely, Business Process Management Competency, Human

Resource Management Competency, IT Management Competency, Outsourcing Management Competency, and Relationship Management Competency.

The competencies/capabilities identified above are not exhaustive and indeed there are not many studies that examine the topic in-depth [21], [40], [47]. We have explored key literature that explicitly attempts to identify generic categories that may affect the interaction between client and service provider, whether that service provider is an internal or external entity. Broadly speaking, these competency categories fall into the following areas: (1) human resource skill development, (2) relationship management, (3) technological management, (4) exploitation of business domain knowledge, (5) service delivery management and (6) alignment of core competencies (e.g. client to vendor, business-side to service-centre-side). Although presented as separate areas, these generic categories are in effect, interrelated and overlapping, since they interact with each other to help provide the necessary services. Very few studies, however, examine the relationship between these competencies and the customer's perceived benefits [40]. Although there may be some connection between competencies and value generation, none of the competency categories identified above explicitly address issues concerning creating customer benefit through value co-creation and the customer's perception of the SSCs capability to generate that value. The next section therefore evolves a competency category that we feel is more closely related to providing customer benefit. It looks at the SSC's value proposition and how "service competency" may be developed to help achieve customer benefit.

2.2 Service Competency and Customers' Perception of Value

The specific value proposition of an SSC is related to four broad client objectives: cost reduction, efficiency gains, economies of scope and improved service [1], [7], [32], [63], [68]. By sharing services in a centralized IT location, cost per unit decreases as volume increases [1], [20], [41], [59], [64]. Headcount also decreases across multiple sites [32]. Economies of scope are introduced with services being broadly available to all organisational units especially with regard to knowledge [63], [68], where specialized know-how is more easily distributed through the client network. A shared services approach may also increase opportunities for innovation through better focus on clients' needs [7], [32], [63]. By utilizing standardized services across the organisation and streamlining of business processes, duplicated procedures are eliminated leading to increased efficiencies [59]. Shared services are also argued to improve the cycle time normally associated with functional tasks and to adopt process-centred improvement in quality such as continuous improvement strategies [48], [59]. The process-oriented approach leads to a focus on measurement of outcomes and performance-oriented targets related to a mindset of continuous improvement [1], [63]. Standardization and continuous improvement along with improved opportunities for innovation are expected to lead to improved service quality [63]. A stronger emphasis on core competencies is also envisaged [1], [68].

Generally speaking, the elements of the value proposition of an SSC, as outlined above, are covered by the generic competencies discussed in the previous section. For example, in order to achieve client expectations of cost reduction through shared centralised IT services, competencies such as technological management and service delivery management need to be developed. If the nature or amount of cost reduction needs to be negotiated, then some competency in relationship management would be an asset as well. Since service provision is the raison d'être of the SSC, however, a customer focus should be important in all interactions with the client. We need to explore, therefore, how a competency related to this aspect can be developed. We propose, in this paper, a complementary notion of competence specific to the SSC organisation: "service competency". The term competency, itself, refers to skills, technologies, capacities and knowledge in utilizing firm resources to accomplish given tasks [8], [27], [47], [56]. Services can be referred to as the value creating aspects of business transactions [66] and service provision as the process through which specialised competencies are applied in the realisation of benefits for another entity, where that entity, in some way, participates in the value creating process [67]. Service competency, therefore, would be those skills, technologies, capacities and knowledge that enable the service organisation (e.g. SSC) to provide value (customer benefit) that consistently satisfies customer expectations.

There are existing proxies in the literature for this concept, however, they are inadequate to reflect the notions of service developed above. For example, traditionally, organisations assess service offerings through service quality and customer satisfaction measures [26], [45], [46], [50], [51], [62]. Johnston defines customer satisfaction as the outcome of particular business transactions in an overall encounter with the service provision, while service quality is seen as the overall impression given by the service provider in the whole process of interaction with the customer [35]. Customer satisfaction is thought to be related to measuring outcomes of service as compared with expectations of that service [50], [51]. Service quality can be measured by five dimensions of service: 'reliability' (dependable and accurate service), 'tangibles' (observable and measurable output), 'responsiveness' (timeliness of service execution), 'assurance' (interaction, relationship, and customers confidence), and 'empathy' (understanding of customer's needs) [23], [45], [46], [50]. Customer satisfaction and service quality are often conflated or combined in studies [15], [37], [62]. A critical debate that emerges from the literature is the gap between customer expectations and perceptions of service, that is whether customers actually perceive benefits in the service encounter that match their expectations or whether managers accurately gauged customers' expectations in the first place [34], [35], [65]. Our conceptualisation of service competency tries to avoid these controversies and encapsulates the more recent literature advocating the active involvement of clients in co-creating value within customer/ service provider encounters [25], [33], [67]. As such, it is a competency that is co-developed with customers. It can stand on its own as a separate competency needed by service provider organisations or it can be seen as the customer-facing, value-generating aspects of the other generic competencies reviewed in the previous section.

2.3 Shared Services vs. Outsourcing

According to Janssen and Joha adopting an SSC is a major decision having a long-term strategic impact, which is often in competition with outsourcing [32]. Thus, a brief consideration of some of the similarities and differences is appropriate. Shared Services and Outsourcing models have been differentiated in various ways. A number of authors have differentiated along the lines of service scope, resource ownership, and commercial relationship [14], [16], [32], [52]. Others, e.g. Frost & Sullivan posit four configurations that incorporate both shared services and outsourcing models, distinguishing them on the basis of offshore and onshore, and insourced and outsoured [20]. Insourced arrangements will include SSCs, i.e. service providers that are part of the organisation or controlled units (fully or partially owned) but which may differ in terms of location. Companies who choose to set up an SSC can locate the organisation locally (onshore) or remotely (offshore). Outsourced arrangements typically refer to external service providers, usually with no relation in ownership to their customers (although there are some examples of wholly owned outsourced subsidiaries), and may include those organisations that offer specialised services to particular clients.

Further differences between SSC and Outsourcing have been identified in contract, structure, interaction, behaviour and outcome dimensions [32]. Outsourcing offers faster implementation, rapid cost reduction, low up-front cost, and best practices [16], [52]. Either fully or selectively outsourced, companies can benefit faster due to low up-front costs through the approach of 'lift and shift' to designated vendors. Quality service is assured if the vendor has adopted best practices and has extensive experience.

In contrast, SSC formation is based purely on the internal arrangements of the organization. As an internal operation, SSCs are often cost centres rather than profit centres [52]. Services charges are based on usage and there is evidence of service agreements between the SSC and its customers, SLAs for instance. SLAs are also often seen in outsourcing contracts [22] but typically an outsourcing contract would address much more than purely service level issues and be a more formal and legally binding contract [32]. The SSC acts as a business partner for its customers that are composed of different units and divisions of the same company (more complex forms of SSCs may act for a range of organisations). The SSC, in general, addresses relationships between many clients and one vendor, as does outsourcing, while the risks in outcome are shared within the organization. The SSC is effective in imposing standards and rules and is an important risk reduction technique. It also offers more control and transparency of costs [32] whereas with outsourcing risks are typically transferred to the vendor. Different configurations determine the achievability of differing goals and involve different risks [14], [16], [52] and there is probably a range between vertical integration of an activity or function and total outsourcing of the whole function, with trade-offs inherent in each case.

Previous studies show that 70% of outsourcing clients have negative experiences with up to 25% of clients bringing outsourced services back in-house [2]. However, there is a significant association between SSC insourcing and the nurturing of IT-enabled business processes [48]. This is due to the internal coordination related to an in-house centre which has the potential to enhance strategic alignment and knowledge management. Tasks carried out in an SSC are meant to retain and consolidate core in-house processes. Outsourcing poses risks in this domain (typically in business process outsourcing) where clients lack the skills and understanding of the activities performed by the vendor [2]. Furthermore, keeping the core processes in-house will secure control and privacy. According to Lowes,

"Outsourcing tends to make the most sense when an organization is looking for fundamental change, wants to move quickly, and views cost reduction as a top priority. The organization acknowledges the vendor's superior systems, processes, talent, and scale economies, and wants to take advantage of them. A shared services approach tends to make the most sense when control is a top priority, and when the activities in question are unique to the organization. However, success hinges on having adequate systems, processes, talent, and scale. If these are not on par with what an outsourcing vendor offers, it is hard for shared services to be competitive." (Lowes, P., Deloitte [16] *, p. 3).*

Combining the benefits from two types of business model of in-house centralization and decentralization means inheriting the disadvantages as well [29]. Whoever runs the service delivery activities must be sufficiently competent to provide services to another party. A service provider (as in 'an employee of an SSC') must acquire the service oriented mindset to satisfy customer's needs and create a professional service organisation as a whole.

Having looked at the SSC literature and the similarities and differences with outsourcing we now turn to the SSC case and the lessons learnt.

3 Methodology

In the following sections, the context of the research is explained and the case study organization is described. The research methods used in the study are then detailed.

3.1 Research Context

The case study presents an SSC organisation located in Malaysia that operates as the regional headquarters in business and IT/IS services for a European chemical company serving the Asia Pacific region. Core activities in the SSC consist of back-office functions of an Enterprise Resource Planning (ERP) system implemented by the organisation. Malaysia has recently been gaining a reputation as a global ICT hub. In 2005, Malaysia was ranked third and second in Shared Services and Outsourcing (SSO) hubs for the financial and energy sectors respectively [20]. With the status as one of world's top ranked SSO locations, Malaysia is the choice for many global and regional operations of top international companies such as ACS, BMW, DHL, HSBC, IBM, Intel, Motorola, Nokia, Shell and Unisys [42], [43].

Malaysia's key strengths in attracting investors are affordable costs, modern infrastructure, a skilled labour force, and a favourable business environment. The inception of the Multimedia Super Corridor (MSC) has been regarded as the biggest contributor to Malaysia's development in the IT industry. Developed in multiple areas spanning approximately 15x50 km^2 south of downtown Kuala Lumpur, the MSC is expected to be a hub for global and/or regional operations in Asia and for global test beds and solutions [42], [43]. The investment in designated "cyber cities" is also supported by the government's 10-point Bill of Guarantees. Among other benefits, this initiative brings competitive financial incentives such as Pioneer Status (100% exemption of taxable statutory income for the first 5 years) and Investment Tax Allowances. The freedom to source capital and funds while being offered globally competitive telecommunication tariffs in a world class infrastructure also attracts big players in the industry.

The low and attractive labour costs impact the cost efficiency of SSC operations. In 2004, Malaysia was ranked second lowest among seven other countries in terms of loaded cost per person which only amounted to 20% of an equivalent worker in the USA [60]. Malaysia also enjoys low wage inflation rates (around 5.5%) which is important in considering cost of labour over a period of time [20]. However, despite the notable lower costs, Malaysia claims to offer unique characteristics and quality in human capital. Malaysia's multi-racial society has provided the nation with a multi-lingual workforce, typically with proficiency in more than one language besides English, which proves to be crucial in SSC operations, particularly in managing the dynamic nature of global project management operations [20].

The nation's political stability and continuous government support also generate confidence among global companies to set up their SSC operations in Malaysia. For example, in 2010 the MSC initiative started its third phase with a target to establish 500 world-class companies under the MSC brand [42], [43]. Shared Services is one of the key business areas expected to contribute to the MSC milestones. The services sector in Malaysia is divided into two types; SSC-Insource where services are provided and delivered internally (i.e. DHL, HSBC, BAT and Shell SSCs), the traditional SSC model and what they term SSC-Outsource which involves partnerships with external providers (i.e. EDS, IBM, Satyam and Unisys)[42].

3.2 Case Study Organisation

The case study was carried out in an SSC in Kuala Lumpur, Malaysia. Due to confidentiality agreements, it will be referred to as SSC-A in this paper. SSC-A is an IT Services regional hub of a European chemical company for the Asia Pacific region. The company produces chemical solvents, plastics, performance chemicals, agricultural products, and oil and gas for various industries such as automotive, pharmaceutical, manufacturing, fabric and petroleum. In 2004, the company's sales in Asia Pacific amounted to €5,300 million with production in Malaysia accounting for 57% of sales.

The company hosts plants, factories, offices, and operation hubs in the Asia-Pacific region comprising 30 subsidiaries and 23 joint ventures with over 11,000 employees and is engaged in ongoing mergers and acquisitions. SSC-A was formed in 2005 as part of an initiative to centralize business operations and processes via an ERP system, the chosen ERP system being SAP. At about the same time, the company also launched a similar SSC operation for finance and accounting, human resources and information technology to service Europe in East Berlin, Germany. According to the company, both SSCs were scheduled to be in full operation by the end of 2005 and were to replace services provided by more than 150 local units across the two regions.

With investment of over €21 million, the company's board of executives responsible for the Asia-Pacific region hoped that the regional SSC would increase the firm's flexibility and strengthen their overall competitiveness. At the point of SSC-A's inception, its staff of 130 were estimated to expand to 400 when fully operational, by 2007. At the point of this study (as of July 2010), SSC-A employee headcount was recorded at 428 consisting of staff from the main functional areas of Finance and Accounting, Human Resource Services and IT/IS and Service Management. As of the end of 2009, the company's overall business in Asia Pacific included 51 subsidiaries and 33 joint ventures, 13,700 employees, more than 100 production sites, 15 research and development facilities and customers located in 15 countries across the region.

3.3 Methods

In-depth case studies of shared services centres are limited [6], [44], therefore it was decided that an exploratory case study research approach [69] should be undertaken. A mixed methods approach combining both qualitative and quantitative methods [10] was adopted in order to triangulate findings and increase credibility of the results. The case study organisation, SSC-A, was selected based on three criteria that fit this research topic: (1) the SSC in the study should be a hub of business functions with multiple numbers of customers, (2) the SSC in the study should use a functionally integrated system (such as an ERP) in their service delivery, and (3) the SSC in the study should promote a customer-oriented focus to their operations.

Several sets of data were collected: a survey of 50 SSC-A employees, 5 semi-structured interviews of key personnel, 3 months worth both of error log data on issues related to customer satisfaction and data from SLA reports in addition to document analyses of company guidelines and procedures. The survey was designed to provide demographic data and to cover all aspects relevant to the research topic. Emphasis was placed on the reaction and behaviour of employees towards the training program and relied on Kirkpatrick Model of employee satisfaction toward training [39], as well as questions regarding training programs, learning curves, business process understanding, and customer service skills. The survey was exploratory in keeping with the exploratory nature of the case study and was not designed to confirm or test any hypotheses about the case. Participants were asked to answer on a voluntary basis and a research information sheet was handed out to each respondent. Participants were aware of the objectives of the study and that details given would remain confidential. A consent form was also sent out to each team leader to obtain permission to conduct the survey. 46 survey questionnaires were returned with a response rate of 92%. Frequency and correlation analysis were done in SPSS (Version18.0) on the results of the survey.

The error log is a historical list of problems encountered in the daily tasks of the SSC. It records data such as root cause, issue owner, resolutions and countermeasures related to a particular customer incident. In the error log, mistakes in processing by employees are recorded daily for improvement and audit purposes. These have been extracted and analyzed by issues' root causes. A particular country with an obvious amount of error could have issues, for example, with the business process, data quality, customer's behaviour or system compatibility. Alternatively, a particular team within SSC-A handling certain business processes might register more errors than the others.

The Service Level Agreement (SLA) report is a measure of performance for the service organization, with data related to the output achievement of the service based on the agreed levels of response with customers. SLA analysis shows the amount of ERP transactions executed by SSC-A each month and the percentage accuracy and timeliness of the processing. With reference to the agreed SLA with each customer, the report shows which function, transaction, company and country was responsible for breaching the SLA. In total, 3 months (April, May and June 2010) of error logs and SLA reports were analysed. Analyses are done based on frequencies and cross-referenced by customers/countries and ten categories of error root cause.

To complement and further investigate the core issues pertaining to the quantitative data analysis, qualitative interviews were undertaken [10]. Semi-structured interviews, lasting on average 30 minutes, were carried out with SSC-A staff at managerial and/or higher levels (4 Managers and 1 Senior Manager). The interviews covered the service provider perspective on operational aspects of an SSC, training initiatives and improvement in service quality. Awareness of SAP and business processes, data quality, and knowledge gaps were some of the important factors that were addressed. Participants were asked to answer on a voluntary basis and were informed of the purpose of the research. Documents related to the company's strategy and guidelines concerning service delivery were analysed. Valuable insights were gathered from all interview sessions and document analyses and the thematic analysis method [10] was used to identify themes within the data.

Through the analytical frameworks of service competency and models of sourcing developed in the paper, the case study reveals how service competency is achieved by this organization and illustrates the extent to which organizational arrangements are leveraged to manage typical problems associated with dispersed models of sourcing. These insights give a rich picture of SSC operational issues in one particular context but are also useful for contributing to our understanding of SSC organizational arrangements in general.

4 Results

In this section, the results of the data analyses are presented in three main categories: data pertaining to the SSC-A's arrangements for supporting service delivery obtained from document analyses; survey and error log data analyses; and interview analyses.

4.1 Organisation Structure and Support for Service Delivery

Through detailed analysis of the company's documentation and the interviews the following picture of how the company has structured itself as a service delivery organisation has been evolved. Figure 1 shows the service scope, organisation structure and overview of service delivery in SSC-A.

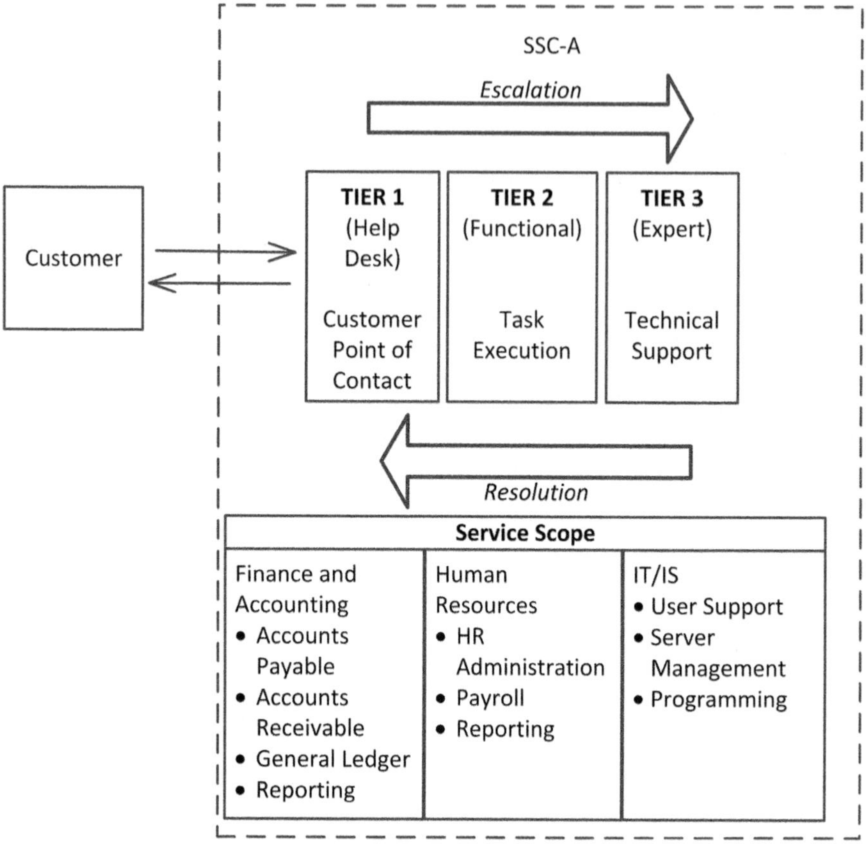

Fig. 1. The organization of service delivery at SSC-A

The analysis also revealed the following mechanisms to be in place which measure and promote a culture of service competency within the organisation. SSC-A has developed their own competency framework which consists of three main categories, with 14 personal competencies derived from the company's characteristics and business requirements. Five of these are considered highly connected to the service environment of SSC-A: Analytical Thinking, Striving for Achievement, Communication and Interpersonal Understanding, Customer Focus, and Intercultural Orientation. According to the company, the rationales of the competency framework are to provide guidance in terms of roles and responsibilities of employees, to identify skill sets and requirements for a job, to prepare the organisation's training and development needs, and as a guideline for performance improvement and assessment.

In SSC-A, the Balanced Scorecard (BSC) approach [36] is used as a means of organising and managing the company. The BSC is defined as an integrated framework for describing strategy through the use of linked performance measures in four balanced perspectives: financial, customer, internal process and employee [36]. It is largely used as a tool in the organisation for business performance evaluation, strategic management and as an internal (management and employees), and external (customers and partners), communication tool. The financial perspective focuses on the financial aspects of the operation: operational costs, costs per service and revenues. The customer perspective provides information on service interaction between SSC-A and its customers, service accessibility and timeliness. The internal process perspective deals more with the operational side of the service delivery: volume, accuracy, and timeliness. Finally, the employee perspective provides the latest status on human resources such as recruitment and attrition figures. Through the BSC, key information can be observed in a systematic way. It also permits observation on trends and changes over time of each agreed service deliverable with each customer.

A comprehensive training program is implemented in SSC-A to fully prepare its employees with related skills prior to involvement with actual service execution. Each new employee undergoes SAP functional or technical training depending on the job descriptions throughout the first week of employment. Here, system-related training such as navigation, business processes and system transactions are carried out in the training simulation environment of SAP. Employees will then be assigned to 'buddy training' where they learn and practice specific tasks assigned to them from a more experienced colleague for a probationary period of at least three months. This may involve simulations in SAP, extracting and processing data in worksheets and progress to running transactions and processing data and requests by customers with high supervision from trainers. Only then, the new joiners are considered ready to "go-live"; they are allowed to handle actual tickets, data and requests from customers.

4.2 Quantitative Results

The employee survey sample amounted to about 10.7% of the total headcount. Figure 2 illustrates the characteristics of the surveyed population. Based on a 5-point likert

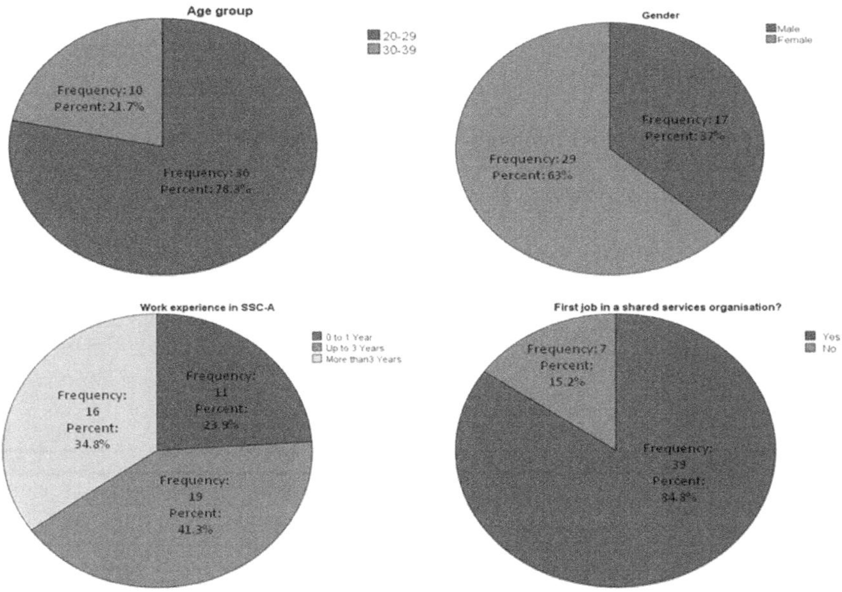

Fig. 2. Survey respondents' profiles

scale, 84.8% (Mean=4.07, Std. Dev. =.389) of respondents considered themselves competent in handling their tasks. 73.9% (Mean=3.76, Std. Dev. =.639) agreed that the BSC helps in better translation of strategy into operational terms. 69.6% (Mean=4.26, Std. Dev. =.491) considered tools such as the SLA, reports and error logs help in their work organisation and continuous development.

More variable results are observed with regards to service delivery. While 54.3% (Mean=3.41, Std. Dev. =.805) considered themselves well-informed on customers' business processes, 17.4% of respondents disagreed with this. Meanwhile, only 50.0% (Mean=3.33, Std. Dev. =.845) rated themselves as fully equipped with customer service knowledge. As illustrated in Table 1, although there are correlations between the two variables (skilled in customer service and competent in handling tasks), a large number of respondents considered there was still a gap in customer service skills (with 21.7% disagreement).

Also, in their opinion, 'constant desire for continuous improvement' (37%) would be the most important aspect of competency they would need to acquire apart from 'strong background in system and business process' (32.6%), 'customer service' (19.6%) and 'language ability' (10.9%).

From the employee survey results, 60.9% (Mean=3.49, Std. Dev. =.895) agreed that the training in SSC-A was sufficient to provide necessary skills in their designated positions. 63.0% (Mean=3.61, Std. Dev. =.745) considered that they have successfully applied what they learned in training into practice. There is also a correlation observed between the responses on competency and training. As observed in Table 2 below, most respondents who considered themselves as competent in handling tasks agreed that they have applied training lessons into practice. In terms of self-rating on understanding of ERP (SAP) system processes, the results show that 45.6% of respondents rated themselves from 'weak' to 'moderate' levels. Ratings on the user-friendliness of SAP system show that 58.7% selected 'moderate' to 'hard'. These prove that although their daily tasks are highly related to the system, the responsibility and accountability of understanding the processes affected end-user acceptance of the ERP system.

Table 1. Crosstabulation (Competent in handling tasks X Skills in customer service)

		Skills in customer service?				Total
		Disagree	Undecided	Agree	Strongly Agree	
Competent in handling tasks?	Undecided	1	1	0	0	2
	Agree	8	10	20	1	39
	Strongly agree	1	1	3	0	5
Total		10	12	23	1	46

		Value	Asymp. Std. Error	Approx. T	Approx. Sig.
Interval by Interval	Pearson's R	.137	.143	.916	.365
Ordinal by Ordinal	Spearman Correlation	.141	.143	.943	.351

Table 2. Crosstabulation (Competent in handling tasks X Training lessons put into practice)

		Training lessons put into practice?				Total
		Disagree	Undecided	Agree	Strongly Agree	
Competent in handling tasks?	Undecided	1	0	1	0	2
	Agree	4	7	26	2	39
	Strongly agree	0	3	2	0	5
Total		5	10	29	2	46

		Value	Asymp. Std. Error	Approx. T	Approx. Sig.
Interval by Interval	Pearson's R	.013	.161	.089	.930
Ordinal by Ordinal	Spearman Correlation	-.066	.165	-.436	.665

From the employee survey, the majority of respondents (32.6%) selected "system issues" as the most common difficulty in executing their daily tasks. "Customer's behaviour" (30.4%) and "lack of business and/or system process knowledge" (26.1%) ranked second and third respectively. When questioned about which aspects of national difference impacted the execution of their tasks, 37.0% selected "difference in regulations or legal requirements" as having a direct impact on their tasks as shown in Figure 3 below.

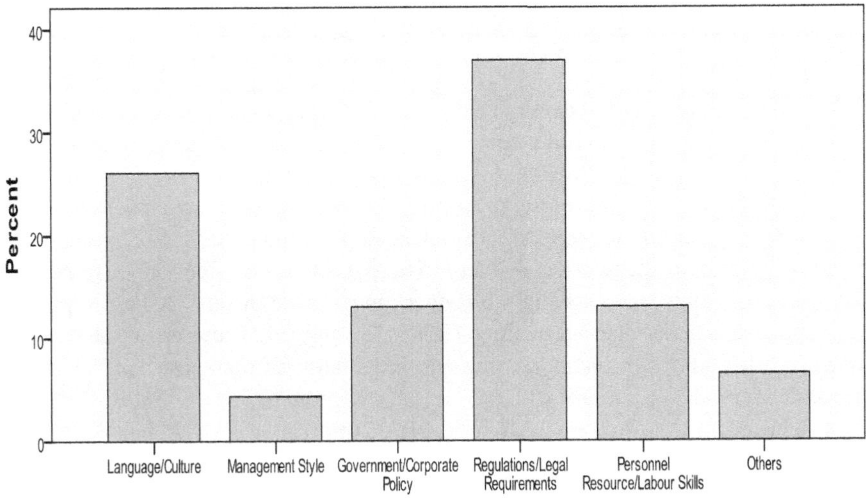

Fig. 3. Aspects of transnational difference which had direct impact on tasks

'Others' in this figure includes a combination of several items and non-applicability due to the fact that some employees only liaise with companies from Malaysia. When asked, however, whether transnational differences have an impact towards delivering quality services, 47.8% (Mean=2.78, Std. Dev. =.987) of respondents disagreed with the statement.

A frequency analysis of issues raised in the error log revealed common mistakes and difficulties in the service delivery of SSC-A. As shown in Table 3 (consolidated from a department in SSC-A), the majority of recorded defects were attributed to customers.

Table 3. Analysis of error root cause issues at SSC-A from April to June 2010

#	Error Root Cause	April	May	June	Total	%
1.	Late Request Submissions	96	41	34	171	26.47
2.	Careless Mistakes	47	41	50	138	21.36
3.	Incorrect Information from Customer	44	39	45	128	19.81
4.	Non-compliance to Standard Process	9	12	29	50	7.74
5.	Knowledge Gap	13	18	17	48	7.43
6.	Incomplete Information from Customer	12	17	18	47	7.28
7.	System Configuration	16	15	5	36	5.57
8.	Others	7	3	7	17	2.63
9.	New Requirements	3	3	3	9	1.39
10.	Timeline Management	0	0	2	2	0.31
	Totals	247	189	210	646	

The "knowledge gap" category which included lack of awareness of certain processes and misunderstandings only rounded up to 7.43% of total errors. 21.36% errors were due to careless mistakes, which were attributed to mass data processing and needed to be monitored closely. Although services were governed by the SLA, and employees needed to support customers at any time, SSC-A customers also played a big role in the service delivery. Their positive contribution, responsibility and task ownership were crucial. Stronger governance needs to be in place to overcome errors in service interactions (Items 1, 3 and 6). These errors also suggest customers' difficulties in understanding and acceptance of the end-to-end process of service delivery.

As depicted in the error analysis in Table 3, training in SSC-A has managed to develop the understanding and capabilities of employees in handling tasks. Further analysis of the error log also shows that, although a small figure, the amount of defects recorded by five new joiners decreased through time.

Table 4. Non-compliance to Standard Process error type categorised by country

	April	May	June	Total
Non-compliance to Standard Process (Totals)	9	12	29	50
Australia	-	1	1	2
China	2	-	2	4
Hong Kong	-	-	9	9
India	-	2	1	3
Indonesia	-	-	1	1
Japan	2	4	5	11
Korea	2	3	2	7
Malaysia	2	1	4	7
Singapore	-	1	4	5
Thailand	1	-	-	1

With reference to previous analysis (Table 3), while errors such as "careless mistakes", "late request submission", "incorrect and incomplete information from customers" did not show any particular relation with countries, patterns can be observed in "non-compliance to standard process" and "system configuration errors". As illustrated in Tables 4 and 5, countries such as Japan, Korea, India and Hong Kong are observed being repeatedly recorded and contributed to a large portion in both types of errors in all three months. System issues are, for example, errors in mapping between input fields and outputs such as reports, system limitations and calculation errors, and errors due to changes in configuration resulting from recent roll-out of projects. These errors and the incompatibility of the system to cater for each country's requirements led to manual handling of requests.

Table 5. System Configuration Issues error type categorised by country

	April	May	June	Total
System Configuration Issues (Totals)	16	15	5	36
Australia	-	2	-	2
China	-	3	2	5
Hong Kong	4	2	-	6
India	2	4	1	7
Japan	1	1	-	2
Korea	5	1	1	7
Malaysia	1	-	-	1
Singapore	2	2	-	4
Taiwan	1	-	1	2

4.3 Qualitative Results

Results from the interviews show that a mixed set or combination of competencies from technical, business and customer service backgrounds are important for service delivery in SSC-A. For example, a quality manager stated:

> *"It is really a big scope to say what type of competencies [are] required. It pretty much depends on the roles and responsibilities of [a] particular person. For the one who is in direct contact with customers, customer service would be the essential key. For those who are back-end they might need other areas of competencies; critical, analytical and strategic thinking. Same goes with management level employees. You can't direct all to master all competencies. It is continuous learning and comes through experience" (Interviewee #1).*

As an SSC which processes transactions via an ERP system, SSC-A requires teams with extensive technical competency and functional knowledge. However, at the same time, a senior manager in operations stated that these two aspects need to complement each other to facilitate growth and improvement:

> *"In our case, people with IT competencies and skill sets will definitely have certain advantages. But it doesn't mean we only need this group of people. We also need to think from the perspective of how the process could drive the system. IT personnel can tell you how the system can run the processes. Our intention is also to think from the functional side; how we can leverage the system. There were always arguments between these two; should process fit the system or system drive the processes? Initially, in most cases we always tried to accommodate processes to fit into the system. IT used to have higher voices on this and that's why there were processes changed to fit in the system. But now, we are trying to revisit this issue to further enhance the operation. So, from that perspective I think it's fair to say that we need the right mix and balance of competencies. Like in HR Services for example, we need to have people with both skill sets to support HR personnel in local units. Human resource perspective of the job is equivalently important with system knowledge" (Interviewee #5).*

In another perspective, a team that deals directly with customers (as the main point-of-contact) emphasises more customer service skills. A manager in the service desk operation mentioned that:

> *"In terms of the service desk team, I think the most important one might be 'customer service skills'. System, process and technical knowledge can be built through training, but not everyone has people skills and abilities to handle customers nicely. During hiring, we put the advantage to people who were previously involved in customer service. If not, we will see their interests so we can cultivate it through time. As service providers we need to have good interpretation of information. Customer communication skills should be one of the essential skill sets; how employee should react in certain situations, like to convince people and to win the situation" (Interviewee #4).*

When asked what was the most important factor in building a competent service organisation, most respondents mentioned company practices such as the competency framework, structured training program and performance assessment tools. There was also a response related to focusing on retaining the pool of talent in the company:

> *"I would say a good retention strategy is an important factor. I think competencies could be built up through time; over training, projects, and workshops. It is more about the difficulties on how to retain these skilful people. As the SSC market is a growing market in Malaysia right now, there are lots of head-hunters around. So retaining our group of competent people is the most challenging part for the organisation. Our development program also supports the retention strategy, lateral and vertical moves, for example, are important in nurturing the pool of talent. Programs like sending our employees on projects on customers' sites show that we are eager to give them chances and to create the awareness that we are in a culture of building up a competent centre. Benefits will be in both ways; customers will see that we have the necessary talent and our employees can share and distribute the knowledge to develop our services to another level" (Interviewee #5).*

Interview results show satisfaction with the current training program of SSC-A. Most interviewees agree that compared to the initial stages, current training activities are considered more objective. The respondents report, that through time, the SSC-A training module has been improved to address various areas of service delivery including SAP functional training, Microsoft Excel training, and quality improvement tools such as Six Sigma. Other skill sets are planned for each group of employees depending on their needs.

> *"I think now we have a more structured training program. Structured in the sense that in the past, without competency assessment we just select certain employees to go to certain training with no clear objectives and follow up actions. Now we have structured the training to accommodate employees' needs. Objectives are set with subsequent tasks and assignments. For new joiners, a series of training modules are planned; in class rooms or on-the-job with assessment or dialogue sessions in a certain period of time to ensure whether these candidates are competent enough and suitable for the jobs" (Interviewee #5).*

However, some responses are not in total agreement with these viewpoints. Aligned with the employee survey results, there seems to be evidence from the interviews of a lack of emphasis on customers' requirements, as mentioned by a manager:

> *"I see the training as more in general terms. Specific knowledge, for example, on a certain country or company's requirement (which logically have more impact in daily tasks), would benefit more" (Interviewee #3).*

For SSC-A, customer service is a necessary skill regardless of the type of customers, and there is still room to improve.

> *"I think we are still lacking in training on customer service skills; how to handle difficult customers, how to provide best solutions. Different to other companies*

like the telecommunications industry, they handle various groups of customers. Here, we handle our own group of customers (from the same organisation). I think in that sense the training here is not customized to meet needs on how to handle our customers. I think because we are from the same group / organisation, we should know our rights; to what extent we need to entertain them, to what extent we should highlight to them that a certain request is not doable" (Interviewee #4).

As SSC-A progresses, evidence of effective training can be seen through SLA figures, extension of service volume and knowledge documentation. While the company may organise necessary training and development efforts, the effectiveness can only be realized if employees are willing to develop their career.

"There's no full stop in training. Learning is always ongoing. Managers are also learning from their staff. Today SAP is also upgrading and functions differ in characteristics. The company may provide training to a certain extent. Individuals also need to have own initiative on how to progress. If they are willing to initiate with management, we may develop future career plans for them. Each function such as HR, Finance and IT (with availability of accreditation and certificates) has lots of angles. It all depends on how the employee wants to pursue further" (Interviewee #1).

System difficulties due to the transnational operation of SSC-A are also evident in the interview sessions. On most occasions, during the initial stage of operation, local units are obliged to follow standard procedures applied by the SAP system. This led to problems like incompatibility with their practice and system acceptance. Non-standard items and manual handling of requests are examples of the outcomes.

"Although we are using a well-known ERP system, it still has weaknesses in some areas. Asia is a unique market with diverse and dynamic countries. They are countries with rapid changes. There are occasions when our system could not cope with the changes. For example, although there are patches updated to accommodate changes, there are still mismatches in their understanding of the rules or legal requirements. As a result, we are always stuck in the centre where we have to argue with system suppliers and our customers. I agree we do have these problems largely in our operations in Asia" (Interviewee #2).

Similarly, language ability and cultural understanding are claimed as challenges in delivering services. Customers of SSC-A which are diverse in nationalities demand employees gain expertise in language and sensitivity to cultural differences. Capabilities to bridge these differences ensure better relationships with customers as demonstrated by this response:

"There is definitely some issue of understanding the culture of certain customers. For example, Japanese are cultured people and comparably they have higher expectations than others. Simple issue of writing emails and verbally communicating in their language might bring difficulties at our end" (Interviewee #3).

5 Discussion

SSC-A reflected aspects of both onshore and offshore sourcing models [20]. It served clients both locally in Malaysia and remotely in neighbouring Asian locations, some as far away as India. It was similar to traditional insourcing models, since it was a part of, and under the governance of the overall organisation [20]. In opting for an SSC solution as opposed to an outsourcing option, retention of key skills is cited as an advantage [16]. The threat of SSC failures due to lack of sufficient resource pools [63] as opposed to the flexibility of outsourcing models is more evident, however, in the concerns expressed by the case study respondents.

SSC-A developed competencies identified previously as being critical for service providers. Hence, human resource skill development and technical competency are realized in the rigorous SAP training programs and "buddy" schemes deployed in the organisation. Service delivery management is evident in the operational functionality of the ERP system, with the BSC to monitor its effectiveness, and the Error Log to audit the process. Less evident is any concerted effort to match core competencies of the SSC with its client business units. There is evidence of the SSC's existence being aligned with the organisation's overall goal of achieving competitiveness, but specific practices leading to that objective at the level of SSC-A have not been identified. Rather, SSC-A tried to develop a service-oriented, customer-facing culture.

In the case study, SSC-A conceptualised and implemented its own interpretation of "service competency" and supported it through processes and procedures such as the BSC, SLA, structured training programs, targeted recruitment, structured workflows, audits of customer satisfaction (Error Log) and a competency framework. The development of competencies through skills, knowledge and capacity [47] should have matched customer expectations. The results nevertheless, reflect previous findings that there is a gap between the service provider's perception of customer requirements and satisfying customer expectations [34], [35], [65]. Both interviews and survey results revealed inconsistencies in the implementation of the organisation's service competency approach. Training did not necessarily seem to be related to confidence in using the ERP system. Employees did not all perceive their knowledge of customers' business processes to be sufficient, however error logs indicated no problems with knowledge gaps. Interviews revealed that there is considerable variation at the employee level in who benefits from which aspects of the service competency model. Those closer to the customer (help desk) were identified as needing more customer-service related skills, e.g. communication skills, while those at the back-end (technical support) needed to develop technical capabilities. Although, this in itself, is not surprising, respondents seemed to suggest that even though employees may develop competency skills such as technological know-how, communication skills were paramount to promoting the service-based culture developed by SSC-A. The organisation therefore promoted the primacy of service competency over other types of competency generally thought beneficial to a service provider in their interactions with customers.

Similar to a study by Soh et al., as analysed from the error log, technical misfits of the ERP system were observed in the data relating to functional and system outputs of certain demanding countries with unique requirements [61]. As identified by Sheu et al., differences in nationality, law, values, traditional cultures, and languages also can be regarded as challenges in SSC operations with regard to realising customer benefits [57]. From all these differences, there are various aspects to consider in terms of service competency, e.g. language, inter-country or inter-cultural understanding, relationship management competency, as well as technical competencies in country-specific data and processes. Evidence from the survey suggests that these aspects may not necessarily be an obstacle in perception of service quality.

Regardless of SSC-A's emphasis on building the service-oriented culture, there were still issues related to serving the customer. Acquiring business domain knowledge is perceived as an important service provider competency [18], yet, SSC-A failed to convincingly portray confidence in this area as seen in the study results. Employees also did not consider themselves equipped with skills to meet customers' requirements. Employees privileged those aspects of the service competency model that developed their personal and professional skills rather than their interpersonal skills in dealing with customer issues. There was also evidence of tensions between the service providers and customers with many issues being laid squarely at the feet of the customer. The competency framework appeared to meet generic service provider competencies well, such as human resource skills development and technical management, but seem not to have adhered to this paper's conceptualisation of service competency from the perspective of value co-creation and customer collaboration.

SSC-A have realised aspects of an SSC's value proposition such as cost efficiency, standardised operations, specialization, and flexibility to the company in the region. These match results of the study of SSC motives by Janssen and Joha that include 'strategic and organisational', 'technical' and 'economic' categories [32]. Operational results have also shown that SSC-A service quality outcomes may be said to have met the five dimensions of service [45], [46], [50] reliability, tangibles, responsiveness, assurance, interaction, and empathy. Accuracy and timeliness of service execution observable through the BSC and SLA output also suggest dependable service delivery. These results would tend to affect customer relationship and confidence. The results, however, do not resoundingly support a successful service competency model for SSC-A. Two main issues appear to contribute to this outcome: (1) no concerted correlation between the core competencies of SSC-A and the parent organization (as advocated by [40]) and (2) no evidence of collaborative efforts between customer and service provider to develop a mutual understanding of service competency, to better understand customer expectations and contribute to mutual generation of customer benefits.

6 Conclusion

The paper has discussed the shared service organisational arrangement or model and compared it with the earlier, but related, concept of outsourcing. Shared services achieve economies of scale through the creation of separate specialized entities where services are provided to clients. Although there is now some research on shared services with regard to its conceptual underpinnings, implementation strategies and rationales, there are still limited studies on its implementation, operation and challenges. This paper has sought to help fill that gap by reporting on a particular instance of a shared services centre located in Malaysia. Findings from the study reveal rich detail concerning their objectives and rationales, their resources, the skill pools, the cultural issues, and their successes and failures. The case findings, using a range of data sources, including error logs, are hopefully a useful contribution to the SSC literature.

Further, the case reflects previous findings of a gap between the service provider's perception of customer requirements and satisfying customer expectations and the difficulties of solving this. It reveals inconsistencies in the implementation of the organisation's service competency approach. It illustrates that the generic service provider competencies are relatively well addressed and achieved. Indeed, they are deemed to have met the five dimensions of service; reliability, tangibles, responsiveness, assurance, interaction, and empathy, but they do less well in achieving service competency from the perspective of value co-creation and customer collaboration to better meet customer expectations and contribute to mutual generation of customer benefits. Thus, although, the low level attributes of service competency have been achieved, the higher level, more strategic objectives, of supporting the organisation in collaborating to achieve longer term mutual benefit and business value, have not. This is a significant finding and emphasises the importance of ensuring that both the low and high level aspects of service competency are addressed and that the achievement of one does not necessarily lead directly to the other and that specific objectives and mechanisms must be established to ensure both are achieved.

References

1. Aksin, O.Z., Masini, A.: Effective Strategies for Internal Outsourcing and Offshoring of Business Services: An Empirical Investigation. Journal of Operations Management 26, 239–256 (2008)
2. Atesci, K., Bhagwatwar, A., Deo, T., et al.: Business Process Outsourcing: A Case Study of Satyam Computers. Int. J. Inf. Manage. 30, 277–282 (2010)
3. Bardhan, I.R., Demirkan, H., Kannan, P.K., et al.: Special Issue: Information Systems in Services. J. Manage. Inf. Syst. 26, 5–12 (2010)
4. Barrett, M., Davidson, E.: Exploring the Diversity of Service Worlds in the Service Economy. In: Barrett, M., Davidson, E., Middleton, C., et al. (eds.) Information Technology in the Service Economy: Challenges and Possibilities for the 21st Century, vol. 267, pp. 1–10. Springer, Boston (2008)
5. Bassellier, G., Reich, B.H., Benbasat, I.: Information Technology Competence of Business Managers: A Definition and Research Model. J. Manage. Inf. Syst. 17, 159–182 (2001)
6. Becker, J., Niehaves, B., Krause, A.: Shared Service Center vs. Shared Service Network: A Multiple Case Study Analysis of Factors Impacting on Shared Service Configurations. In: Wimmer, M.A., Scholl, H.J., Janssen, M., Traunmüller, R. (eds.) EGOV 2009. LNCS, vol. 5693, pp. 115–126. Springer, Heidelberg (2009)
7. Bergeron, B.: Essentials of Shared Services. Wiley & Sons, New Jersey (2003)
8. Bharadwaj, A.S.: A Resource-Based Perspective on Information Technology Capability and Firm Performance: An Empirical Investigation. MIS Quarterly 24, 169–196 (2000)
9. Bharadwaj, S.S., Saxena, K.B.C.: Service Providers' Competences in Business Process Outsourcing for Delivering Successful Outcome: An Exploratory Study. Vikalpa: The Journal for Decision Makers 35, 37–53 (2010)

10. Bryman, A., Bell, E.: Business Research Methods, 2nd edn. Oxford University Press, Oxford (2007)
11. Bryson, J.R., Daniels, P.W., Warf, B.: Service worlds: People, Organisations and Technologies. Routledge, London (2004)
12. Chesbrough, H., Spohrer, J.: A Research Manifesto for Services Science. Communications of the ACM 49, 33–40 (2006)
13. Child, J.: Organizational Structure and Strategies of Control: A Replication of the Aston Study. Administrative Science Quarterly 17, 163–177 (1972)
14. Cullen, S., Seddon, P.B., Willcocks, L.P.: IT Outsourcing Configuration: Research into Defining and Designing Outsourcing Arrangements. The Journal of Strategic Information Systems 14, 357–387 (2005)
15. Das, A., Soh, C.W.L., Lee, P.C.B.: A Model of Customer Satisfaction with Information Technology Service Providers: An Empirical Study, pp. 190–193 (1999)
16. Deloitte: Which is Better: Outsourcing Or Shared Services? Deloitte Debates (2009)
17. Donaldson, L., Child, J., Aldrich, H.: The Aston Findings on Centralization: Further Discussion. Administrative Science Quarterly 20, 453–460 (1975)
18. Feeny, D., Lacity, M., Willcocks, L.: Taking the Measure of Outsourcing Providers. Sloan Management Review 46, 41–48 (2005)
19. Feeny, D., Willcocks, L.: Core IS Capabilities for Exploiting Information Technology. Sloan Management Review 39, 41–48 (1998)
20. Frost and Sullivan: Shared Services and Outsourcing (SSO) Hub Potential Analysis (Abridged by Select Verticals), 1–53 (November 2005)
21. Goles, T.: Vendor Capabilities and Outsourcing Success: A Resource-Based View. Wirtschaftsinformatik 45, 199–206 (2003)
22. Goo, J., Kishore, R., Rao, H.R., et al.: The Role of Service Level Agreements in Relational Management of Information Technology Outsourcing: An Empirical Study. MIS Quarterly 33, 119–145 (2009)
23. Gorla, N., Somers, T.M., Wong, B.: Organizational Impact of System Quality, Information Quality, and Service Quality. The Journal of Strategic Information Systems 19, 207–228 (2010)
24. Grant, G., McKnight, S., Uruthirapathy, A., Brown, A.: Designing Governance for Shared Services Organisations in the Public Service. Government Information Quarterly 24, 522–538 (2007)
25. Grönroos, C.: A Service Perspective on Business Relationships: The Value Creation, Interaction and Marketing Interface. Industrial Marketing Management 40, 240–247 (2011)
26. Grover, V., Myun, J.C., Teng, J.T.C.: The Effect of Service Quality and Partnership on the Outsourcing of Information Systems Functions. J. Manage. Inf. Syst. 12, 89–116 (1996)
27. Hamel, G., Prahalad, C.K.: Competing for the Future. Harvard Business School Press, Boston (1994)
28. Janssen, M.: Managing the Development of Shared Service Centres: Stakeholder Considerations. ACM International Conference Proceeding Series 113, 564–570 (2005)
29. Janssen, M., Joha, A.: Issues in Relationship Management for Obtaining the Benefits of a Shared Service Center. In: Proceedings of the Sixth International Conference on Electronic Commerce, pp. 219–228 (2004)
30. Janssen, M., Joha, A., Zuurmond, A.: Simulation and Animation for Adopting Shared Services: Evaluating and Comparing Alternative Arrangements. Government Information Quarterly 26, 15–24 (2009)

31. Janssen, M., Wagenaar, R.: An Analysis of a Shared Services Center in E-Government. In: Proceedings of the 37th Hawaii International Conference on System Sciences, pp. 1–10 (2004)
32. Janssen, M., Joha, A.: Motives for Establishing Shared Service Centres in Public Administrations. International Journal of Information Management 26, 102–115 (2006)
33. Johnston, R., Kong, X.: The Customer Experience: A Road-Map for Improvement. Managing Service Quality 21, 5–24 (2011)
34. Johnston, R.: Internal Service – Barriers, Flows and Assessment International Journal of Service Industry Management 19, 210–231 (2008)
35. Johnston, R.: The Determinants of Service Quality: Satisfiers and Dissatisfiers International Journal of Service Industry Management 6, 53–71 (1995)
36. Kaplan, R.M., Norton, D.: The Balanced Scorecard: Translating Strategy into Action. Harvard Business School Press, Boston (1996)
37. Kettinger, W.J., Lee, C.C.: Perceived Service Quality and User Satisfaction with the Information Services Function. Decision Sciences 25, 737–766 (1994)
38. King, W.R.: The Post-Offshoring IS Organisation. Information Resources Management Journal 21, 1–11 (2008)
39. Kirkpatrick, J., Kirkpatrick, W.: The Kirkpatrick Model: Past, Present and Future - Chief Learning Officer, Solutions for Enterprise Productivity, http://clomedia.com/articles/view/the_kirkpatrick_model_past_present_and_future
40. Levina, N., Ross, J.W.: From the Vendor's Perspective: Exploring the Value Proposition in Information Technology Outsourcing. MIS Quarterly 27, 331–364 (2003)
41. McDowell, J.: Achieving Strategic Cost Advantages by Focusing on Back-Office Efficiency. Healthcare Financial Management, 98-104 (June 2010)
42. MSC Malaysia: MSC Malaysia Company Directory, http://www.mscmalaysia.my/topic/Company+Directory
43. MSC Malaysia: MSC Malaysia National Rollout, http://www.mscmalaysia.my/topic/12073013095558
44. Murray, J.G., Rentell, P.G., Geere, D.: Procurement as a Shared Service in English Local Government. International Journal of Public Sector Management 21, 540–555 (2008)
45. Parasuraman, A., Zeithaml, V.A., Berry, L.L.: SERVQUAL: A Multiple-Item Scale for Measuring Consumer Perceptions of Service Quality. J. Retail. 64, 12–40 (1988)
46. Parasuraman, A., Zeithaml, V.A., Berry, L.L.: A Conceptual Model of Service Quality and its Implications for Future Research. J. Market. 49, 41–50 (1985)
47. Peppard, J., Ward, J.: Beyond Strategic Information Systems: Towards an IS Capability. Journal of Strategic Information Systems 13, 167–194 (2004)
48. Qu, W.G., Oh, W., Pinsonneault, A.: The Strategic Value of IT Insourcing: An IT-Enabled Business Process Perspective. Journal of Strategic Information Systems 19, 96–108 (2010)
49. Ross, J.W., Beath, C.M., Goodhue, D.L.: Develop Long-Term Competitiveness through IT Assets. MIT Sloan Management Review 38, 31–42 (1996)
50. Russ-Eft, D.: Customer Service Competencies: A Global Look. Human Resource Development International 7, 211–231 (2004)
51. Rust, R.T., Miu, C.: What Academic Research Tells Us about Service. Commun ACM 49, 49–54 (2006)
52. Sako, M.: Outsourcing Versus Shared Services. Commun ACM 53, 27–29 (2010)
53. Sambamurthy, V., Zmud, R.W.: At the heart of success: organization wide management competencies. In: Sauer, C., Yetton, P.W. (eds.) Steps to the Future: Fresh Thinking on the Management of IT'Based Organizational Transformation, pp. 143–163. Jossey-Bass, San Francisco (1997)

54. Sambamurthy, V., Zmud, R.W.: IT management competency assessment: A tool for creating business value through IT. Financial Executives Research Foundation, Morristown, NJ (1994)
55. Schulz, V., Hochstein, A., Uebernickel, F., et al.: Definition and Classification of IT-Shared-Service-Center. In: Proceedings of the Fifteenth Americas Conference on Information Systems, pp. 1–9 (2009)
56. Shee, D.Y.: An Analytic Framework for Competence Set Expansion: Lessons Learned from an SME. Total Quality Management & Business Excellence 17, 981–997 (2006)
57. Sheu, C., Chae, B., Yang, C.: National Differences and ERP Implementation: Issues and Challenges. Omega 32, 361–371 (2004)
58. Shih, Y., Wu, Y., Wang, Y., et al.: Competence Maps for the Information Service Industry. International Journal of Human Resource Management 20, 1618–1633 (2009)
59. Sia, S.K., Soh, C., Weill, P.: Global IT Management: Structuring for Scale, Responsiveness, and Innovation. Communications of the ACM 53, 59–64 (2010)
60. SiliconIndia: Silicon Island of the East - Si Team - SiliconIndia Magazine, http://www.siliconindia.com/magazine_articles/Silicon_island_of_the_East-YWQ137624955.html
61. Soh, C., Kien, S.S., Tay-Yap, J.: Enterprise Resource Planning: Cultural Fits and Misfits: Is ERP a Universal Solution? Commun. ACM 43, 47–51 (2000)
62. Song, H.M., Wong, S.F.: Understanding Customer Satisfaction in the IT Outsourcing Environment: A Classification of Quality Attributes. Journal of Outscoring and Organizational Information Management, Article ID 102114, 1–5 (2009)
63. Strikwerder, J.: The Shared Service Centre: Change, Governance and Strategy. Business School – Universiteit van Amsterdam, Nolan Norton Institute (2006)
64. Su, N., Akkiraju, R., Nayak, N., et al.: Shared Services Transformation: Conceptualization and Valuation from the Perspective of Real Options. Decision Sciences 40, 381–396 (2009)
65. Urban, W.: Service Quality Gaps and their Role in Service Enterprises Development. Technological & Economic Development of Economy 15, 631–645 (2009)
66. Vargo, S.L., Lusch, R.F.: Evolving to a New Dominant Logic for Marketing. J. Market. 68, 1–17 (2004)
67. Vargo, S., Lusch, R.: Why "service"? Journal of the Academy of Marketing Science 36, 25–38 (2008)
68. Wang, S., Wang, H.: Shared Services Beyond Sourcing the Back Offices: Organizational Design. Human Systems Management 26, 281–290 (2007)
69. Yin, R.K.: Case study research: Design and methods, 3rd edn. Applied Social Research Methods Series, vol. 5. Sage Publications, Thousand Oaks (2003)

Innovation in Outsourcing: Towards a Practical Framework

Ilan Oshri[1] and Julia Kotlarsky[2]

[1] Rotterdam School of Management Erasmus University
Burg. Oudlaan 50, Rotterdam 3000 DR, The Netherlands
ioshri@rsm.nl
[2] Warwick Business School, University of Warwick,
Gibbet Hill Road, Coventry CV4 7AL, United Kingdom
julia.kotlarsky@wbs.ac.uk

Abstract. The outsourcing industry is now up for a new challenge: to understand how innovation can be realized from outsourcing engagements. While innovation has been explored and prized within businesses for decades, it is a relatively new topic in the context of outsourcing. And, as such, the perceptions regarding what innovation in outsourcing is, what inhibits or enables innovation in outsourcing, and what client firms are willing to do to ensure they benefit from innovation in outsourcing are still being defined.

This paper provides insight into some of the critical aspects in innovation in which both client firms and vendors have taken interest in recent years. We go beyond the simplistic approach we have seen in some recent reports that advocates for the development of trust and close relationships between client firms and vendors as the main enablers of innovation in outsourcing. In our view, innovation in outsourcing can be properly understood only when both contractual and relational aspects are examined as well as the nature of the innovation, i.e. incremental or radical, is explored. Further, we posit that the sourcing model applied has also an impact on the ability to innovate.

Keywords: Outsourcing, radical and incremental innovation, contract type, client-supplier relationship.

1 Introduction

Recent years have witnessed an unprecedented growth of the outsourcing industry. By the end of 2010, the market for information technology outsourcing (ITO) worldwide was reported as $270 billion and for business process outsourcing (BPO) $165 billion. Recent estimates predict that in the 2011-14 period ITO growth will be 5-8% per annum and BPO growth will be 8-12% per annum. Soon the BPO market size worldwide will overtake the ITO market[1]. It is common to talk of Brazil, Russia, India and China as the BRIC inheritors of globalization, offering both offshore IT and back-office services, and also, with their vast populations and developing economies,

[1] Oshri I., Kotlarsky J. and L.P. Willcocks (2009) 'The Handbook of Global Outsourcing and Offshoring', *Macmillan*, London.

J. Kotlarsky, L.P. Willcocks, and I. Oshri (Eds.): Global Sourcing 2011, LNBIP 91, pp. 201–217, 2011.

huge potential markets. However, the phenomenon of offshoring and offshore outsourcing is certainly expanding, with, on our count, some 120 centres developing around the world. Furthermore, as firms become more savvy consumers of outsourcing services, they apply various sourcing models. The multi-vendor sourcing model is still by far the most popular trend among client firms[2], though some client firms experiment with bundled outsourcing services[3]. Also, we have reported recently on a surge in setting up offshore captive centres in India and Central and Eastern Europe and the dynamic nature of goals pursued by such centres, despite some ongoing media reports about the 'death of the captive centre'.[4,5]

In this regard, we have seen a shift in decision-makers' mindsets from focusing on low costs, which was typically considered as the main reason for firms to engage in outsourcing, to accessing talent and skills not available in-house. Results of our research indicate that saving costs has become a secondary driver of outsourcing[6]. Clearly, the outsourcing industry has entered a new phase in its evolutionary path in which clients are shifting from focusing only on costs saving to realizing value. In this journey, client firms need to develop tools that will allow measuring the returns on their outsourcing investments beyond the one-off costs saving and vendors are required to demonstrate how long-term commitments translate into value-adding organizational outcomes. Our 2009 study confirmed that the vast majority of client firms have not yet embarked on a systematic approach to measure the returns on their outsourcing investments[7].

2 Innovation in Outsourcing: The Challenges

As the ongoing search for real benefits in global sourcing shifts from costs saving to adding value, and from the operational to the strategic level, client firms are also raising their expectations regarding the potential to benefit from innovations delivered by their vendors. In management terms, innovation can take the form of a new product or service offered to clients or a new process through which an organization develops products or delivers services. Innovation can also be anything that is state-of-the-art and also anything which is new to the organization. For example, setting up a network of suppliers for certain business processes previously provided from in-house.

---

2 Oshri I., Kotlarsky J. and L.P. Willcocks (2009) 'The Handbook of Global Outsourcing and Offshoring', *Macmillan*, London.

3 Willcocks L.P., Oshri I. and J. Hindle (2009) "Client's propensity to buy bundled IT outsourcing services", White Paper for Accenture.

4 Oshri I. (2011) "Offshoring Strategies: Evolving Captive Center Models", MIT Press, Boston, MA.

5 Captive centre strategies are discussed in detail in Oshri I. (2011) "Offshoring Strategies: Evolving Captive Center Models", MIT Press, MA. In this regard, we argue that the captive centre has been one sourcing model within a broad range of strategic options that client firms utilize in order to maximize the return on their outsourcing and offshoring investments.

6 Oshri I. and J. Kotlarsky (2009) "The Real Benefits of Outsourcing", A WBS white paper for Cognizant. http://www.quantifyingoutsourcingbenefits.com/default.asp

7 Oshri I. and J. Kotlarsky (2009) "The Real Benefits of Outsourcing", A WBS white paper for Cognizant. http://www.quantifyingoutsourcingbenefits.com/default.asp

Innovation does not come easy, whether as an in-house process or through external partners. When in-house, inertia forces often obstruct attempts to innovate and break away from old ways. And when sought through relationships with external partners, innovative efforts face additional challenges, for example, agreeing and monitoring how each party involved in a collaborative venture should contribute to the partnership as well as benefit from the value created.

The outsourcing context poses additional challenges to achieving innovation between a client firm and a vendor. One of the main reasons often cited by CIOs for failing to achieve innovation in outsourcing is the uncertainty about the nature of innovation desired from the vendor and also the inability to design a contract that is on the one hand mitigating the client's exposure to be exploited by the vendor and at the same time offers compensation for extra work and innovation delivered by the vendor. Put simply, most outsourcing contracts do not accommodate these often contradicting requirements properly.

Despite this contractual challenge, client firms still seek innovations from their outsourcing engagements. Among the key drivers for innovation in outsourcing are limited resources and capabilities within the client firm, shortage of specialist talents, management of multiple risks, attracting talent in the company's non-specialized areas, and reducing time-to-market. As globalization intensifies and many more firms quickly become global players, the influence of these drivers will only have a bigger impact on the firm's performance, pressing executives to seek innovation through partnerships.

So how can companies innovate through various ways of sourcing? Very often client firms have an ad hoc approach to achieving innovation from outsourcing arrangements. Such an approach often fails to leverage organizational learning and may also result in the unintended loss of knowledge. An ad hoc approach also cannot create a culture in which external contributions are accepted or welcomed. Moreover, it is very difficult to measure innovative processes and outcomes when companies innovate on an ad hoc basis. As academics with over 20 years of combined experience in the field of outsourcing, we observed that the topic of innovation in outsourcing is poorly understood. For this reason, this study is set about understanding (i) what client firms expect to receive from vendors in terms of innovation and (ii) what the key factors are that influence the extent to which innovation can be delivered in outsourcing relationships.

3 Research Approach

This research, conducted in collaboration with Cognizant, focuses on understanding whether CIOs and CFOs achieve innovation through their outsourcing arrangements. We also examine the factors that positively affect innovativeness in outsourcing.

The ideas presented in this paper are based on original research carried out by Dr. Ilan Oshri and Dr. Julia Kotlarsky. The researchers also conducted semi-structured interviews and held discussions with experts in the field of outsourcing, including CIOs and CFOs from leading multinationals with headquarters based in Europe. The ideas in this paper are also based on a quantitative survey, which was carried out in partnership with research organization Vanson Bourne. The quantitative survey sampled 250 CIOs and CFOs from companies with revenues from $500m up to over $1bn (51%) from financial services, manufacturing, logistics, retail, utilities, telecom and other leading sectors in the UK (50%) and other European countries such as France, Germany, Denmark, Sweden, Switzerland, Belgium, Netherlands and Luxemburg.

4 Innovation in Outsourcing: What Have We Learnt?

4.1 What Functions Have Been Outsourced?

In our previous study, carried out in 2009[8], we analyzed the functions outsourced recently. Table 1 brings together the results from the March 2009 and the recent study to allow a comparison in trends and therefore make some conclusions about the expected growth of specific outsourcing segments.

Clearly, BPO has grown strongly between the two studies. While only 33% of the 2009 respondents reported that they outsourced business processes, 47% of the later study's respondents have done so. This result corresponds with other studies which predict that BPO will overtake ITO by 2015[9].

As Table 1 shows, IT and IT-enabled business processes are still the most popular candidates for outsourcing. Based on the later study, among the vast range of services outsourced, IT infrastructure and data management is on the top of the list, being outsourced by 58% of the surveyed companies, followed by IT and technology consultancy and ERP support (53% each).

We also observe a significant increase in BPO projects, in particular, in ERP implementation and integration. In the later study, 53% of the respondents reported that they engaged in such projects against only 41% in 2009. Other business processes, such as Finance and Administration, HR, Payroll and many others which in the past were largely moved offshore to captive facilities because of data security and control issues, nowadays are increasingly outsourced to third parties. For example, compared with the results of the 2009 survey, in the more recent study we observe a significant increase in outsourcing of such business processes (from 33% to 47%). Furthermore, large European firms tend to outsource more knowledge-intensive processes such as CRM and business analytics (i.e. data warehousing and business intelligence systems), which were not so popular in 2009. We see a significant increase in the outsourcing of these processes compared to early 2009 (29% outsource CRM in 2010 compared to 22% in 2009, and 26% outsource data warehousing and business intelligence compared to 18% in 2009).

While IT infrastructure and data management is still the most popular function to outsource, we have observed a small drop between the earlier and later surveys in the number of firms reporting on such engagements. While these results are surprising, we do not think that they represent a long-term decline trend. Consistent with Gartner's recent report, we agree that the ITO market is maturing and will probably maintain a 5% compounded annual growth in the next five to seven years.

---

[8] Oshri I. and J. Kotlarsky (2009) "The Real Benefits of Outsourcing", A WBS white paper for Cognizant. http://www.quantifyingoutsourcingbenefits.com/default.asp

[9] Oshri I. and J. Kotlarsky (2009) "The Real Benefits of Outsourcing", A WBS white paper for Cognizant. http://www.quantifyingoutsourcingbenefits.com/default.asp

Table 1. Functions outsourced in 2009 and 2010

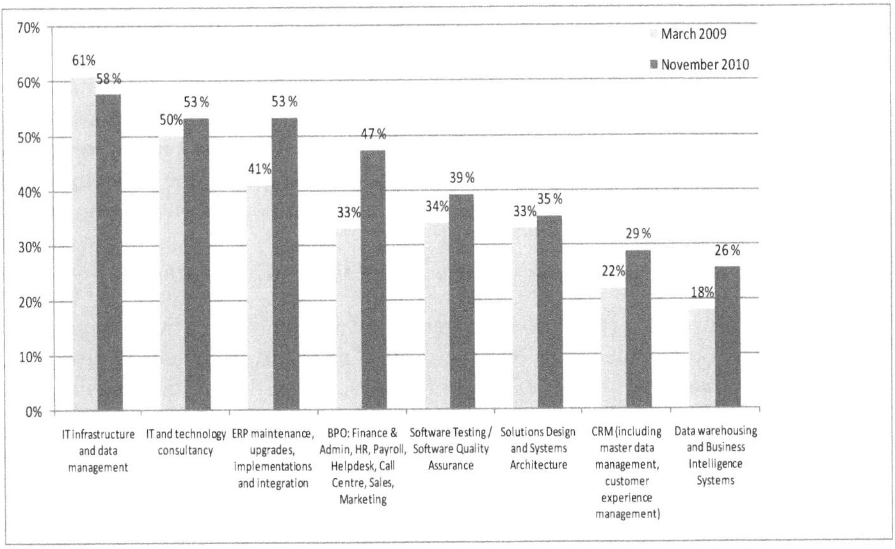

4.2 The Importance of Innovation to Business Success

Traditionally innovation has been perceived as one of the sources of competitive advantage in fast changing industries. To keep up with market forces and changing consumer tastes, firms need to be innovative by tapping into both internal and external knowledge. Indeed, 64% of the responding firms believed that their ability to be more innovative contributes to the financial performance of their organization. Seventy per cent of the respondents also thought that the innovation they have achieved through outsourced business arrangements had contributed to the financial performance of their organization. And 53% of the respondents indicated that innovative capabilities demonstrated by the vendor are either important or very important in their vendor selection criteria.

However, selecting a vendor capable of innovating successfully, either incrementally or in a radical manner, requires a robust, methodological approach that turns not only ideas into successful products, but also ensures the appropriation of value created through the innovation.

Indeed, research has persistently identified the management of innovation as one of the key weaknesses in a firm's ability to build an innovation capability. It seems that firms have a flow of ideas generated either internally or through external change agents; however, translating these ideas into a successful commercial product or service has always been the challenge. When asked: 'Would you benefit from an innovation framework that could guide all your stakeholders through the journey of translating an idea to a defined product or service?', 58% of the respondents replied that they would like to have such an innovation framework. And, 67% of the respondents also believed that it is possible to formalize, repeat and maintain innovation within their industry. However, when asked regarding their willingness to invest in such a service, only 50% of the respondents indicated that they were willing to pay for an outsourced service which will formalize, repeat and maintain innovation within their industry, and only 45% were willing to pay rates higher than standard for an innovation framework that would be provided as a service by their outsourcing partner and that would demonstrate a return on investment.

Clearly, client firms value innovation and acknowledge its impact on business performance. Furthermore, they also see the importance in obtaining a framework that will allow them to build and retain an innovation capability that outperforms their competition. However, the majority of firms still do not see the value in paying extra for such services, even if the vendor is able to show a return on the investment.

4.3 The Innovation Challenge in Outsourcing: Clients' Expectations

Client firms expect their vendors to help them innovate. Innovation in this regard can be delivered not only through the offering of new products, services and processes, but also via the transformation of existing processes. According to the results of this study, the majority of the client firms in this survey expect vendors to either turn ideas into improved processes (56%), transform existing products (55%), help transform existing processes (53%) or help turn ideas into new products (see Table 2). However, when asked how such expectations would come into effect, 66% of the client firms indicated that an engagement with an outsourcing vendor should free up in-house resources that could focus on higher value activities (see Table 3). Clearly, such a belief implies that the vast majority of client firms still believe that innovation is core to the firm's value chain and as such should be carried out in-house. Therefore the majority of client firms still rely on their own knowledge-base for innovation, failing to recognize that innovation can in fact be a service. Often such a shift in mindset requires not only an extensive change management process within the client firm but also a re-skilling exercise of the retained talent and expertise to realize their ability to focus on managing relationship for innovation rather than just managing supply contracts.

Table 2. Expectations from the outsourcing partner in terms of innovation

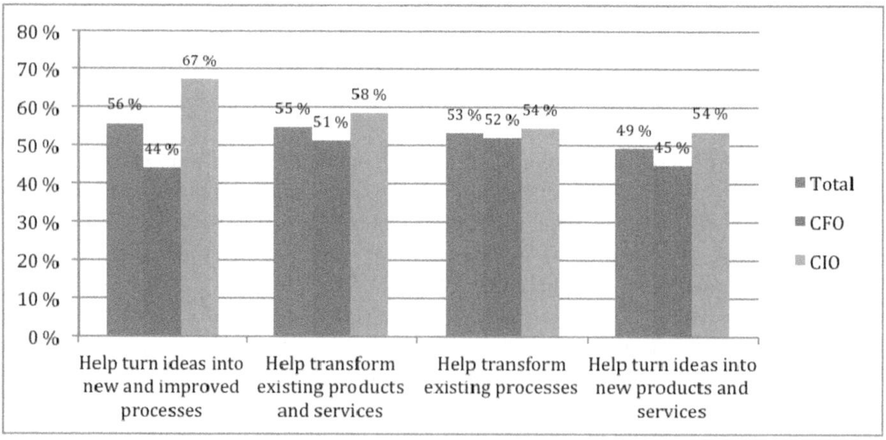

Table 3. How your outsourcing engagement will result in innovation

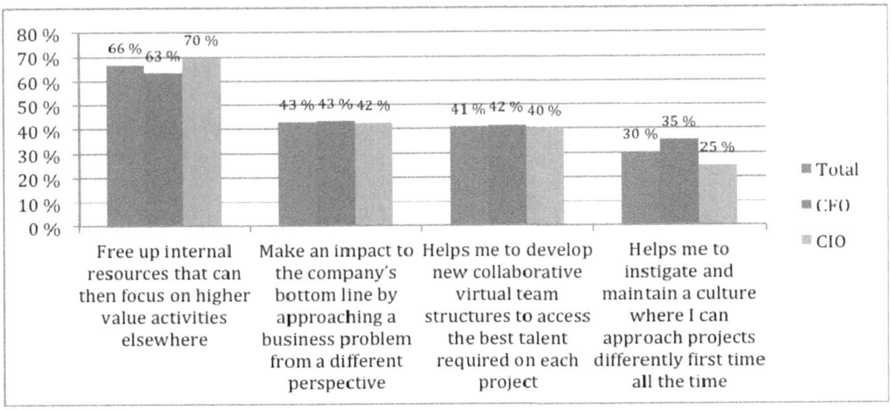

4.4 Enabling Innovation in Outsourcing: The Role of the Contract

Outsourcing arrangements are based on contracts and therefore understanding which contract is more likely to accommodate innovation is key. To our knowledge, the link between contract types and innovation in outsourcing has never been studied before and the implication for how firms set up contracts to achieve innovation is therefore poorly understood. To start with, in order to achieve innovation in outsourcing, both clients and vendors need to craft contracts that offer incentives and that nurture innovation. In this regard, contracts should include clauses that incentivize vendors to think about innovations regardless of the nature of the process or system outsourced. There is a misperception that some contracts are not designed for innovation, such as ticket-based contracts or fees for service. However, we came across several examples that demonstrated the wide possibilities available to the vendor to innovate, despite relatively unfavourable contract terms. For example, in one ticket-based contract, the vendor improved the service provided, a process innovation that resulted in a reduction in the number of tickets generated by the client firm's clients. The vendor was motivated to innovate by the contract that offered higher margins per ticket should the number of tickets dropdown, while the client firm was satisfied with this improvement as their customer satisfaction feedback had significantly improved.

Our study shows that the vast majority of contracts are fee for service (78%) and ticket-based (47%), suggesting that most deals are based on fixed fees for a specified service. Non-fixed price contracts, such as time and material account for 42% of all outsourcing contracts[10]. Considering that the vast majority of the firms opt for fixed price contracts, we see a challenge to achieve innovation in outsourcing engagements. One executive we interviewed discussed the challenge as one that is similar to the chicken and egg analogy. He explained that setting up a collaborative environment for innovation depends very much on the steps each side take. But because of resource management, there will always be the issue of 'who is paying for all the goodwill'?

[10] Total percentage of contracts is higher than 100% because some client companies surveyed engaged in several outsourcing relationships, some with different types of contracts.

Yet, this scenario does not mean that innovation in outsourcing cannot be achieved in relatively rigid and inflexible clauses in the contract. We would expect that clients would include clauses in the contract that would improve flexibility in payments when the vendor 'went the extra mile'. However, when asked, our results show that 53% of the respondents either did not include or were not aware if such clauses were included in their contract to compensate vendors for innovation introduced in the outsourcing project.

4.5 Types of Innovation and Contractual and Relational Governing Approaches

There are numerous types of innovations that the academic and professional literature has discussed in recent years. Among the more popular innovation types are incremental, radical, systemic, architectural, autonomous, disruptive and discontinuous innovation. At the same time, innovation can be in the form of a new product, service or process. Incremental and radical innovations have, by far, been at the centre of academics' and practitioners' attention. For this reason, we have focused in this study on how either incremental or radical innovation can be achieved in outsourcing. There are two governing approaches to manage outsourcing arrangement: one is a contractual approach that emphasizes the formality of the relationships between the client firm and the vendor through the relatively high dependence on the contract as a governing mechanism. The second is a relational approach which brings to the fore the interpersonal relationships between staff from the client and vendor firms that drive collaboration between the parties and form partnership as the cornerstone of the outsourcing governing structure. We actually see contractual and relational governing approaches as complementary rather than substitutes, which means that client firms will seek to leverage on relational aspects to promote a collaborative attitude while ensuring that the outsourcing project meets the clauses specified in the contract. In this regard, our study sought to understand the link between innovation types and the governing approaches.

Our results show that radical innovation is strongly associated with both contractual and relational governing approaches. The results of this study also suggest that client firms seeking radical innovations in outsourcing should first develop strong contract management capabilities and then complement those with relationship management capabilities to ensure that the parties shift their attitudes from a transactional approach to a collaborative mode.

An example provided by the CIO Downstream of Shell illustrates how innovation in outsourcing can take place. We have learned that the most acute and contemporary challenges are shared with the vendors of Shell's outsourcing ecosystem, with the hope that one or more vendors will come up with a proposal on how to tackle such challenges. Once a proposal is made, Shell's management will seek funding for the solution and will form a joint venture with the vendors to arrive at a contract that clearly defines the investment required by each party and also the appropriation of value created and intellectual property issues. In this regard, Shell's approach confirms our results that joint venture contracts are more likely to lead to radical innovation.

4.6 Sourcing Models and Innovation in Outsourcing

There is an ongoing debate as to which sourcing model is more likely to deliver innovation to the client firm. This debate has centred around two sourcing models: Bundled services and multi-sourcing. On the one hand, a bundled service sourcing model, in which the client outsources multiple business functions to a single vendor, implies strong relationships between the client firm and the vendor, a trait which is imperative for the collaborative innovation attitude in outsourcing settings. However, bundled services also pose a threat to client firms lacking strong sourcing capabilities in the form of being 'locked in' and therefore not being able to switch vendors when performance deteriorates and innovation is not delivered. The alternative, which is now the dominant sourcing model, is multi-sourcing, in which the client firm outsources part of its value chain to multiple vendors.

The results of the survey show that multi-sourcing settings are more likely to deliver client firms radical innovation from their vendors than any other sourcing models.

4.7 Measuring Innovations in Outsourcing

In the end, executives will invest in partnership with vendors when the returns on innovation in outsourcing are clear. In our 2009 survey, we observed that 57% of the CIOs and CFOs surveyed either did not measure or did not know whether they quantify the returns on their investment in outsourcing. In the present study, 64% of the respondents never measured or did not know whether they measured innovation delivered by their vendors (see Table 4).

Table 4. Do you measure the value or the innovation delivered by your vendor (CIOs and CFOs perspective)?

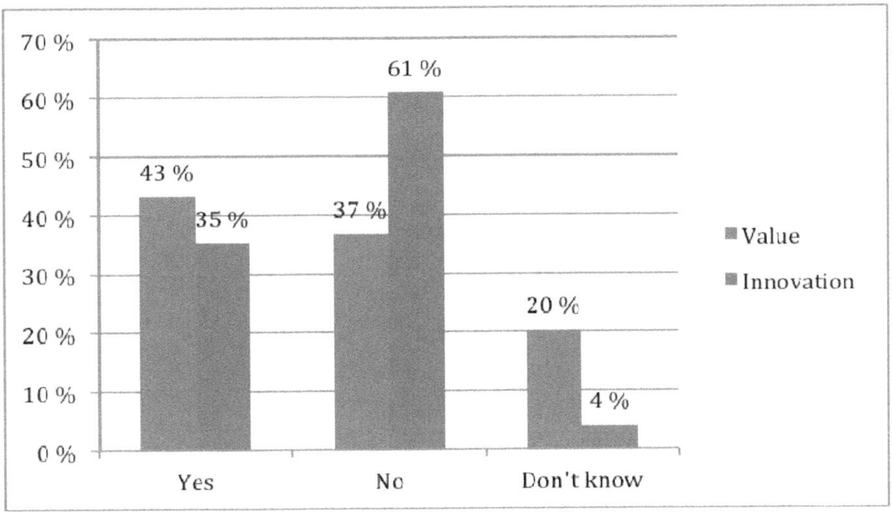

From the above results, it is evident that the vast majority of C-level executives fail to measure the returns on either outsourcing or innovation investments made in their relationships with vendors. From interviews we have held, we learned that many client firms do not quantify the value that a business function contributes to the competitiveness of the firm but rather prefer to compute the cost-base of this business function. Such an approach drives client firms to focus on cost reductions as the main objective sought from vendors while expressing desires to see value and innovation delivered in outsourcing engagements, yet without building a capacity that allows them to properly manage and measure innovation outcomes and impact. This attitude is in particular a source of concern as 64% of the respondents in this study confirmed that they are now investing more in outsourcing partnerships than they did three years ago, hinting that client firms seek to tighten relationships with vendors and leverage on the relational approach in order to incentivize the vendor to innovate. Such a combination of desires and deeds calls for the examination of required steps that we believe will lead clients firms to benefit from innovation in outsourcing.

5 How to Achieve Innovation in Outsourcing: The Innovation Ladder

We developed a framework that we call The Innovation Ladder (Figure 1) to help client companies to incorporate innovation in their outsourcing strategy. The emphasis in our approach, as opposed to some other studies we have seen, is that we believe that the innovation strategy should be integrated into the outsourcing strategy of the client firm. We acknowledge that some firms, such as Shell, prefer to execute innovation with their outsourcing vendors outside the ongoing outsourcing relationship; however even such firms should consider implementing some of the steps described below. In this regard, The Innovation Ladder is a full cycle approach

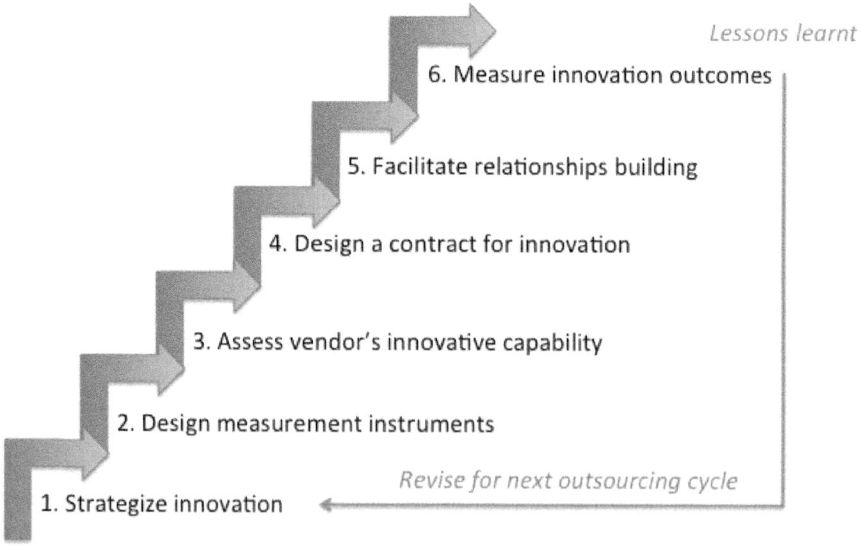

Fig. 1. The Innovation Ladder in Outsourcing

from the beginning of the outsourcing relationship until the delivery of innovation. Yet, client firms can pick and choose some steps depending on the breadth of innovation sought and on the nature of the relationship they establish with their vendors.

Step 1: Strategize Innovation

A journey into innovation in outsourcing should start at the early stages of strategizing the outsourcing project. These early stages of the outsourcing lifecycle often involve the identification of objectives and the potential areas for improvement derived from the outsourcing engagement. At that point in time, it is imperative that executives consider the impact expected on the firm, from operational or strategic perspectives, and the two levels of innovations: incremental and radical (see Figure 2).

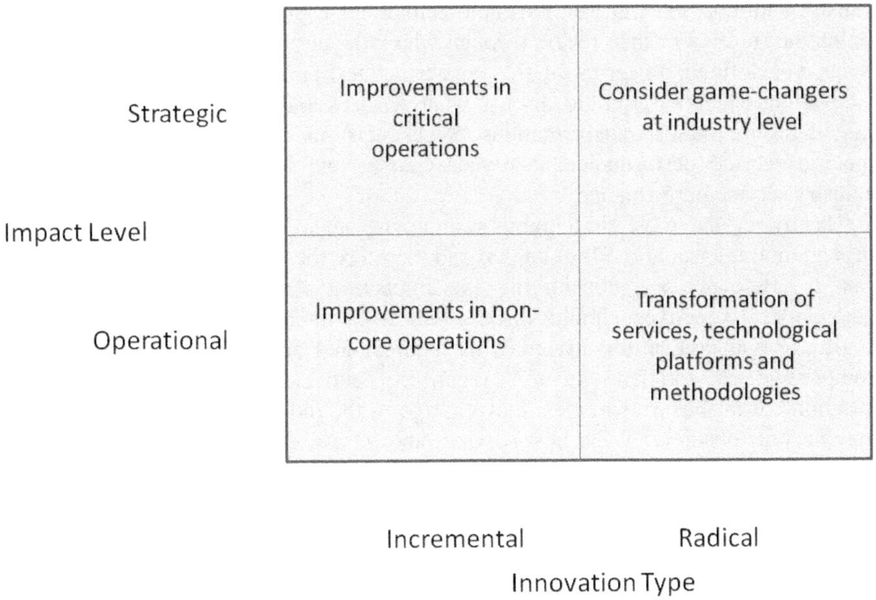

Fig. 2. Impact of Incremental and Radical innovation on the Operational and Strategic levels of the client firm

In principle, executives should consider the four areas of improvements when strategizing innovation in outsourcing. To start with, executives should discuss the incremental improvements expected at the operational level in business processes that are considered to be non-core to the firm's competitive position. Such business processes can be, for example, finance and accounting, human resource management and procurement, which are becoming prominent candidates for outsourcing; however, with little attention to the improvements sought to be achieved from the vendors.

Client firms should also seek incremental improvements in critical operations outsourced to a third party service provider. One example of such business process is business analytics. Our study reports that 26% of the respondents outsourced business intelligence to a third party service provider. In this regard, executives should consider incremental innovations in a critical business function that benchmark with best practices in the industry. For example, executives can ask: what gaps exist between our level of critical operations and the industry best performer's level of these critical operations?

Combining the areas of improvements in non-core and critical business operations will allow executives to form their 'wish list' of the incremental improvements which can be clearly specified and described in any type of contract and that corresponds with the enhancement of the firm's operational competitiveness. Including in the contract rewards, such as the sharing of savings achieved from improved processes,would motivate vendors to put efforts into such improvements.

Executives should also consider radical innovation that can be achieved in their outsourcing engagements. This would require executives to consider not only the transformation of existing services and technological platforms but also scenarios in which the solution or the process through which the desired outcome will be achieved is not yet defined. In terms of the impact at the operational level through radical innovation, executives should discuss what services and technological platforms are candidates for major transformations. Such decisions can be made by considering specific service performance, cost/value ratios, and benchmarking against cross-industry service performance.

The fourth and most challenging strategizing stage should be about problems or strategic moves that are still unknown and therefore the solutions for them are still to emerge. Here we are considering the impact at the strategic level of radical innovation. Executives should discuss scenarios of major shifts in the industry landscape and competitor strategies as a threat and an opportunity to shape their competitive environment. In this regard, executives should ask the following questions: what business models may emerge in the industry? What business models may become obsolete? What new services and service delivery methods may emerge and how prepared are we to either shape the environment or benefit from such changes? Decision markers at this stage may also consider entry to new markers and/or new industries as a strategic move of the firm, or as a result of mergers and acquisitions that create a need for executives to re-consider how to maximise benefits from new markets/industries. The purpose of such discussions is two-fold: first, to shift executives' attention from focusing on the operational/transformative level in outsourcing to considering strategic issues that are still to emerge, as a response to the dynamic and highly competitive environment, and second, to discuss and formulate a framework within which such challenges will be shared with trustworthy vendors.

By bringing together these four aspects of innovation in outsourcing during the early stages of the planning, the client firm will be able to devise an approach to realizing the innovation potential from each setting. Below we describe in depth each of the following steps.

Step 2: Design Measurement Instrument

As a second step, client firms need to develop the measurement instruments for the incremental innovation expected to be delivered by the vendors and design a framework for which radical innovation will be pursued with selected vendors. The measurements for incremental innovation should be developed against the benchmark in the industry. With this, the objectives captured in step 1 will be translated into specific expectations regarding incremental improvements expected from their prospective vendors. While designing measurements for incremental innovation (e.g., percentage of cost reduction, percentage of improvement in time-to-marker or a percentage reduction in process duration), it is important to relate these targets to Key Performance Indicators (KPI) of the client's firm and to Key Success Factors (KSF) at the industry level. In this stage executives should ask the following questions: which of our services/technological platforms/methodologies are lagging behind the standard performance in the industry? Which of our business functions candidates for outsourcing are key for our operational excellence? The answers to these questions will assist executives in identifying the services and technologies that are candidates for incremental innovation and also to realize the expected improvement measurement as benchmarked against industry performance. This analysis will address the design requirements of incremental innovation in the early stages of the outsourcing engagement. The contract should also have a clear reference to how the vendor will be rewarded if it improves the measurements further (e.g., a bonus as apercentage of the additional cost savings that result from the process improvement).

The design of a collaborative framework for radical innovation should take a different approach. As the challenge is not clearly defined at the operational and strategic levels, client firms should devise a radical innovation framework to create conditions within which preferred vendors will be introduced to significant and game-changing challenges that require radical innovation. The radical innovation framework includes procedures and processes within the client firm that scout threats from competition and markets, and translate those into descriptive scenarios that can be shared with external partners. The radical innovation framework should also outline the knowledge sharing platforms, their participants, structure and frequency of interactions between the participants, to ensure that vendors bidding for the outsourcing project are aware of the commitment required from them in exploring radical innovation opportunities, which would allow them to budget for additional resources required for such activities. Last but not least, the radical innovation framework will include a proposed contractual approach once the client firm and vendor(s) have agreed on the approach to tackle transformative and game-changing challenges. Our recommendation is that a joint venture arrangement, separate from the ongoing outsourcing engagement, should be the main vehicle through which radical innovation is carried out.

Step 3: Assess Vendor's Innovation Capability

Having carefully crafted the measurement requirements for incremental innovation and devised a plan (and a framework) for achieving radical innovation, it is now the time to develop a set of criteria upon which the innovativeness of the bidding vendors will be assessed. While the results of this study suggest that most client firms consider the innovativeness of their vendors as one of the vendors' selection criteria, to our best knowledge, no study has so far revealed what these criteria were as well as how they should be applied in the context of incremental and radical innovation.

Based on research we have conducted and input from leading consumers of outsourcing services, we come to the conclusion that in incremental innovation the relevant selection criteria should seek proven evidence of improvements made in the same scope, complexity and criticality to operational excellence of business processes, services and IT platforms. This proven evidence can be in the form of referral letters from the vendor's existing and past clients, the vendor's case studies about improvements made in business processes and IT platforms and an outline of the approach to meet improvement measurements submitted as a project plan. Further, the vendor should also provide similar evidence for their relationship capabilities, which, in the case of incremental innovation, are complementary to proven abilities to provide solutions according to the specifications. These inputs will allow the client firm to systematically compare between the various bidders concerning their incremental innovation capabilities.

Assessing capabilities to carry out radical innovation is far more challenging. Based on our research we argue that client firms should put the emphasis on understanding the relationship capabilities developed by the potential vendors and then seek complementary delivery capabilities in the form of technical and service development capabilities. We advocate for this approach for two reasons: first, as the challenges requiring radical innovations at the operational and strategic level are still not clearly defined, and because the success of setting up a collaborative framework depends to a large extent on the relationship developed between the client and vendor, client firms should focus on clearly mapping out the relationship capabilities developed and applied by the vendor firm. Second, in many examples of radical innovations we have come across, it was the result of a 'consortium' of several firms (usually the client and several vendors) that were able to bring together expertise and knowledge from various domains to arrive in a game-changing product or service. Once again the relationship aspect is coming across as imperative for facilitating a collaborative framework between multiple vendors that are part of the 'consortium' of firms that bring together distinct expertise and capabilities.

The relationship capability implies the supplier's willingness and ability to align its business model to the values, goals, and needs of the customer[11]. For example, this capability is evident in the vendor's attitude to continuously educating existing customers about state-of-the-art developments in the areas related to the client's business; flexibility to accommodate changing or additional clients' requests, and adapting organizational design and governance structures to those of the client[12]. To assess the relationship capabilities of the bidding vendors, client firms should seek evidence from past projects regarding the procedures, processes and personal interactions set up and used by the vendor. We believe that only by examining the wide range of communication channels between clients and vendors, can one in fact understand how the relationship side has been accommodated. Therefore, client firms should seek evidence about weekly and bi-weekly meetings set and held between the vendor and its clients; evidence regarding forums, portals and databases as knowledge-sharing mechanisms; and evidence regarding interpersonal relationships between the

[11] Feeny D., Lacity M. and L.P. Willcocks (2005) "Taking the measure of outsourcing providers," *MIT Sloan Management Review*, 46(3): 41–48.

[12] Oshri I., Kotlarsky, J. and L.P. Willcocks (2007) "Managing dispersed expertise in IT offshore outsourcing: Lessons from TATA Consultancy Services" MIS Quarterly Executive, 6(2): 53–65.

vendor's staff and the client's personnel. This information can be gathered through referrals to the existing customer and information available on the Internet such as blogs, social media websites (e.g., LinkedIn) and professional magazines.

Step 4: Design a Contract for Innovation

Once the vendor selection phase has been concluded, the attention of the parties involved is shifted to the contract and its content. One very clear result from this study is that most outsourcing contracts are not designed to accommodate innovation. Many of these contracts focus on defining service levels, pricing and penalties, tilting the attention of the vendor to a 'maintenance' mentality as well as the client's mindset to monitor outsourcing performance based on well defined SLAs. Accommodating innovation in outsourcing contracts requires a different attitude.

Contracts that accommodate incremental innovations should elaborate on both improvement targets and innovation processes that will commit both the client and vendor to follow and monitor, including desired targets and rewards if these targets are outperformed. In this regard, and often beyond the regular SLA clauses, the incremental innovation clauses should be specific regarding the relationship mechanisms put in place by both the client and vendor that will support the vendor's effort to deliver incremental innovation according to the improvement measurements.

The clauses in the contract that refer to radical innovation should provide an elaborative description of the methodology through which vendors will become partners. In this regard, the contract should describe the process put in place to share transformative and game-changing challenges with the vendors, the expected participation from the vendors in such forums and the preferred legal agreement to pursue solutions in the form of radical innovation by one or more vendors. Our recommendation is that this kind of partnership should be established on the basis of a joint venture agreement in which a clear specification of resources and capital is defined as well as the approach to appropriate value and manage intellectual property is outlined.

While our guidelines for tailoring clauses for incremental and radical innovation stand in various contexts, we also took note of a general approach by client firms regarding fixed price contracts and innovation. For example, client firms refrain from offering open-ended clauses in the contract that incentivize vendors to innovate. Such clauses could have been in the form of bonuses for innovation delivered beyond the scope of the project or 'a time and materials' pricing component for innovation within a fixed price contract. Our study provides additional support to such client's tendency to refrain from offering incentives to actual innovation delivered by the vendor. We examined this matter in view of contract types and have come to the conclusion that such an approach harms the relationship aspect in the outsourcing engagement. Indeed, the client firm's concern, which is anchored in the belief that client firms should avoid having loosely-defined clauses, is well justified; however, it is also a risk that clients can mitigate. For example, we have learned that in a ticket-based contract, the client and vendor devised a pricing model which incentivized the vendor to reduce the number of tickets logged onto the system through significant end-to-end service improvements and as a return the vendor gained from higher margins per ticket processed. We view this example as radical innovation at the operational level which was mitigated based on the actual outcomes delivered by the vendor.

Step 5: Facilitate Relationships Building

It is without doubt that building relationships between the client firm and the vendor is imperative for the success of either incremental or radical innovation. However, as opposed to some recent studies on innovation in outsourcing which advocated for an investment in trust regardless of the type of innovation sought, we posit that relationships play a different role in incremental and radical innovation. We have already discussed the various ways client firms can represent the potential leverage for innovation through relationship management. At this point in time, we wish to discuss how relationship management should be executed in incremental and radical innovation.

Our results indicate that, in the case of incremental innovation, the relationship between client and vendor comes second to the contract regardless of the contract type (all but joint venture). We therefore advise client firms seeking incremental innovation to focus on developing relationships with their vendors as a complementary element to monitoring the contract. Further, we argue that relationships in incremental innovations should in fact be facilitated through the formal channels, which are already captured in the contract. Some examples of such mechanisms include the regular meetings, shared portals and communication procedures which are elementary in each outsourcing project; however, becoming imperative for incremental innovation.

Radical innovation, however, begs for a different approach according to which client firms need to invest in the interpersonal side of the relationship with the vendor, as a complementary step to the contractual approach. Our extensive research about outsourcing suggests that it is imperative that trust and rapport between senior managers (e.g., relationship manager) should be developed and renewed to encourage a collaborative atmosphere between client and vendor staff[13]. While personality clashes and cultural differences might play a negative role in developing rapport and trust between individuals from the client and vendor teams, there are always opportunities to enhance the relationship dimension by organizing informal social events, the use of social media tools and through open and preferably face-to-face communication channels. Clearly, it takes a major commitment from senior managers to develop a collaborative atmosphere, which in our view is only one enabler among many to set up and launch a radical innovation project.

We also see opportunities in harnessing social media and open source platforms to support relationship building between clients and vendors. Social media platforms that serve as collaborative tools will enhance the collaborative experience of the client firm in particular when vendor and client teams are remote. Similarly, Web 2.0 platforms will enable stakeholders to co-innovate and co-create services regardless of their physical location.

Step 6: Measure Innovation Performance

As reported above, client firms fail to measure the return on innovation delivered by their vendors. In the academic literature there is general agreement that innovation improves business performance. It flows from this that client firms should invest more

---

[13] Oshri I., Kotlarsky J. and L.P. Willcocks (2007) "Global Software Development: Exploring Socialization in Distributed Strategic Projects", Journal of Strategic Information Systems 16 (1), pp. 25-49.

in understanding the nature of innovation delivery, its impact on the operational functions within the value chain, as well as on the firm's strategic positioning within the market. Such an exercise will allow decision-makers to realize the value delivered by partners and will inform executives regarding the opportunities that emerge in outsourcing relationships. We think that most firms can, in fact, measure the return on the outsourcing investment, in a quantifiable form, should they follow steps 1 and 2 of The Innovation Ladder. For incremental innovation at the operational and strategic level, client firms should have developed clear measurement instruments as part of steps 1 and 2. These measurement instruments may have to be revisited during the project lifecycle. Using the measurement instruments as reference points, the client firm should seek to evaluate whether its incremental innovation targets have been met.

Radical innovation is more challenging to measure; however, the client firm should seek both qualitative and quantitative inputs regarding performance. In terms of qualitative feedback, the client firm should seek input regarding the quality of the network created to arrive in radical innovation. Periodical surveys among members of the joint venture consortium regarding the quality of collaboration, motivation to contribute, assessment of each partner's contribution and intention for future collaboration can provide an indication regarding the 'health' of the joint venture consortium and the potential to tap into this pool of expertise in future projects targeting radical innovations. Quantifiable measurement tools to assess the impact of the radical innovation on business performance should be in the form of benchmark against industry performance. In particular, as radical innovation was sought to improve the competitiveness of the firm either through operational excellence or strategic positioning, the client firm should judge the impact of the radical innovation through industry-wide performance indicators. For example, the quality of service provided, represented through various measurable indicators such as customer satisfaction, is one performance indicator that can be used by service firms.

Step 6 is not the last step in the innovation ladder. If anything, it is a step that calls for reflection and a stage that offers an opportunity to redesign the innovation framework. Feedback collected during these six steps should serve the client firm in its journey to achieve innovation in outsourcing.

6 Conclusions

As the outsourcing industry matures and the range of outsourcing services extends to higher value activities, client firms raise the bar regarding their expectations, seeking the delivery of high impact innovation from their vendors. This paper brings together the expectations of client firms regarding innovation in outsourcing as well as the willingness of client firms to invest in creating the conditions for innovation in outsourcing. In our view, pressure from client firms on outsourcing vendors to deliver both incremental and radical innovation will only increase in the coming years. In a similar vein, both client firms and outsourcing vendors will be faced with far more complex outsourcing arrangements which will require a systematic approach to achieve innovation, one that integrates relationship building with a methodical contractual approach.

Author Index